LINCOLN

Authoritarian Savior

D1572127

Alexander J. Groth

University Press of America, Inc.
Lanham • New York • London

Copyright © 1996 by
Alexander J. Groth
University Press of America, ® Inc.
4720 Boston Way
Lanham, Maryland 20706

3 Henrietta Street
London, WC2E 8LU England

Library of Congress Cataloging-in-Publication Data

Groth, Alexander J.
Lincoln : authoritarian savior / Alexander J. Groth
p.   cm.
Includes index.
l. Lincoln, Abraham, 1809-1865. 2. United States--Politics and
government--1861-1865. 3. Democracy--United States--History--19th
century. I. Title.
E457.4.G76   1996   973.7'092--dc20   96-33245 CIP

ISBN 0-7618-0478-1 (pbk: alk. ppr.)

⊖™The paper used in this publication meets the minimum
requirements of American National Standard for information
Sciences—Permanence of Paper for Printed Library Materials,
ANSI Z39.48—1984

Dedication

To the memory of Dr. Maksymilian Zirler,
physician and sage, martyred in Warsaw, 1944.

PREFACE

The Presidency of Abraham Lincoln is a subject to which posterity has returned many times, and, because of its great significance in American politics and world history, it is likely to be visited many more times in the future as well. This study examines the Lincoln presidency in relation to the notion of democracy. It reexamines the role of the sixteenth president of the United States as the savior of a virtually bankrupt political system c.1860. It also attempts to put Lincoln into a political perspective with some leaders and some situations of the twentieth century to which the Lincoln experience of 1861-1865 seems especially relevant.

The focus of this work is an interpretation, and to a degree, a reinterpretation of the Lincoln experience. It is based on the premise that who Lincoln was, what he did, and what he meant to do, is best discovered from the testimony of Lincoln himself, certainly insofar as any one source can shed light on the matter. Additional information for the study comes from generally mainstream Lincoln scholarship accumulated over the years.

The purpose here is not to present hitherto unknown facts of the President's life and career. It is rather to reexamine the traditionally accepted perspective on what Lincoln did and how he did it. Naturally, the author assumes all responsibility for errors of commission and omission.

TABLE OF CONTENTS

I

THE UNION IN CRISIS: AN OVERVIEW.

During the decade preceding Lincoln's election, the American political system moved on a path of precipitous decline seemingly in the direction of some momentous catastrophe. The decline coincided, paradoxically it might seem, with tremendous expansion in population, territory, and, above all, the economic capabilities and the technological powers of the nation. But as aggregate wealth, land and people multiplied to new, unprecedented levels, so did also profound underlying divisions and disabling conflicts. As the nation approached the 1860's, it began to resemble a huge vessel whose steering mechanisms were no longer functioning to keep it on a steady course in any particular direction. The passengers and the crew were increasingly at odds with one another. No captain seemed capable of commanding the ship through the hitherto established processes and institutions. In fact, the ship seemed about to founder on the rock of disintegration, as Civil War -- and Abraham Lincoln -- approached.

One of the principal underlying dimensions of the American political crisis was contextual: economic, social, and cultural. While the nation grew bigger and richer, the gap between the South and the North continued to develop disproportionately. In the North, population was increasing at a dramatic pace, much of it fueled by waves of immigration from western and central Europe. By 1860, 87 percent of the foreign-born population resided in the Northern states. To most of these people, the South's basic institution -- slavery -- was a repugnant anachronism. Industrialization, urbanization, and the adaptation of new technologies was progressing quickly and massively in the North. While distinctions of place and degree are certainly in order, there was an undeniable Northern dynamism confronting an equally undeniable, even if relative, material and social stagnation in most of the South. And material and social differences tended to reinforce cultural differences.[1] In the South, there was an increasing sense of isolation, fear, and vulnerability.

Although several slave holding states were added to the Union after 1789, the institution of slavery did not have a comparable importance in all the states. Slavery was not nearly as "solid" an institution in Missouri, Delaware, or Kentucky on the eve of the Civil War as it was in the Deep South. In Missouri, according to the 1860 census, only ten percent of the population was non-white; in Delaware about 19 percent, and in Kentucky 20. In eight southern states -- South Carolina, Mississippi, Louisiana, Alabama, Florida, Georgia, North Carolina and Virginia, this percentage ranged between 58.6 and 34.4. (Note Table 1 below)

Table 1

Slave States with the Largest Percentage of
Black Population According to the 1860 U.S. Census*

Rank	State	Percentage Black Pop.	Entered Union
1	South Carolina	58.6	1789
2	Mississippi	55.3	1817
3	Louisiana	49.5	1812
4	Alabama	45.4	1819
5	Florida	44.6	1845
6	Georgia	44.0	1789
7	North Carolina	36.4	1789
8	Virginia	34.4	1789
9	Texas	30.3	1845
10	Arkansas	25.6	1836
11	Tennessee	25.5	1796
12	Maryland	24.9	1789
13	Kentucky	20.4	1792
14	Delaware	19.3	1789
15	Missouri	10.0	1821

*The original 6 states are listed at 1789.

2

Meantime, California, Illinois, Indiana, Iowa, Maine, Michigan, Minnesota, Ohio, Oregon, Vermont and Wisconsin were added as free states. Kansas was admitted as a free state in January 1861.

According to the U.S. Census figures for 1860, the white population of the 15 slave holding states was only 8,038,000. The so-called colored population was 4,202,000. Together, this amounted to 12,240,000 persons living in the slave states as compared with 19,203,000 in the 19 free states. Since the Constitution allowed each state only three-fifth vote value for each slave or person other than a citizen, the political power ratio between the slave states and the free states was, in one sense, about 10.6 for the former and 19.2 for the latter, a gross decline from the near parity enjoyed by the slave holders of 1790.

In regional terms, this meant that the South was now hopelessly outnumbered in the presidential electoral college; it could control only about 35 percent of the seats in the House of Representatives. In the Senate, the South's margin declined from a 14-12 split of seats in 1790 to a 38-30 division at the beginning of 1861, with the admission of Kansas as a free state in January. Other political consequences, threatening the South's great political influence in the American system were bound to follow. The balance of power, in virtually every imaginable way, in wealth, population and political "clout", which underlay the original American system of 1789 during the Presidency of George Washington, was shifting dramatically, and, to all appearances, inexorably, away from the South in the ensuing decades, and especially during the Presidencies of Millard Fillmore, Franklin Pierce and James Buchanan.

Between 1789 and 1861 fifteen men had filled the office of the President of the United States. Nine of the fifteen were southerners and slaveholders. It is of particular interest that in terms of incumbency, the six northerners, John Adams, John Quincy Adams, Martin Van Buren, Millard Fillmore, Franklin Pierce, and James Buchanan, served a total of only 23 years, while Southerners occupied the position 49 years or, roughly, four fifths of the time.[2]

3

During the Presidency of George Washington, according to the 1790 census, of the three most populous states in the Union, two were slave-holding states: Virginia with 747,610 persons and North Carolina with 393,751. As Isaac Lippincott notes:

> "The center of [the American] population at the time of the first census was 23 miles east of Baltimore, Maryland; during the next seventy years it moved westward more than 356 miles to a point about 20 miles south of Chillicothe, Ohio."[3]

This was a symbolic as well as substantive change of great importance. Between 1790 and 1860, U.S. population increased from 3,929,214 to 31,443,321.[4] In 1790, the population balance between North and South was virtually even, with those living south of Pennsylvania at 1.961 million and those north of Maryland at 1.968 million.[5] By the time of the Civil War, the balance had swung to virtually 2 to 1 in favor of the North.

In 1790, agriculture was the occupation of about 95 percent of the American labor force and the percentage of people living in places of 8000 inhabitants or more was only 3.2 percent.[6] According to the 1860 census, the population of cities over 10,000 (a more demanding standard than that of 1790) was 4,763,757, or roughly 16 percent of the total. Among the top 15 cities of America, in terms of population size, only two were southern -- New Orleans (6) and Louisville (12). By 1860, among the many other changes, the four largest states in the Union were all free states: New York, Pennsylvania, Ohio, and Illinois. Virginia dropped to fifth largest.[7]

By 1860, there was also an increasing economic developmental imbalance. The eastern and midwestern states accounted for some eighty percent of all American capital invested in manufacturing. Between 1840 and 1850, a great upsurge in railroad construction had swept the United States, but virtually eighty percent of it was outside the South. In the same decade, New York City grew by 200,000 to the size of half a million as the nation's largest city. Buffalo and Cincinnati more than doubled during the decade. Chicago and St.

4

Louis grew fivefold. But New Orleans, the only large city in the Deep South, "grew only slightly" and dropped from fourth to fifth among American cities.[8] As Professor James A. Rawley has written recently:

> ..."if one critically examines those eleven states that formed the Confederacy, one finds, certainly from the 1840's on, a distinctive region. It grew nearly all the nation's cotton, owned nine of every ten slaves, held three of every four plantations, was intensely rural, had poor canal and rail connections, was more homogeneous in its population than the rest of the nation, and favored the Democratic ticket. Moreover, what was portentous for the future, it was determined to preserve its way of life based on black servitude."[9]

As economist Isaac Lippincott has observed:

> "The varied industries of [the North] held out great opportunities for laborers of all descriptions. The demand was great, wages were high, and the thrifty, ambitious, resourceful individual enjoyed advantages which he could find in no other part of the country. This applied particularly to immigrants who came to America to better their conditions.... To a large degree the plantation system, with slavery as its outstanding characteristic, inhibited the settlement of immigrants in the South...[as] the newcomer encountered either direct or indirect competition from the...slave [and where] stigma attached to work."[10]

With increasing opportunities of industrialization and urbanization, the North greatly outpaced the South in attracting foreign immigrants. By 1860, the percentage of foreign-born persons in the population was 15.0 in New England; 20.8 in the

5

Middle Atlantic region; 17.3 in the East North Central; 16.0 in the West North Central; 13.8 in the Mountain, and 34.9 in the Pacific.

Meantime, in the three southern regions, South Atlantic, East South Central and West South Central, it ranged from a low of 2.5 to a high of 7.3.[11] From the standpoint of social stability, the rate of immigration was probably no less important than its numbers. For the first thirty years after the establishment of the Union, average annual immigration to the United States was probably only slightly more than 7,700 persons per year.[12] Beginning with the decade of the 1820's, when reasonably accurate figures began to be kept, 151,824 foreign entrants were recorded in the United States in the years between 1821 and 1830. By way of stark contrast, 1,713,251 entered the country between 1841 and 1850, and 2,598,214 between 1851 and 1860.[13] The territory of the United States increased from 892,133 square miles in 1790 to 3,026,000 square miles in 1860.

The number of persons engaged in manufacturing, within enterprises producing output valued at $500 a year or more, rose from 349,000 in 1820 to 1,311,000 in 1860. The value of U.S. manufactured products rose from 483 million dollars in 1840 to about 1.9 billion in 1860.[14] Almost all of this great increase occurred outside the South. In fact, the Southern states accounted for only 8.2 percent of the value of all American manufactures in 1860.[15]

According to Stanley H. Engerman, "the percentage of population in urban areas in 1860 was 36 percent in the Northeast, 14 percent in the North Central states, and 7 percent in the South. Of the total national employment in manufacturing in that year, 72 percent was in the Northeast, 14 percent in the North Central states, and 10 percent in the South."[16]

Economic and social changes in the North brought about new kinds of cultural and political awareness. In 1852 a remarkable cultural and political event took place in the North with the publication of Harriet Beecher Stowe's *Uncle Tom's Cabin*. The

6

book sold some 300,000 copies in the first year of its appearance. It was subsequently turned into a highly popular, widely performed theater play. As John Hope Franklin remarks:

> "Its story of abject cruelty on the part of masters and overseers, its description of the privations and suffering of slaves, and its complete condemnation of Southern civilization won countless thousands over to abolition.... when Southerners counted their losses from this one blow, they found them to be staggering indeed."[17]

One aspect of the developing American society -- North and South -- was the growing self-awareness among the African-American victims of slavery. Fugitive slaves from the South joined in increasing numbers the ranks of abolitionist movements in the North. The reach of new abolitionist efforts within the South itself, the spread of literacy among the slaves, the links with various forms of white-sponsored and supported abolitionism, all these had their important practical effects as mounting challenges to the prevailing Southern institution.[18] There was also significant change of socio-economic roles for many African slaves within the new industrial and commercial establishments of the old South, and these, in a variety of ways, through new exposures, new skills, and new expectations tended to undermine the acceptance of one's lot on the part of the slave.[19]

While the so-called Compromise of 1850 worked out in Congress sidestepped the issue of slavery extension into new American territories, the Kansas-Nebraska Act of 1854 dangerously reopened the whole question. Stephen Douglas' popular sovereignty idea was the guiding light of this piece of legislation which gave the voters of the new territories the right to decide for or against the institution of slavery. The geographic division agreed upon in 1820 was set aside, and abolitionist opinion was greatly alarmed at this development.

Given the great, developing schism in the underlying context of American life, what were the evidences of the political system's malaise? Among the major ones, we find quite a few observed in the histories of other nations in crisis. Germany and Spain in the 1930's; Chile in the 1970's, France and Italy, at various times, all come to mind. Clearly, one element of the American malfunction was radical polarization.

In the North, this was manifested in the increasing strength of militant abolitionism and alternately, of course, the declining proportion of people who might regard the South with benign indifference. The symbolic expression of the North's increasingly militant attitude was highlighted by John Brown's famous raid on the federal armory at Harpers Ferry, Virginia, on October 16, 1859. Though a singular event, it served as a catalyst of Southern fears and suspicions about the future course of North-South relations within the framework of the federal Union. And in the South, polarization expressed itself both in increasing support for secession and also in more assertive, aggressive, militant defenses of the institution of slavery. Here, too, fewer people tended to view the "basic institution" as merely a given, to be used and tolerated simply because it had been there for a long time. More and more, the spokesmen of the South sought to justify and promote slavery on the basis of racial and religious arguments, moving it from the status of tolerated evil to one of desirable principle.[20] Above all, the new Southern militancy demanded the political, moral and legal recognition and sanction of the institution of slavery by the North as the explicit, or implicit, price of further common association.

These sorts of views were illustrated by the bold statement made by John C. Calhoun in a 1854 speech:

> "...I fearlessly assert that the existing relation between the two races in the South, against which these blind fanatics are waging war, forms the most solid and durable foundation on which to rear free and stable political institutions."[21]

And, likewise from the lips of Alexander H. Stephens, Vice-President of the Confederacy in March of 1861:

"The prevailing ideas entertained by [Jefferson] and most of the leading statesmen at the time of the formation of the Constitution were that the enslavement of the African was in violation of the laws of nature, that it was wrong in principle [and that it] would be evanescent and pass away...

...These ideas, however, were fundamentally wrong. They rested upon the assumption of the equality of races.... Our new government is founded upon exactly the opposite idea... that the negro is not equal to the white man; that slavery -- subordination to the superior race -- is his natural and normal condition."[22]

For both sides, the phenomenon of polarization could be described as the decreasing number of participants in the political system willing to "let sleeping dogs lie" and a decreasing number willing to trust the good intentions of the other side. As Rawley reminds us, in 1840 an abolitionist Party calling itself the Liberty Party drew only 7,609 votes in the free states out of some 2.4 million cast in all the states of the Union.[23] By the next decade, the clearly abolitionist vote increased fifty fold. By 1845, the American Methodist Church had split into Northern and Southern branches over the slavery question. The Baptist Church split likewise in 1845. In 1857, the Presbyterians divided analogously.

Polarization in the 1850's was also associated, as in other historic situations, with increasing partisan fragmentation, volatility, and incoherence. The major political parties, Democrats and Whigs, suffered from numerous internal schisms. New parties and factions, such as the American Nativist Party, the so-called Know-Nothings, tended to surface with their various political leaders fishing in troubled waters of a disenchanted, alarmed and confused public opinion. Thus, the conflict "between" was also a conflict "within" or "among."

When the House of Representatives voted in 1848 on the so-called Wilmot Proviso, banning slavery from any of the territories to be acquired from Mexico, 52 Northern Democrats voted for it, all 50 Southern Democrats voted against it, and only 4 Northern Democrats joined them in this opposition. A sectional split was obvious. Pennsylvania's David Wilmot and the Northerners abandoned the old compromise setting the 36 30' line of division between the slave territories and the free. In response to this "radicalization" from the North, John C. Calhoun introduced a resolution in the Senate which denied to Congress the power to exclude slavery from any newly acquired territories. Calhoun called for the South to stand together in protecting its interests and "foresaw" civil war on the course demanded by Wilmot.

Soon, the great Democratic Party was split in three: followers of Polk and the old territorial compromise; supporters of Wilmot seeking total exclusion of slavery from new territories; and the followers of Calhoun altogether denying to Congress the power to exclude slavery. Indeed, the Party shortly split even further as Lewis Cass of Michigan and later, of course, Stephen Douglas, propounded the popular sovereignty idea, i.e., the right of voters in each locality (and it was often a matter of deliberate confusion whether such an entity was any new territory or only a state found out of new territory...) to decide for itself whether it would, or would not, have slavery.

On the eve of the 1848 election, the Democrats' main competition, the Whig Party, was split between so-called "Conscience Whigs" supportive of the Wilmot proviso, and "Cotton Whigs" sympathetic to the Southern cause. The Party nominated a slave owner, General Zachary Taylor, and ignored all pending political issues by offering no platform at all. Partly in reaction to the Whigs' evasion, a Free Soil Party was created, and at its first national convention in Buffalo, New York, it nominated former Democratic President, Martin Van Buren, as its standard bearer. It opposed the extension of slavery and ran on the platform of "Free soil, Free speech, Free labor and Free men." The Free Soil Party captured 10 percent of the national vote, roughly fifty times more than the Liberty Party of 1840. Neither major party was able to control the Congress elected in 1848. The Democrats controlled the Senate. The House of Representatives was nominally controlled by Whigs against Democratic and Free Soil Party opposition. The Presidency was won by the Whigs' Zachary Taylor, the man without a program.

The 1850's witnessed the rise of a kind of mass politics described by William Kornhauser in his 1959 classic, *The Politics of Mass Society*. As Michael Holt has noted recently:

> "...between 1853 and 1856, Know-Nothingism was the fastest growing political movement in the country, though these were also the years that the rival antislavery Republican party began. In an atmosphere of popular hysteria about Catholics, hundreds of thousands of men joined the lodges, including thousands who had never bothered to vote before... by 1855 [the Know Nothings] controlled all the New England states except Vermont and Maine... Only three years after the party began its political activity, Fillmore received a larger share of the popular vote (over 21 percent) than any other third party candidate for president in our history except Theodore Roosevelt in 1912."[24]

On the other hand, the Whigs, who in 1848 not only won the Presidency with Zachary Taylor but controlled 57 percent of the membership of the House of Representatives and 71 percent of the country's governorships, by the end of 1856 "had ceased to exist as a functioning organization."[25] The political conflicts produced another unfortunate and observable phenomenon. They tended to poison political discourse, with more vicious, mutually threatening, angry rhetoric and violent behavior characterizing the exchanges of participants, whether in the media, "on the stump," in the countryside, or in the legislative halls and public meetings of the states and the Union.[26]

11

Inasmuch as fear and anger are not conducive to the processes on which democracy prides itself -- negotiating and bargaining and compromising -- the phenomena of division and embitterment spilled over into the functioning of the formal institutions of government, especially at the federal level.[27] Stalemate and conflict, in a variety of ways, became characteristic of the American Congress during the decade, while the executive branch seemed to exhibit all the qualities of drift, lethargy, and despondency.

Neil McNeil in his book, *Forge of Democracy, The House of Representatives* (New York: David McKay, 1963) describes the House during the 1850's as an institution in crisis, reflecting the crisis of the nation. "Factionalism broke out in the old political parties, splintering Northern and Southern partisans. Violence became common on the floor of Congress. ...Partisanship rankled so bitterly that the chamber at times simply became unmanageable. More than once, there appeared grave danger that the House could not even organize itself by choosing a Speaker." (P. 28)

Ronald M. Peters, Jr. in his book, *The American Speakership: The Office in Historical Perspective* (Baltimore: The Johns Hopkins University Press, 1990) explains the situation as follows:

> "It was the breakup of the party system that caused the paralysis of government reflected in these Speakership elections. During the 1850's America had something like an Italian parliamentary system, divided by numerous splinter parties. The choice of Speaker was tantamount to a vote to organize the government... Under the circumstances, no party could gain a majority, and no coalition of parties adding up to a majority could be formed..."

> Even with a Speaker in place maintaining a minimum degree of order in the House was the most a Speaker could accomplish. Lacking the ability to unite the House for constructive action, the Speakers in the 1850's all sought to prevent it from coming

apart. In an environment in which invective drowned out deliberation, the preservation of a minimal sense of fairness was no small achievement." (P. 48)

According to George B. Galloway's *History of the House of Representatives*, Second Edition (New York: Thomas Y. Crowell Company, 1976) it took 133 ballots and two months' time in 1855 to decide who would be Speaker. Professor Galloway describes the process of election of the Speaker in the 36th Congress which first met on December 5, 1859 but did not elect its Speaker until February 1, 1860 as follows:

"Voting for Speaker proceeded very slowly, amid scenes of uproar and confusion, as the clerk who was presiding declined to decide any questions of order. All such questions were submitted to the House and debated, so that it was impossible to expedite the proceedings. Sometimes only one vote would be taken during a day, the remainder of the time being consumed in passionate arguments. The galleries were packed with partisans of both sides, whose applause and hisses goaded the gladiators on the floor. Members came armed with revolvers and bowie knives, and it looked as if the Civil War might begin in the House itself. Filibustering by the Southern Democrats was chiefly responsible for the long delay in the organization of the House." (P. 49)

A dramatic example of the violent temper afflicting America's legislature of that period was the 1856 caning of Senator Charles Sumner of Massachusetts by Representative Preston Brooks of South Carolina. The beating was sufficiently severe to cause Sumner to pass out in his seat.[28] As Congressmen and Senators literally brandished revolvers and sticks on the floor of the respective legislative chambers, Presidents wrung their hands and generally confined themselves to the most timid uses of their statutory and constitutional powers. The more unsteady the political boat became, the more fearful of rocking the boat became the elected and executive leaders of the American Union.[29]

Millard Fillmore, who became President on July 9, 1850, on the death of Zachary Taylor, was one of those leaders who privately detested, or at least in some sense professed to detest, slavery, but publicly supported its existence for reasons which combined fear of upheaval and disintegration of the Union with a certain dose of one's own political self-interest.

In a letter to Daniel Webster, Fillmore even made the argument once that slavery had to be tolerated ('an evil to be endured') because otherwise the ""last hope of a free government in the world" would be destroyed. Fillmore signed into law the Fugitive Slave Act which, among other things, committed the Federal Government to lend its support, including its military, to recover fugitive slaves escaping from the South to their "rightful owners." The Whig Party split in response to Fillmore's leadership on this issue, and in the 1856 election he became the candidate of the so-called "Know-Nothing" Party. To be sure, some have credited Fillmore with delaying for a decade the break-up of the Union but whatever may be said about the "delay," there was unmistakable evidence that tension continued to increase ominously during and after his administration. In this sense, Fillmore was hardly a successful peacemaker.

When Franklin Pierce ran for President in 1852, the Democrats whom he led, and the opposition Whigs, too, were so badly fractured that hardly any substantive issues were discussed before the voters during his presidential campaign. The eastern elements of the Democratic Party with which the President was identified tended to support slavery in order to keep the peace and to encourage continuing national prosperity. They opposed anti-slavery agitation and sought to appease the South. As Herbert Agar remarks:

> "Instead of insisting on men who upheld the Union
> and the election promises, Pierce put into his

14

Cabinet able and forceful representatives of every diverse opinion. So his Administration was doomed to become a minor civil war within itself."[30]

Agar also supports the view that of "all presidents...none was more insignificant than Mr. Pierce."[31] Pierce included in his Cabinet both Northern businessmen and Southern planters, seeking to pacify by a policy of broad inclusion.[32] He interpreted his election as a mandate to somehow defuse the slavery issue. In this effort, Pierce attempted to mollify the South. He was behind the so-called Ostend Manifesto of 1854 seeking to obtain the island of Cuba from Spain for the U.S. He also supported the Kansas-Nebraska Act of 1854 which opened two new territories for settlement and allowed the popular vote to decide on slavery. Among the opponents of slavery, this was, of course, seen as an unacceptable departure from the Missouri Compromise. It led to the rise of the Republican Party and was instrumental in Pierce being denied renomination by the Democratic Party in 1856.[33]

James Buchanan, the Democrat who succeeded Pierce, was a presidential leader who valued compromise and feared violent conflict. Though a Pennsylvanian, he was ambitious for high office and he, too, coveted Southern support. In 1846 he had opposed the Wilmot proviso because it offended the South by its prohibition of slavery in the territories acquired from Mexico. As a diplomat, he sought to have the U.S. seize Cuba to prevent a slave take-over there, much feared in the South. Buchanan, in office in 1857, attempted to dampen anti-slavery agitation in the North and enforce the 1850 Fugitive Slave Act. He favored the extension of slavery to Kansas under the so-called Lecompton Constitution, not really popular with the bulk of Kansas settlers.

At the very beginning of Buchanan's Presidency, on March 6, 1857, came the fateful Dred Scott decision handed down by the United States Supreme Court. Although -- characteristically for situations of socio-political disarray each of the nine justices wrote a separate opinion -- the majority, by 6 to 3, denied Dred Scott his freedom. Scott and his lawyers had argued that he could not remain

15

a slave since he was being held as such within a free territory. But the Supreme Court disagreed. It declared the Missouri Compromise unconstitutional, claiming that Congress was not empowered to exclude slavery anywhere. Slaves were property and property was protected by the Fifth Amendment to the Constitution. No slave master could be deprived of his property "without due process of Law."

A widely held interpretation of the Dred Scott decision (including Lincoln's) was that it nationalized slavery.[34] No Congress or state legislature could stop it. Justice Taney declared that no Negro had any right "which a white man was bound to respect." Buchanan hoped, naively, that the Court decision would put an end to anti-slavery agitation.[35] In fact, this action by at least one governmental institution in the U.S. which was still capable of making decisions ran contrary to quickly rising currents of Northern public opinion. Instead of calming the waters, the Dred Scott judgment helped to propel the onset of the great storm. Even Stephen Douglas with his popular sovereignty objective, was backed into a political corner by the Court's judgement since the people's right to say "no" to slavery was now being judicially denied.

John Brown's raid on the federal arsenal at Harpers Ferry, Virginia in October 1859 also occurred on Buchanan's watch, and both highlighted and symbolized the gathering tension of the American system on the eve of the Civil War.

> "As John Brown was being hanged, the new Congress met. Once again it took two months to arrange the coalition that finally organized the House under a Republican Speaker. Once again there was a legislative deadlock..."[36]

On February 8, 1861 seven southern states, led by South Carolina, in anticipation of the Lincoln presidency, seceded from the Union. Buchanan adopted the perfectly ambivalent position of opposing secession as unconstitutional but at the same time claiming a lack of means to stop it. The President professed to opt for the maintenance of Union forts and garrisons in federal hands but, typically, when he sent reinforcements in January of 1861 to Fort Sumter, and the secessionists fired on the federal supply ship attempting to provision the fort, Buchanan simply accepted its withdrawal from the scene. He was prepared to hand the problem over to Lincoln.[37]

Buchanan's hand-wringing attitude was reflected in his last message to Congress on December 3, 1860:

> "Apart from the execution of the laws, so far as this may be practical, the Executive has no authority to decide what shall be the relations between the Federal Government and South Carolina..."[38]

Given the occurrence of a grave political crisis -- in the case of the United States in the 1850's -- rising polarization[39]; increasing fragmentation; incoherence and behavioral volatility, embitterment and mounting violence in public discourse; and a consequent enfeeblement of governmental institutions, a new and urgent demand upon the polity was implicitly created.[40] A diagnosis of the situation and application of remedies were urgently required.

In a remarkably perceptive work written a century after the American Civil War, political scientist Chalmers Johnson described the circumstances under which conceivably any society could experience revolutionary tensions. The fundamental condition of such tension in Johnson's view was a dissynchronization between the role structure of the society and its value system. Recognizing that the causes of dissynchronization may be either internal (endogenous) or external (exogenous), or indeed both, Johnson saw the potential for violent upheaval in those societies where roles and values were substantially at odds with one another.

The United States of the 1850's constituted a classic example of such a society. For many years after 1789, the South was able to win fairly dependable Northern acquiescence in the institution of slavery, and, to an impressive degree, it was, in fact, able to impose its leadership upon the American federal system. But what was possible in a largely agrarian society of the late eighteenth century, with relatively limited connections to the external world, and a powerful South, was hardly tenable sixty or seventy years later under very different circumstances of economic, social and cultural change and the relative decline of the South. Washington's Union required the establishment of new socio-political relations, a new equilibrium, in Johnson's phrase. Whether this could be accomplished peacefully and gradually, or violently, or not at all, was a challenge to the American political leadership of Lincoln's time. The Civil War may not have been inevitable but, in retrospect, it was preceded by many portents and warning signals.[41]

What characterized the views of many people in the 1850's and most "run-of-the-mill" politicians, as is the case always, was an inability to recognize that, somehow, the "political game" all around them, the whole process of political interaction within the system, had changed, and that only drastic remedies could bring about a new condition of relative equilibrium. Conventional politicians, precisely men of the caliber of Fillmore, Pierce and Buchanan, were prone to "keep plodding," i.e., continue to apply old methods and old concepts to the management of a fundamentally new situation. The tendency to do this may be seen as a prevalent human inclination to incrementalism. Politicians, as brokers of various group interests, were not especially eager for innovation on a grand scale. Far from it. Innovation imposed costs and risks. The tendency was always to fall back on old methods and established channels in dealing with freshly arising challenges.

In the case of the American politicians of the 1850's, the tendency was to play the game as it had been played heretofore. The leaders attempted to continue democratic politics of earlier years. Bring everyone under one big tent, if possible. If not possible, provide outlets, new parties, for example, for the representation of new shades of public opinion. Appease those with the loudest and most threatening demands, in this case the Southern secessionists or would-be secessionists. Pretend that a fundamental conflict does not exist and perhaps it might go away. Provide some distractions.

Distribute offices. Above all, keep the old political market place going through the conventional processes of elections and legislative assemblies, even if these do no more than bring gun-toting antagonists face to face with one another. Do it hoping that, sooner or later, the shouting matches will subside. It is always very difficult to believe that "normalcy" cannot be maintained, or, if disturbed, that it cannot be restored.

One must have compassionate sympathy, to be sure, for the ordinary participant in the political process and for the ordinary politicians. The diagnosis of an acute crisis is not, and can never be, as simple as taking a patient's temperature. Everyone can use a thermometer and interpret what a reading of it means. The political process is much more complicated and some of its dimensions are, unfortunately for would-be diagnosticians, very qualitative. A correct reading of them may require insight beyond the capabilities offered by a thermometer, a seismograph, or a computer. It may require great quality of statesmanship.[42]

In summary, one might say that the situation confronted by Lincoln on his assumption of the Presidency of the United States was one in which, to use his own words, the government of the people, by the people and for the people -- as it had been constituted up to 1860 -- could no longer function effectively. It had become too dangerous for some and too weak for others. Its services were seen as increasingly unsatisfactory by mutually opposed, seemingly ever larger popular constituencies. It had, in effect, broken down.[43]

Given the understanding that "normalcy" cannot be maintained, the question of remedies involves many possible alternatives, dictated, in part, by a variety of socio-political conditions, but also by the character and insights, and aspirations, of the leader who takes on the role of the principal agent of change. In the twentieth century, different solutions for variously disequilibriated societies were provided by such leaders as Lenin, Mussolini, Hitler, Franco, Mao Tse Tung, Pinochet, Ataturk, and de Gaulle.

Lincoln's understanding that the American system had reached a crossroads beyond incremental tinkering was expressed in his public utterance that the nation could not permanently remain half slave and half free, and that sooner or later it would have to become all one thing or all the other. Here, Lincoln parted company not only with Fillmore, Pierce, and Buchanan, but all fifteen of his predecessors. His publicly professed view that the principles of the Declaration of Independence required that the United States must become all free, delineated the task and made it fit into what we recognize today as a fundamental American ideal.[44] The Civil War represented a second American Revolution, almost certainly much more profound in its domestic, social consequences than was the original War of Independence.

In order to realize the objective of that second revolution, Lincoln was, from the moment of his election, willing to use force if necessary, and he was also willing to depart from the constraints of democratic majoritarianism represented in the old system by the electorate, the Congress, and the states. He was also willing to give a new interpretation to the federal Constitution, one which, with virtual certainly, did not accord with the interpretations of a majority of American voters and politicians of his time.[45]

In doing all this, however, Lincoln intuitively realized the power of a great moral principle, and he sensed that he would likely receive the strong support of an all important plurality (and simultaneously probably, at times at least, majority of the people in the Northern states). He somehow understood that on the great issues of American nationhood and freedom, keeping the Union together while opposing the institution of slavery, he would be able to generate sufficient public support to bring about the necessary changes in the American system.[46] From the evidence of his public pronouncements, it is clear that he was willing to offer his life and career to this great purpose.

Lincoln understood that if, after his election in 1860 or early 1861, the proposition he supported -- an indissoluble federal union with public condemnation of slavery to extinction -- were put to the

20

judgement of the whole American electorate, directly or through its legislative organ, the Congress, it would be rejected. In all likelihood, it would have been rejected because the major implications of this policy, secession of the South *and* Civil War, were becoming increasingly clear. In addition to obvious Southern opposition to his policy, Lincoln would have had to contend with powerful forces of Northern opinion willing to give way on the issue of slavery simply to keep the South in the Union. And if the South could not be appeased, a probably even greater body of Northern opinion would have favored peace over war. It would have been only human.

Faced with the prospect of calamitous losses and the unfathomable risks of war, it would have been quite reasonable for many Northerners, including probably quite a few among that 40 percent who had voted for Lincoln in November, to prefer secession to a bloodbath. If given a choice, they might have been only too glad to embrace the policy of President Buchanan: We deplore secession but we do not believe that we should or can oppose it by violence. One way or the other, the victory would have gone to the Chamberlains of their time.

If in consequence of a majoritarian decision by the "American People," or their representatives within the meaning of the franchise in effect in 1860, slavery became nationalized so as to appease the South, a very short respite from conflict might have been won. In the long run, however, even greater turmoil and unrest throughout the country would have been virtually certain. Free labor within an increasingly modernized Northern economy and society would not have acquiesced in the transplantation of slavery. The rising consciousness of the slaves themselves and their black and white advocates in the North would have continued to grow. There were too many obvious incompatibilities; and if slavery was a grave irritant in the American system even when it only existed in the several southern and border states, it would have been a far more incendiary irritant if it had spread or attempted to spread, pell-mell, North and West.[47]

If, on the other hand, secession had been sanctioned either by Congress or a popular referendum, the prospect of a great, powerful and prosperous American nation would have been fatally undermined. As Lincoln had said in his First Inaugural Address, the path of secession, once entered, would have likely attracted many replicators and imitators: very likely it would eventually attract them not only in the South but in the North as well. Every difference in policy or outlook among and within all the states would have been tempted by the prospect of independence as a fairly obvious way of getting what one wants, when one wants it, just the way one wants it. Could a truncated, fragmented America continue to be the land of opportunity and freedom for all its millions?

In terms of the great American ideals set forth in the Declaration of Independence, either alternative would have been, as Lincoln clearly recognized, fatal. If slavery became nationalized, the principles of freedom and equality of men enunciated by Jefferson would have been rendered total mockery. They might well have become the subject of world ridicule. The dissolution of the Union, on the other hand, would have been a testimonial to their impracticality. Of course, Lincoln was the only American President up to his time to publicly recognize the fact that the maintenance of the United States half-slave and half-free had exposed it to a justified charge of hypocrisy. He proposed to remove the anomaly and to bring the Declaration closer to living reality. In struggling against his own personal, racial prejudice, Lincoln advocated a moral and political rectification of the American Union.

During the 1850's, in the person of Stephen Douglas, Lincoln had encountered a truly modern democrat -- within the franchise laws of the time. Douglas' popular sovereignty doctrine was equivalent to modern conceptions of the "political process" which is alleged to ultimately know all, judge all and settle all. This was a view that the people could have whatever they wanted. Their judgement collectively rendered, and expressed by a majority, was beyond appeal. To this Douglas conception of the omnipotence of political democracy, Lincoln opposed the notion of immanent right, a transhistorical ideal, derived, as with John Locke and Thomas

Jefferson from a certain basic understanding of the nature of humanity. The right to liberty and the pursuit of happiness could presumably no more be denied to a human being by eighty percent of the people than by twenty percent, or even a hundred percent. Ideologically, Lincoln stood on a platform of absolute values of right and wrong.

Whatever may have impelled Lincoln to act as he did, his actions as President were remarkably consistent with the objectives of an indissoluble American Union and the condemnation of slavery to eventual extinction. Lincoln's democratic rhetoric, insisting on ballots not bullets, was ideologically faultless, and with the highlights of the Gettysburg Address and the Second Inaugural, it has become part of a historic treasury of the democratic faith.

In the eyes of posterity, Lincoln saved the Union in the name of democracy. But the content of Lincoln's activity as chief executive, his actual role, was far more contradictory. Even if justifiable in terms of the ends which the means were presumably intended to serve, the President's methods were far more authoritarian than they were democratic.[48] To be sure, Lincoln had some excellent skills in creating certain democratic appearances. He was very good in hearing people out. He was easily approached. It was not difficult to get to talk to the President. Lincoln tended to treat people with a certain genuine sympathy and kindness which were always likely to convey the impression to his interlocutors that the President was taking them seriously. He was good in observing certain minimal proprieties, such as holding Cabinet meetings, even if these had little to do with the determination of his most important policies. Lincoln had an excellent sense of priorities. He dedicated his presidency to the resolution of some great issues.

On matters which lay outside the critical presidential interests, Lincoln was always willing to let appropriate officials, including legislators, do as they might like. He was a large-minded, extraordinarily generous character. He was therefore relatively indifferent to personal criticism. His presidency was free of the kind of suffocating sycophancy characteristic of dictators. He had an

23

extraordinary ability to distinguish between principles and particular, individual cases. Thus, he could be relentless in waging brutal war upon the Confederacy while indulging individual acts of mercy toward various specific persons who may have suffered injury and misfortune during the conflict. This promoted the President's reputation for humaneness.

And Lincoln was certainly thoroughly democratic in his origins and his rhetoric. He was a genuinely poor and obscure son of the people brought to the pinnacle of executive power by the franchise of the American multitudes. He was certainly also one of the most brilliant exponents of the democratic creed in world history.

Avoiding the fallacy of anachronism, i.e., judging nineteenth century actors in terms of criteria accepted in the final years of the present century, Lincoln may still be seen as an authoritarian innovator of the American political system. In brief outline, Lincoln's departures from the "democratic method" may be summarized as follows. The President denied to a substantial number of legitimate participants in the American polity as it existed in 1860, in this case the secessionists, the right of self-definition, including the right of self-determination. With respect to these same participants Lincoln rejected the methods of negotiation and compromise in favor of the alternatives of submission or the use of force.

Faced with the prospect of war and the fact of acute national division, Lincoln prepared his course between November 1860 and March 4, 1861 in autocratic solitude and secrecy. He refused to share the elaboration or even discussion of relevant national policies with any genuinely representative body of opinion, such as the Congress, the leaders of the major political parties, the national media, the state legislatures, or the electorate as a whole in the form of a proposed referendum. The President kept all the cards in his own hands. There was no public dialogue as a precursor to policy enunciated in the First Inaugural. The main features of what may be described as Lincoln's policy in 1860-1861 were all based not on the foundation of majority rule in any genuine sense of the term, but rather on the basis of a very narrowly drawn

Presidential plurality whose validity, as a basis for national policy, even Lincoln himself, in earlier years, had thoroughly rejected.[49]

Lincoln's failure to convoke Congress until July 4, 1861 was only a further indication of the executive's determination to keep the decision-making process very much in his own hands. The President's relief of Fort Sumter, his response to the Confederate attack on it; the series of extraordinary measures ranging from expansion of the Union's military forces and blockade of Southern ports to the Emancipation Proclamation: all this not only lacked the prior approval of Congress; it was not even discussed by the President with the Congressional leaders of his own party.

The suspension of habeas corpus throughout the war in areas outside of immediate military operation provided Lincoln with formidable leverage against domestic opponents of his conduct. The President's disuse of the Cabinet as a collective policy-making body, his refusal to respond to strong demands of American public opinion, North and South, for some form of amicable settlement of the conflict, especially during the bleak times of 1861, 1862 and 1863, and significant election "management", constitute the remaining major elements of the paradoxically authoritarian character of the Lincoln presidency.

REFERENCE

1. See Edward Pessen, "How Different from Each Other Were the Antebellum North and South?" The American Historical Review, vol. 85, No. 5, December 1980, pp. 1119-1149. Note p. 1147 on the "balance". See also Lyle W. Dorsett and Arthur H. Shaffer, "Was the Antebellum South Anti-urban? A Suggestion" in The Journal of Southern History, vol. 38, No. 1, February 1972, pp. 93-100. Jon C. Dawson, "The Puritan and the Cavalier: the South's Perception of Contrasting Traditions" The Journal of Southern History, vol. 44, No. 4, November 1978, pp. 597-614. As the author notes, "Contributors to the major antebellum southern journals ultimately believed that the divided moral and religious heritage of the nation rested upon different philosophical orientations." P. 599. Note Ian R. Tyrell "Drink and Temperance in the Antebellum South: An Overview and Interpretation," The Journal of Southern History, vol. 48, No. 4, February 1982, pp. 485-510, for a discussion of an interesting cultural vector in differentiating between Northern and Southern societies.

2. Note Don E. Fehrenbacher, The South and Three Sectional Crises (Baton Rouge: Louisiana State University Press, 1980) pp. 45-46 on the preponderance of southern influence in other federal political institutions until 1861. Some of the relevant illustrations included 23 speakers of the House of Representatives out of 35; presidents pro tem of the Senate, 24 to 11; attorneys general, 14 to 5; ministers abroad 86 to 54. P. 46. See also Barbara R. de Boinville, Origins and Development of Congress, Second Edition (Washington, D.C.: Congressional Quarterly, Inc., 1982) for an institutional testimonial to the political power of slavery in the first half of nineteenth century America. She notes that former President John Quincy Adams in 1836 offered a petition in the House of Representatives on behalf of some of his Massachusetts constituents to abolish slavery in the District of Columbia. This challenged a practice followed since 1792 of "refusing to receive petitions or memorials on the subject of slavery." The House response to this attempt, apart from abortive impeachment, was to pass a resolution by a vote of 117-68 essentially reasserting the 1792 principle. In 1837, the House of Representatives approved by a 163-18 vote the proposition that "slaves do not possess the right of petition secured to the people of the United States." As late as 1840, the House adopted rules forbidding the consideration of any measure "praying the abolition of slavery." Pp. 112-113. See also W.E.B. DuBois, The Suppression of the African Slave-Trade to the United States of America 1638-1870 (New York: Shocken Books, 1969). This book, first published in 1896, casts a somber light on America's indulgence of the slave trade in the first half of the nineteenth century, Congressional prohibition notwithstanding. Note the

author's reproving conclusion. Pp. 198-199. Obviously, in pre-1860 America it was difficult to divorce the policy from the policy makers and policy implementors...

3. See Isaac Lippincott, Economic Development of the United States (New York: D. Appleton and Company, 1922), p. 130.

4. Ibid, p. 129.

5. Ibid.

6. Ibid, p. 131.

7. Ibid, pp. 131-132.

8. See James A. Rawley, Secession: The Disruption of the American Republic, 1844-1861 (Malabar, Fla.: Robert E. Krieger Publishing Company, 1990) p. 5.

9. Ibid, p. 13.

According to the United States Census Bureau in its Eighth Census of 1860, the fifteen slave holding states, including the rapidly expanding Texas, increased in population between 1850 and 1860 by an aggregate of 27.33 percent. The nineteen free states and seven territories, however, increased by 41.24 percent. Note also Rawley op. cit., pp. 185-188.

As Woodrow Wilson noted, the North changed much more economically, socially, and politically than the South, which seemed to change very little... Epochs of American History, Division and Secession, 1829-1909 (New York: Longman's Green and Co., 1909). Pp. 104-108.

10. Lippincott, op. cit., pp. 134-135. See also Allan Nevins, Ordeal of the Union, A House Dividing, 1852-1857, volume II (New York: Charles Scribner's Sons, 1947) Chapter 7 "The Rising Industrialism," pp. 242-271. "Year by year it rendered the North more powerful in relation to the South..." Pp. 270-271.

11. Ibid, p. 135.

12. Ibid, p. 136. See Donnal V. Smith, "The Influence of the Foreign-Born of the Northwest in the Election of 1860," The Mississippi Valley Historical Review, Vol. 19, No. 1, June 1932, pp. 192-204. Smith's

27

conclusion was that "without the vote of the foreign-born, Lincoln could not have carried the Northwest, and without the Northwest, or with its vote divided in any other way, he would have been defeated." P. 204. In a more narrowly focused study Andreas Dorpalen, "The German Element and the Issues of the Civil War," The Mississippi Valley Historical Review, Vol. 29, No. 1, June 1942, pp. 55-76, argues that for German commercial and financial circles, "secession meant loss of the vast southern market" and they were bitterly opposed to Republicans and Lincoln." P. 65. The author concludes, however, that among German immigrants, support for Lincoln more generally approximated that of "their American-born neighbors." P. 76.

13. Lippincott, op. cit., p. 137.

14. Ibid, p. 198.

15. Ibid, p. 207.

16. See Stanley L. Engerman, "The Effects of Slavery Upon the Southern Economy: A Review of the Recent Debate" Pp. 295-327 in H.G.J. Aitken, Did Slavery Pay? Readings in the Economics of Black Slavery in the United States (Boston: Hougton Mifflin, 1971) p. 320.

17. See John Hope Franklin, From Slavery to Freedom: A History of Negro Americans, Third Edition (New York: A.A. Knopf, 1967) Pp. 266-267. Note the provocative essay by Charles W. Ramsdell, "The Natural Limits of Slavery Expansion" in The Mississippi Valley Historical Review, Vol. 16, No. 1, June 1929, pp. 151-171, in which the author concludes that slavery was an economic system on the way to extinction by the time of the Civil War. "It had reached its limits in both profits and lands. The free farmers in the North who dreaded its further spread had nothing to fear. Even those who wished it destroyed had only to wait a little while -- perhaps a generation, probably less." P. 171. He implies that the Civil War was an unnecessary, very expensive, conflict.

To Ramsdell's judgment one might add just a single qualification, equally applicable, of course, to all of humanity's past conflicts -- if only everyone had been reasonable about everything....

18. Note the account of Nicholas Halasz, The Rattling Chair, Slave Unrest and Revolt in the Antebellum South (New York: David McKay Company, Inc. 1966). According to Halasz, between 1835 and 1840, antislavery "societies" in the North inspired by William Lloyd Garrison alone increased from 200 to 2000. P. 199.

28

19. Note especially Robert Starobin's essay "Race Relations in Old Industries" in Allan Weinstein and Frank O. Gatell (eds.), <u>American Negro Slavery</u> (New York: Oxford University Press, 1968), pp. 299-309.

20. An extensive account is given by Peter Kolchin, "In Defense of Servitude: American Proslavery and Russian Proserfdom Arguments, 1760-1860," <u>The American Historical Review</u>, vol. 85, No. 4, October 1980, pp. 809-827.

21. Rawley, <u>op. cit.</u>, p. 155.

22. <u>Ibid</u>, pp. 248-249.

23. <u>Ibid</u>, p. 4.

24. Michael F. Holt, <u>Political Parties and American Political Development from the Age of Jackson to the Age of Lincoln</u> (Baton Rouge: Louisiana State University Press, 1992) Pp. 113-114.

25. <u>Ibid</u>, p. 237.

26. See Jay Monaghan, <u>Civil War on the Western Border (1854-1865)</u> (Boston: Little Brown and Company, 1955). As the title implies, sporadic fighting between pro-slavery and anti-slavery forces in Kansas predated the outbreak of the Civil War of 1861 by several years. A resident of Lawrence, Kansas, Mrs. Hannah Anderson Ropes, wrote her sister-in-law in Boston on December 2nd of 1855: "Everybody is armed and everybody sleeps with their arms about them and clothes on." P. 39. In May of 1856, Lawrence was sacked, burned, and looted by armed pro-slavery forces. Pp. 56-59. Note especially also Clement Eaton, "Mob Violence in the Old South," <u>The Mississippi Valley Historical Review</u>, vol. 29, No. 3, December 1942, pp. 351-370. As the author observes, "mob violence in the South reached a climax in 1859-1860 after the John Brown raid. "So many acts of violence against anti-slavery men and Northerners in the South took place that Garrison could fill a large pamphlet with Southern atrocities in these two years..." P. 366. Cf. Phillip S. Paludan, "The American Civil War Considered as a Crisis in Law and Order," <u>The American Historical Review</u>, vol. 77, No. 4, October 1972, pp. 1013-1034. Also Harvey Wish, "The Slave Insurrection Panic of 1856," <u>The Journal of Southern History</u>, vol. 5, No. 2, May 1939, pp. 206-222. The author describes the considerable upsurge in the "crop of individual slave crimes reported" and the insecurity of the slave-owning society. He concludes that the "South, attributing the slave plots to the inspiration of Northern

abolitionists, found an additional reason for the desirability of secession..."
P. 222.

27. According to Don E. Fehrenbacher, The South and Three Sectional Crises, op. cit., when Congress convened on December 5, 1859, just after the execution of John Brown, there was such bitterness, that, as one senator put it, "the only persons not carrying a revolver and a knife were those carrying two revolvers." P. 62. See also James Redpath, Echoes of Harper's Ferry (Boston: Thayer and Eldridge, 1860) whose work, celebrating the effort of John Brown, included this observation so relevant to his time: "Agitation is good when it ultimates in action; but not otherwise. Sarcasm, wit, denunciation, and eloquence are excellent preparations for pikes, swords, rifles, and revolvers; but, of themselves, they yet never liberated a Slave Nation in this world, and they never will." P. 6.

28. James T. Currie, op. cit., p. 37; note also N. McNeil, op. cit., p. 314.

29. See Roy F. Nichols, The Disruption of American Democracy (New York: The Macmillan Company, 1948), pp. 306-322 on the disintegration of the Democratic Party and pp. 474-491 on "stalemate in Washington." Also Roy F. Nichols, The Stakes of Power, 1845-1877 (New York: Hill and Wang, 1961) pp. 1-46. Also see Ollinger Crenshaw, "The Speakership Contest of 1859-60, John Sherman's Election a Cause of Disruption?" The Mississippi Valley Historical Review, vol. 29, No. 3, December 1942, pp. 323-338. The author concludes that, on the whole, "historians have been unaware of the extreme gravity of the situation during the speakership struggle, of the bare escape of the American Congress from an indescribable holocaust." P. 333.

30. Herbert Agar, The Price of Union (Boston: Houghton Mifflin, 1951) p. 357.

31. Ibid, p. 356.

32. See Larry Gara, The Presidency of Franklin Pierce (Lawrence: The University of Kansas Press, 1991) p. 79: "Pierce undoubtedly believed that the South had always been the victim of aggression from certain northern interests." And also: "He did not regard slavery as a moral or ethical question; slaveholders had a right to their property, and slaves had no rights at all." P. 78.

33. "Those who play the presidential ratings game have always assigned to Franklin Pierce a below-average score. Thomas A. Bailey rated Pierce 'less than a success, not wholly a failure.' That is about the best one can say about his presidency. He had the bad fortune to come to office at a time when the political system of the founding fathers, with the addition of the two parties, was starting to unravel." Ibid, p. 180.

34. Note the interesting study by F. H. Hodder, "Some Phases of the Dred Scott Case" in The Mississippi Valley Historical Review, vol. 16, No. 1, June 1929, pp. 3-22, which discusses the different, basically fragmented, attitudes of the several justices behind the ultimate, fateful decision. Note Steven Hahn, "Class and State in Postemancipation Societies: Southern Planters in Comparative Perspective," The American Historical Review, vol. 95, No. 1, February 1990, pp. 75-98. The author advances the view that "were it not for secession, the Supreme Court might have effectively 'nationalized' slavery by invalidating all obstacles to slave transit." P. 83. Also Walter Ehrlich, "Was the Dred Scott Case Valid?" The Journal of American History, vol. 55, No. 1, June 1968, pp. 256-265. The author suggests that the case was politically "contrived," but it put the nation on a course to war... Pp. 256-257.

35. Eric Foner and Olivia Mahoney, A House Divided, America in the Age of Lincoln (New York: W.W. Norton, 1990) p. 60. President Buchanan took the position that slavery, after the Dred Scott decision, must be considered legitimate in all territories by "virtue of the Constitution." Note pp. 65-67 on John Brown's raid.

36. Roy F. Nichols, The Stakes of Power 1845-1877 (New York: Hill and Wang, 1961) p. 75.

37. A reasoned defense of Buchanan is offered by Frank W. Klingberg in his study "James Buchanan and the Crisis of the Union," The Journal of Southern History, vol. 9, No. 4, November 1943, pp. 455-474. It is also an implicit reproach to Lincoln. Klingberg says: "In line with his heritage of compromise, with his concept of the importance of congressional representation of public opinion, with his belief in the bargaining rights of a minority, and his conviction that the Union could not be cemented by the blood of its citizens, it is difficult to see how Buchanan could have chosen another course." P. 474. Also Horatio King, Turning On the Light: A Dispassionate Survey of President Buchanan's Administration from 1860 to Its Close (Philadelphia: J.B. Lippincott Company, 1895) pp. 130-142. King, who had served as Postmaster-General in the Buchanan Cabinet, cites the opinion of James Madison, expressed in May of 1787, denying to the federal government the right to use force in order to coerce compliant behavior of individual states, p. 132.

38. Cited by Rawley, op. cit., p. 234.

39. See especially Arnold Whitridge, No Compromise! The Story of the Fanatics Who Paved the Way to the Civil War (New York: Farrar, Straus and Cudahy, 1960). "It is characteristic of fanatics to be so intoxicated by their own logic as to ignore the evidence on the other side." P. 66. Note, however, Whitridge's observation that "Lincoln's inaugural address made it perfectly clear that he had no intention of compromising on any of the critical issues." P. 172. On America's growing polarization of the 1850's, see also William Henry Smith, A Political History of Slavery, volume I (New York: G.P. Putnam's Sons, 1903) Chapter 8, pp. 214-241.

40. Most of these symptoms of crisis are identified in the interesting, lucidly written, book by Norman Stamps, Why Democracies Fail? (Notre Dame, Ind.: Notre Dame University Press, 1957). Stamps discusses the symptoms primarily in relation to European political systems of the twentieth century. As is frequently the case with perceptive conceptual and theoretical constructs, the categories employed by Stamps are readily applicable not only elsewhere, but also both earlier as in the United States c. 1860, and later, as in Chile in 1973.

41. See Chalmers Johnson, Revolutionary Change (Boston: Little, Brown and Company, 1966), pp. 53-58 especially. Relevant literature includes Sebastian de Grazia, The Political Community: A Study of Anomie (Chicago: University of Chicago Press, 1948); Wilbert Moore, "A Reconsideration of Theories of Social Change," American Sociological Review, vol. XXV, No. 4, December 1960, pp. 800-819; Ralf Dahrendorf, "Out of Utopia," The American Journal of Sociology, vol. LXIV, No. 3, September 1958, pp. 120-128 and Lewis Coser, The Functions of Social Conflict (Glencoe, Ill.: The Free Press, 1956).

42. Elbert B. Smith in his The Presidency of James Buchanan (Lawrence: University of Kansas Press, 1975) writes about the fifteenth President: "His blindness to Northern feelings about slavery extension added much to the war spirits that developed in both sections by 1861... His love, admiration, and deep sympathy for Southerners were entirely sincere...but they did not make him an adequate president for all the people... Pierce and Buchanan were elected because most Northern voters were quite ignorant of their pro-Southern views and because the alternatives were [poor]... Was Abraham Lincoln an intelligent choice or a happy accident?" Pp. 196-198.

43. As Professor Ralph Henry Gabriel wrote in 1940: "The roar of the batteries beside Charleston Harbor...announced the defeat of American

political democracy." R.H. Gabriel, The Course of American Democratic Thought (New York: Macmillan, 1940) p. 111.

44. See Legislative Reference Service, Library of Congress, Inaugural Addresses of the Presidents of the United States from George Washington 1789 to Harry S. Truman 1949 (82D Congress, 2nd session, House Document No. 540, Washington, D.C., 1952). Among Lincoln's fifteen predecessors, only James Buchanan mentioned slavery in his inaugural address (pp. 103-105) indicating that while he would abide by the decision of the Supreme Court, popular sovereignty in each territory was his own preference. Lincoln, by his reaffirmation of the Republican platform of 1860 (p. 109), and the reaffirmation of the proposition that slavery is a wrong (p. 114) clearly broke new ground on March 4, 1861. Moreover, Lincoln implicitly asserted the power of a Northern majority over a Southern minority on all issues not expressly settled by the Constitution. He asked "May Congress prohibit slavery in the Territories?... The Constitution does not expressly say." And he went to affirm the majority's right to decide such issues while denying the minority right to either block decisions or secede. (P. 113.)

45. See Douglas J. Hoekstra, "Neustadt, Barber and Presidential Statesmanship: The Problem of Lincoln," Presidential Studies Quarterly, vol. 19, No. 2, Spring 1989, pp. 285-299. He points out that Lincoln's "deepest convictions challenged important aspects of the [American] regime" and suggests that recent so-called models for the understanding of the Presidency in general "are inadequate for this kind of statesmanship." P. 295. Hoekstra observes that "great presidents of extraordinary ambition, such as Lincoln, obviously produce a great strain in a regime which, like our leading analysts of the presidency, is generally oriented to the political behavior of the relatively ordinary." P. 296. Note also, James Chowning Davies, "Lincoln: The Saint and the Man," Presidential Studies Quarterly, vol. 17, No. 1, Winter 1987, pp. 71-94. Davies identifies Lincoln as "a man for all times and places" because "he helped a people think anew and act anew." P. 71. But he also says "If he had not been articulating and if the majority of the American public (!) in the Civil War had not worked with him in acting on egalitarian principles... "the last best hope on earth" would have failed. P. 92.

46. See Paul Findley, A. Lincoln: The Crucible of Congress (New York: Crown Publishers, 1979) who sees Lincoln gradually shifting his position on slavery while in Congress. According to Findley, Lincoln would have been shocked "if one of his colleagues had predicted that most slaves would be freed by executive order in less than twenty years and appalled at the thought that he might give the order." P. 143. According to Findley by 1860 Lincoln "was the voice of moderation. His adamant stand against

extension of slavery coupled with his equally adamant stand against federal interference with slavery where it existed placed him near the broad center of public sentiment." P. 232. Unfortunately, there was no such thing as a "broad center" in 1860, anymore than there was a broad center in Spain in 1936 or in Chile in 1973.

47. See Douglas Dowd, Eli Ginzberg and Stanley Engerman, "Slavery as an Obstacle to Economic Growth in the United States" in Irwin Unger and David Reiners (eds.) The Slavery Experience in the United States (New York: Holt, Rinehart and Winston, Inc., 1970) pp. 195-207.

48. See Stephen John Stedman, "The End of the American Civil War," pp. 164-187, in Roy Licklider (ed.) Stopping the Killing, How Civil Wars End (New York: New York University Press, 1993) for a summary of the argument presented here. Says Stedman: "The historical narratives of McPherson (1982; 1988), Potter (1968; 1975) and Donald (1978) tacitly argue that the Civil War resulted from the inability of American political institutions to resolve conflict as the country's society changed...and the gradual loss of commitment to negotiated settlement and constitutional union." P. 171.

49. See infra, Chapter III.

II

THE LINCOLN PARADOX: ITS MORAL FOUNDATIONS

Although he has been regarded by many as the very embodiment of democratic ideals, Lincoln's moral sense and his personal determination to achieve what is right set him -- the author of the Gettysburg Address -- on a course of unprecedented authoritarian innovation within the context of the American political system. The roots of the Lincoln paradox, its authoritarian content and memorable democratic rhetoric, are to be found -- all confusion to the contrary -- in Lincoln's lifelong aversion to the institution of slavery.

The confusion, it may be noted, arises from the fact that Lincoln's opposition to slavery differed from that of most of the so-called abolitionists of his time; that it was, occasionally, associated with apparent expressions of racial prejudice toward Africans; and that it was also somewhat disguised by Lincoln's own rhetoric, not altogether accurate even if sincere, about the primacy of saving the Union. The latter was most notably put forward in his famous 1862 letter to publisher Horace Greeley where the President said that if it were necessary to save the Union by freeing all the slaves, he would do it, and if he could save the Union by not freeing any of them, he would be willing to do that, too.[1]

In fact, however, Lincoln's willingness to preserve the Union -- amicably -- was always conditioned by his unwillingness to recognize slavery as "rightful," or even "morally indifferent," and by his refusal to see it extended beyond the crest of 1860. It was also predicated on his insistence that slavery be publicly recognized as on its way to ultimate extinction.

From the earliest available evidence, it is clear that Lincoln disapproved of slavery as a moral wrong; that, in so far as he dealt with the subject, he believed that Congress had the power to exclude slavery from new territories and states acquired by the United States, and that indeed Congress ought to so exclude it. Simultaneously, however, Lincoln believed what may be termed the American creed, the fundamental operative values of the American political system, uneasily combined in the Constitution of 1789 and the Declaration of Independence of 1776, as an enormously important ideal of human liberty, betterment, and progress, not only on the North American continent but throughout the whole world; as a derivative or corollary of the latter proposition, Lincoln regarded America's so-called Founding Fathers with exceptional and genuine reverence, most strikingly focusing his intellectual and emotional loyalties upon the figures of Washington, Jefferson, and Madison.[2]

In Lincoln's mind, the evident progress and prosperity of the American Republic, its wealth and population, its territorial extension, its buoyant energy and enterprise, were all linked to the political formula of the Founders. The Declaration and the Constitution were causally associated by Lincoln throughout his life with the great success and seemingly even greater promise of the "American experiment."

But, of course, the great American formula was based on a fundamental contradiction on the very subject which came to dominate Lincoln's career: slavery. The Declaration of Independence declared all men to be born equal and free. The Africans were men. They were human beings. It was difficult to escape the conclusion that the principles of the Declaration applied as much to them as to whites or to any other races. Lincoln himself interpreted the Declaration of Independence in this sense.

But the Constitution of 1789 was quite another matter. It was a completely equal compact between several states in which slavery was a well established institution and several states in which it was not. Within the provisions of the Constitution itself, no disabilities were placed upon slave owners or upon states adhering to the institution of slavery. In the first portion of the document which even alluded to slavery, Article I, section 3, slaves were euphemistically referred to as "other persons" for purposes of determining each state's congressional representation; and this part of the Constitution, in effect, rewarded slavery because it allowed three fifths of the number of slaves ("other persons") to be added to the number of free persons in calculating each state's representation in the lower house of Congress.

Article I, section 9, declared that "the immigration or importation of such persons as any of the States now existing shall think proper to admit, shall not be prohibited by the Congress prior to the year one thousand eight hundred and eight but a tax or duty may be imposed on such importation, not exceeding ten dollars for each person," This provision left the door open to the eventual prohibition of the slave trade by the Congress, but apart from leaving the door open, the provision actually guaranteed the slave states that for about nineteen years after the ratification of the Constitution, the Union would certainly not prohibit the slave trade. Section 9 could not be reasonably construed as *mandating* an obligation upon Congress to stop the slave trade nineteen years thence.

In the third reference to slavery in Article IV, section 3, the Constitution actually obligated all states to deliver up fugitive slaves to their "rightful" masters. If the Constitution had been written by men who were truly hostile to the practice of slavery, it is all but impossible to deduce this from the language of the final product agreed upon in 1787 and ratified in 1789. Not a single phrase or word in the Constitution condemned slavery or indicated that it should be either terminated or limited in any manner whatever.

When Lincoln became President, he, like all other chief executives, took the oath to preserve, protect and defend the Constitution of the United States. Ratified by all the states, the Constitution had a legal-political force not even approximated by the philosophical musings of the great Declaration of 1776. Lincoln's heart, nevertheless, belonged much more to the Declaration than to the Constitution, although he never admitted to any real conflict between the two. Lincoln always attempted to reconcile affinity and obligation.

The practical resolution in Lincoln's mind of the contradiction --
between the Declaration and the Constitution -- manifested itself in
the two absolutes of his career. Lincoln would never countenance
the legitimization of slavery. But he would never countenance the
dissolution of the Union. He sought to end slavery while also
maintaining the Union. He, in fact, refused to sacrifice one
objective to the other. In consequence of this "dual loyalty,"
Lincoln, even as President and at war with the Confederacy, always
lagged in his emancipation policies beyond the demands of radical
abolitionists.[3]

Lincoln first tasted success in the practice of politics when he was
elected to the Illinois legislature in 1834 at age 25. On March 3,
1837, at age 28, Lincoln co-sponsored a protest resolution, with one
Dan Stone, on the subject of slavery. The resolution reads in part:

> "They believe that the institution of slavery is
> founded on both injustice and bad policy; but that
> the promulgation of abolition doctrines tends rather
> to increase than to abate its evils;"

> "They believe that the Congress of the United States
> has no power, under the Constitution, to interfere
> with the institution of slavery in the different
> States."

> "They believe that the Congress...has the power,
> under the constitution, to abolish slavery in the
> District of Columbia; but that that power ought not
> to be exercised unless at the request of the people of
> said District."[4]

For the next quarter of a century, Lincoln remained faithful to the
principles he had espoused at age 28. His 1837 reference to the
consent of the people of the District of Columbia could be only
hastily considered a concession to the later "popular sovereignty"
doctrine of Stephen A. Douglas. In fact, the District of Columbia
was an area in which slavery had already existed at the time of the

adoption of the Constitution, and Lincoln was, characteristically, careful not to deny arbitrarily to anyone whatever the law may have conferred upon them, slave ownership included. He attached great value to law as a means of regulating human conduct, and as an agency of reform; and he urged obedience to law as a necessary American religion.[5]

In a letter to Mary Speed, a friend, Lincoln wrote on September 27, 1841, that he had witnessed the transport, on board of a boat, of "twelve negroes" from Kentucky to a farm farther South. They were chained, Lincoln said, six and six together. He was impressed how cheerful they were even though "they were being separated forever from the scenes of their childhood, their friends, their fathers and mothers, and brothers and sisters, and many of them, from their wives and children, and going into perpetual slavery where the lash of the master is proverbially more ruthless...than any other."

Lincoln reflected that evidently "God renders the worst of human conditions tolerable while He permits the best, to be nothing better than tolerable."[6] These private reflections of the future President did not venture into any policy questions. But they indicated a sense of empathy with slaves as human beings which was to prove very important for the later Lincoln.

More of Lincoln's views about slavery and the American Republic emerges from two communications early in his career. The first of these came in a speech to the Temperance Society at Springfield, Illinois on February 22, 1842. Here, Lincoln said:

> "Of our political revolution of '76 we all are justly
> proud. It has given us a degree of political freedom,
> far exceeding that of any other of the nations of the
> earth. In it the world has found a solution of that
> long mooted problem, as to the capability of man to
> govern himself. In it was the germ which has
> vegetated, and still is to grow and expand into the
> universal liberty of mankind."[7]

and when the victory shall be complete -- when ,re shall be neither a slave nor a drunkard on the ,arth -- how proud the title of that Land -- how nobly distinguished that People..."[8]

And, in a private letter to an abolitionist in 1845, Lincoln, at age 36, wrote as follows:

"I hold it to be a paramount duty of us in the free states, due to the Union of the States, and perhaps to liberty itself (paradox though it may seem) to let the slavery of the other states alone; while, on the other hand, I hold it to be equally clear, that we should never knowingly lend ourselves directly or indirectly, to prevent slavery from dying a natural death -- to find new places for it to live in, when it can no longer exist in the old."[9]

In a speech given in Worcester, Massachusetts, twelve years before his election as President, Lincoln said that:

..."the people of Illinois agreed entirely with the people of Massachusetts...that slavery was an evil, but that we were not responsible for it and cannot affect it in States of this Union where we do not live. But, the question of the extension of slavery to new territories of this country, is a part of our responsibility and care, and is under our control."

Then a Whig Congressman from Illinois, Lincoln publicly declared himself opposed to the extension of slavery in 1848.[10]

On January 10, 1849, Lincoln introduced a Resolution in the House of Representatives, once again, proposing the abolition of slavery in the District of Columbia.[11]

On July 6, 1852, about two weeks after the death of Henry Clay, Lincoln delivered a public eulogy in honor of the great statesman.

Giving every indication that he identified with Clay as his own personal hero, Lincoln commended at length his views on slavery. He admitted that Clay himself had actually been a slave owner. But he praised him for lifelong opposition in principle to the institution of slavery and also for his rejection of militant abolitionism.[12] In a view characteristic of his utterances, Lincoln argued that Clay was ..."cast into life where slavery was already widely spread and deeply seated, [and] he did not perceive, as I think no wise man has perceived, how it could be at *once* eradicated, without producing a greater evil, even to the cause of human liberty itself."[13] That greater evil to Lincoln was in large part, presumably, the rending of the American Constitution and Union. In the same speech he advanced the proposition that "Africa's children" should be returned to Africa, once slavery had been ended. This notion Lincoln also found in views expressed by Henry Clay in 1827, and Lincoln likened the American slaves to the ancient Hebrews who were held in Egypt against their will for four hundred years. He called slavery "dangerous" and expressed the hope that the curses which befell the Pharaoh would not befall the American Republic.[14]

Although he often condemned "abolitionism" and nearly always emphasized that his opposition to the extension of slavery was not the advocacy of its forcible extinction in the South, Lincoln never discussed his reasons with any specificity. He alluded to amorphous dangers and disruptions which radical abolitionism would somehow bring about. In one of his most famous "explanations," Lincoln used highly allegorical reasoning to make his point. In a speech in Hartford, Connecticut on March 5, 1860, Lincoln offered this explanation of why he would not attack slavery in the South head-on:

"for instance, out in the street, or in the field, or on the prairie I find a rattlesnake. I take a stake and kill him. Everybody would applaud the act and say I did right. But suppose the snake was in a bed where children were sleeping. Would I do right to strike him there? I might hurt the children or I might not kill but only arouse and exasperate the snake, and he might bite the children. Thus by meddling with him here, I would do more hurt than good. Slavery is like this. We dare not strike at it where it is... The question that we now have to deal with is, 'Shall we be acting right to take this snake and carry it to a bed where there are children?"[15]

Lincoln's listeners were left to wonder who the children were, and how exactly the snake would hurt them if anyone tried to "attack" the snake, or perhaps "remove" the snake, from the "bed" in which it was allegedly resting.

A remarkable aspect of Lincoln's lifelong argument against slavery was that it was always couched in moral, political and constitutional terms. Never once did Lincoln venture into the presumably important economic aspects of slavery. What effect did it have on the South and the nation as a whole? What might be the likely consequences, and perhaps advantages, of its eventual abolition? How would it affect ordinary workers and farmers, as well as merchants and manufacturers both North and South? To these obvious bread-and-butter issues, Lincoln remained serenely indifferent. He was interested in settling the great question on the basis of right as against wrong, letting other people ponder the economic implications of the problem.[16]

In a document probably drawn up sometime in the summer of 1854, Lincoln wrote that "although volume upon volume is written to prove slavery a very good thing, we never hear of the man who wishes to take the good of it, by being a slave himself."[17] In a contemporaneous paper, Lincoln considered the rationale of slavery by color, intelligence, and interest, grounds commonly advanced by its American proponents. He wrote that if color were to be the criterion of freedom, "By this rule, you are to be slave to the first man you meet, with a fairer skin that your own;" if intelligence, "you are to be slave to the first man you meet with intellect superior to your own;" and if interest, "if you can make it your interest...he can make it his interest...to enslave you."[18]

When Lincoln debated Stephen Douglas in Peoria, Illinois on October 16, 1854, he continued to uphold the views he had now publicly expressed for many years. In Peoria, Lincoln combined two seemingly contradictory but actually reinforcing trends of thought. On the one hand, his repudiation of slavery on moral grounds was unequivocal. He, in fact, declared his attitude toward mere *indifference* to slavery in the following terms:

> "This declared indifference, but as I must think, covert real zeal for the spread of slavery, I can not but hate. I hate it because of the monstrous injustice of slavery itself. I hate it because it deprives our republican example of its just influence in the world -- enables the enemies of free institutions with plausibility, to taunt us as hypocrites...because it forces so many really good men amongst ourselves into an open war with the very fundamental principles of civil liberty -- criticising the Declaration of Independence, and insisting that there is no right principle of action but self-interest."[19]

On the other hand, Lincoln was expressing a certain compassion for the South and an understanding of the predicament, all of which, at first sight, might seem a concession to evil. Lincoln went on to say:

> ..."I think I have no prejudice against Southern people. They are just what we would be in their situation. If slavery did not now exist amongst them, they would not introduce it. If it did now exist amongst us, we should not instantly give it up. This I believe of the masses north and south."[20]

He acknowledged that there were individual exceptions with some people favoring abolition in the south, and some northerners willing to go south and become "cruel slave masters."[21]

He added:

43

"When southern people tell us they are no more responsible for the origin of slavery, than we, I acknowledge the fact. When it is said that the institution exists; and that it is very difficult to get rid of it, in any satisfactory way, I can understand and appreciate the saying. I surely will not blame them for not doing what I should not know how to do myself. If all the earthly power were given me, I should not know what to do, as to the existing institution. My first impulse would be to free all the slaves, and send them to Liberia -- to their own native land. But a moment's reflection would convince me, that whatever of high hope, (as I think there is) there may be in this, in the long run, its sudden execution is impossible. If they were all landed there in a day, they would all perish in the next ten days; and there are not surplus shipping and surplus money enough in the world to carry them there in many times ten days..."[22]

The problem was full of difficulty, Lincoln argued.

"What then? Free them all, and keep them among us as underlings? Is it quite certain that this betters their condition? I think I would not hold one in slavery, at any rate; yet the point is not clear enough for me to denounce people upon."[23]

Lincoln declared himself personally unwilling to make the slave his political and social equal.[24] He did not believe most whites were prepared to see this happen either, but, characteristically, he argued that:

"Whether this feeling accords with justice and sound judgment, is not the sole question, if indeed, it is any part of it. A universal feeling, whether well or ill-founded, cannot be safely disregarded."[25]

It was characteristic of Lincoln, and also very persuasive, and in this sense "politic" of him, that he shunned the stances of zealots and doctrinaire fanatics. To have appreciated the Southern predicament, while declaring the moral evil of slavery, was to have shown himself a reasonable and perhaps even sagacious observer. Human nature was not radically different between north and south, with all those on one side of the line "good" and all those on the other side "bad." Lincoln distinguished between the weight of established institutions and the morality of individuals. He did not idealize Northerners and villify Southerners. In fact, his view of mankind generally was somber. Lincoln was characteristically able to put himself in the position of other "real-life" people.

He did not give himself airs of moral or intellectual superiority. His remark about not knowing what to do if all earthly power were his, was the thoughtful response of a man who refused to rush into judgments of enormously complex problems.[26] It was the sort of statement which set Lincoln apart from political zealots, and it greatly promoted his credibility as a statesman among the more moderate anti-slavery Northerners, who might recoil from deceptively simple and perhaps dangerous solutions of doctrinaire reformers. Lincoln could show that while resettlement of the slaves in Africa *could* be *a* long term solution of the liquidation of slavery in America, it was hardly a ready-made, practical policy option. Still, he insisted that he would not uphold slavery just because the solution to the problem of its abolition was difficult or uncertain.

While Lincoln professed his own prejudices toward the Africans with respect to full social and political equality in the American system, and linked these with the prejudices of others, it was Lincoln's great insight to ask the question whether "this feeling accords with justice and sound judgment...if indeed, it is any part of it." He was a statesman because he understood the enormous importance of public opinion, including its least attractive prejudices, for the possibilities of political action and policy. But he was simultaneously free of a kind of democratic idiocy which identifies prevalent popular opinion, however deeply held, with the summit of human wisdom, and the ultimate boundary of public policy. Lincoln was not a mechanistic democrat of a modern kind whose governing sanction in life is a contrivance called the "political process": a market place arrangement where some tug and others pull, and somehow, something *ipso facto* sacred emerges. Yet, he was not prepared to write off the process as irrelevant either.

It may be fairly speculated upon that Lincoln's great admiration and emotional attachment to the Founding Fathers, especially Washington, Jefferson, Madison, and in a somewhat later period, Henry Clay, influenced his rather peculiarly balanced stand on the slavery question. These were men whom he revered and hoped to emulate. Yet, all these men were also slave owners, and they all, whether formally or practically as in the case of Clay, "signed on" to the compact of 1789. This probably encouraged Lincoln's ambivalence on the slavery question with respect to his oft-repeated "understanding of the practical difficulties" of abolishing slavery; sympathy for southerners more generally; unwillingness to interfere with slavery where it already exited; desire to end slavery gradually rather than suddenly; and with considerable regard to the "property interests" of slave owners.[27]

All these tendencies in Lincoln's thinking, alongside his understated principled rejection of slavery, manifested themselves not only in his rhetoric, but, clearly and importantly, in his conduct as President between 1861 and 1865. It was also one of Lincoln's problems that having identified his heroes, he was always compelled to somehow justify and explain away their failings on the issue which he regarded as so important. They agreed to the maintenance of slavery in 1787 because there was not much chance of a promising American Union without such an agreement. They may have been personally involved as slave owners, but that was because this was a pervasive, well entrenched institution all around them. Actually, the Founders all hoped to see slavery ended, Lincoln argued, and his evidence here rested on pronouncements and, in some cases, votes cast on the issues of prohibiting the further importation of slaves and the extension of slavery into new territories. Lincoln was so taken up with the legacy of the "Fathers" that, in effect, he used his interpretation of what the Fathers really wanted as a counterweight to the naked language of the Constitution itself, and certainly also the interpretations of the Constitution by a majority of his contemporaries and fellow citizens.

Whatever Lincoln's prudential reservations, misgivings, and objections to hasty or radical actions, there is no mistaking his profound moral conviction on the issue of principle. Lincoln would not accept the legitimacy of slavery. In his debates with Stephen Douglass during the 1850's he generally sought to emphasize how he differed from his opponent precisely on the grand question of principle.

Thus, in a speech given on May 18, 1858 in Edwardsville, Illinois, Lincoln reproached Stephen Douglas in the following terms:

> "He tells us, in this very speech, expected to be so palatable to Republicans, that he cares not whether slavery is voted down or voted up. His whole effort is devoted to clearing the ring, and giving slavery and freedom a fair fight. With one who considers slavery just as good as freedom, this is perfectly natural and consistent." ..."Republicans...think slavery is wrong; and that like every other wrong which some men will commit if left alone, it ought to be prohibited by law."[28]

And further on:

> "I am glad Judge Douglas has, at last, distinctly told us that he cares not whether slavery be voted down or voted up. Not so much that this is any news to me; nor yet that it may be slightly new to some of that class of his friends who delight to say that they 'are as much opposed to slavery as anybody.'"[29]

"Nebraskaism," as Lincoln put it, was invented in 1848 and fished out six years later by Judge Douglas who called it the "sacred right of self-government."[30] But the right to make another man one's slave was not self-government, Lincoln said, in his understanding of that term. "To call it so is...absurd and ridiculous."[31]

A key to Lincoln's character and to his quest is contained in a Fragment on the Struggle Against Slavery written sometime in July 1858. Here, Lincoln makes clear that the cause is much more important than office and the contribution to the cause must for him take precedence over success in the quest for public office.

"I have never professed an indifference to the honors of official station; and were I to do so now, I should only make myself ridiculous. Yet I have never failed -- do not now fail -- to remember that in the republican cause there is a higher aim than that of mere office. I have not allowed myself to forget that the abolition of Slave-trade by Great Britain, was agitated a hundred years before it was a final success; that the measure had its open fire-eating opponents; its dollar and cent opponents; its inferior race opponents; its negro equality opponents; and its religion and good order opponents; that all these opponents got offices, and their adversaries got none. But I have also remembered that though they blazed, like tallow-candles for a century, at last they flickered in the socket, died out, stank in the dark for a brief season, and were remembered no more, even by the smell. School-boys know that Wilberforce, and Granville Sharp[e] helped that case forward; but who can now name a single man who labored to retard it? Remembering these things I cannot but regard it as possible that the higher object of this contest may not be completely attained within the term of my natural life. But I can not doubt either that it will come in due time. Even in this view, I am proud, in my passing speck of time, to contribute an humble mite to that glorious consummation, which my own poor eyes may not last to see."[32]

In a speech delivered in Chicago on July 10, 1858, one day after Douglas, Lincoln said that the Union survived eighty two years because people had reason to think that slavery was on its way to extinction.

"I have always hated slavery. I think as much as any Abolitionist. I have been an Old Time Whig. I have always hated it, but I have always been quiet about it until this new era of the introduction of the Nebraska Bill began. I always believed that everybody was against it, and that it was in the course of ultimate extinction."[33]

"I do not claim, gentlemen, to be unselfish, I do not pretend that I would not like to go to the United States Senate, I make no such hypocritical pretense, but I do say to you that in this mighty issue, it is nothing to you -- nothing to the mass of the people of the nation, whether or not Judge Douglas or myself shall ever be heard of after this night; it may be a trifle to either of us, but in connection with this mighty question, upon which hang the destinies of the nation, perhaps it is absolutely nothing..."[34]

On July 17, 1858 in Springfield, Lincoln said that Stephen Douglas was a man of "world wide renown." He was expected by his supporters to become President of the United States soon.[35] And he added: "On the contrary, nobody has ever expected me to be President. In my poor, lean, lank, face nobody has ever seen that any cabbages [of political patronage...] were sprouting out."[36]

But he also said:

"I adhere to the Declaration of Independence. If Judge Douglas and his friends are not willing to stand by it, let them come up and amend it. Let them make it read that all men are created equal except negroes.... I have said...that all men are equal...in their right to 'life, liberty, and the pursuit of happiness.'"[37]

In a document drawn up around August 1, 1858 Lincoln asserted his definition of democracy in these terms:

"As I would not be a slave, so I would not be a master. This expresses my idea of democracy. Whatever differs from this, to the extent of the difference, is no democracy."[38]

On August 17, 1858, Lincoln's remarks in a speech at Lewistown, Illinois, were recorded as follows:

"Think nothing of me -- take no thought for the political fate of any man whomsoever -- but come back to the truths that are in the Declaration of Independence. You may do anything with me you choose, if you will but heed these sacred principles. You may not only defeat me for the Senate, but you may take me and put me to death. While pretending no indifference to earthly honors, I *do claim* to be actuated in this contest by something higher than an anxiety for office. I charge you to drop every paltry and insignificant thought for any man's success. It is nothing; I am nothing; Judge Douglas is nothing. But do not destroy that immortal emblem of Humanity -- the Declaration of American Independence."[39]

Lincoln's concentration on the "moral issue of slavery," beyond all other considerations, and always in the context of the Founding Fathers' Design and the Declaration of Independence, is reflected in all his encounters with Douglas. An outstanding example is the oratorical confrontation between the two on October 13, 1858 at

Quincy, Illinois, roughly within a fortnight of the Senate election. Here, Lincoln once again chided Douglas for his moral indifference to the institution of slavery. He pointedly thumbed the Judge "for his public annunciation here today, to be put on record, that his system of policy in regard to the institution of slavery contemplates that it shall last forever."[40]

Lincoln argued that the founders of the American Union "did not make this nation half slave and half free." They were saddled with the institution of slavery and they "knew of no way to get rid of it at that time."[41] But, Lincoln argued, "when the fathers of the government cut off the source of slavery by the abolition of the slave trade, and adopted a system of restricting it from the new Territories where it had not existed, I maintain that they placed it where they understood, and all sensible men understood, it was in the course of ultimate extinction."[42]

This was the gist of Lincoln's invocation of the Founders on the issue of slavery. Lincoln looked to the Founders not for what they settled, or did not settle, in the Constitution of the United States, but rather to the positions which they had supported on policy issues after the adoption of the Constitution. These positions he linked with his favorite catechism, the Declaration of Independence. On September 16, 1859 in a speech at Columbus, Ohio, Lincoln spoke of the Founders:

> ..."Not only did they [oppose any extension of slavery] but they stuck to it during sixty years, through thick and thin, as long as there was [even] one of the revolutionary heroes upon the stage of political action. Through their whole course, from first to last, they clung to freedom."[43]

Lincoln admired the Founders for their fidelity to the principles of liberty, and argued that the Declaration of Independence was a sum of "definitions and axioms of a free society" -- whose alternative would be ultimately despotism. In a letter written in April of 1859 Lincoln concluded:

51

"All honor to Jefferson -- to the man who, in the concrete struggle for national independence by a single people, had the coolness, forecast, and capacity to introduce into a merely revolutionary document, an abstract truth, applicable to all men and all times, and so to embalm it there, that to-day, and in all coming days, it shall be a rebuke and a stumbling block to the very harbingers of re-appearing tyranny and oppression."[44]

In the October debate with Douglas, Lincoln had said:

"When Judge Douglas asks me why [slavery] cannot continue as our fathers made it, I ask him why he and his friends could not let it remain as our fathers made it?"[45]

Referring to economic changes since the founding of the United States, Lincoln said:

"Judge Douglas could not let it stand upon the basis upon which our fathers placed it, but removed it and put it upon the cotton gin basis."[46]

Lincoln added that he did not mean to interfere with the institution of slavery in any of the states where it was already adopted.[47]   But, he indicated his opposition to the Dred Scott decision of the U.S. Supreme Court prohibiting states from excluding slavery on their territories. Rather tellingly, he said:

..."Judge Douglas understands the Constitution according to the Dred Scott decision, and he is bound to support it as he understands it.   I understand it another way, and therefore I am bound to support it in the way in which I understand it."[48]

On October 15, 1858, Stephen Douglas declared in Alton, Illinois in his last debate with Lincoln, that

..."we live in a confederacy of sovereign and equal States, joined together as one for certain purposes."[49]

..."in my opinion this government can endure forever divided into free and slave states as our fathers made it..."[50]

..."This Union was established on the right of each State to do as it pleased on the question of slavery and any other question..."[51]

And further:

"If the people of any...territory desire slavery let them have it. If they do not want it let them prohibit it.[52] It is their business not mine. It is none of your business in Missouri whether Kansas shall adopt slavery or reject it."[53]

"I hold that there is no power on earth, under our system of government, which has the right to force a constitution upon an unwilling people."[54]

"I hold that it is a violation of the fundamental principles of this government to throw the weight of federal power into the scale, either in favor of the free or the slave States. Equality among all the States of this Union is a fundamental principle in our political system."[55]

"I hold that the signers of the Declaration of Independence had no reference to negroes at all when they declared all men to be created equal. They did not mean negro, nor the savage Indians, nor the Fejee Islands, nor any other barbarous race."[56]

...peace will be achieved when each state minds its own business...

It was in this debate that Lincoln denied any intention of seeking social equality for, or bestowing equal citizenship upon the "Negro;" and it was in this debate, too, that he insisted, interestingly if not altogether convincingly, that the Founders referred to "slavery" and "Negroes" in the Constitution in oblique terms precisely because they "expected and intended the institution of slavery to come to an end."[57] He claimed to "propose nothing more than a return to the policy of the fathers" in which it is understood that slavery "is a wrong and should grow no larger."[58] Lincoln went on to affirm that people do not have a right to do wrong, and that, specifically, "if slavery is wrong one cannot say people have a right to do wrong."[59] By his own definition, however, Lincoln was still willing to let people do "wrong" in those states where slavery had already existed but not do any new "wrong" in freshly acquired territory and states. Once again, fidelity to the constitutional compact seemed a constraint.

On the other hand, given Lincoln's position, it was not really surprising that in their last debate, Stephen Douglas attacked him as follows:

> "Mr. Lincoln proposes to govern the territories without giving the people a representation, and calls on Congress to pass laws controlling their property and their domestic concerns without their consent and against their will. Thus, he asserts for his party the identical principle asserted by George III and the tories of the Revolution."

> "I hold that the people of a territory, like those of a State, have the right to decide for themselves whether slavery shall or shall not exist within their limits."[60]

Lincoln's interpretation of Douglas' Popular Sovereignty was that "if one man would enslave another, neither that other, nor any third man, has a right to object." True popular sovereignty according to Lincoln, could only exist consistent with the principles of the great Declaration.[61]

On October 18, 1858, Lincoln addressed a letter to James N. Brown, a member of the Illinois legislature from Sangamon County. Here, Lincoln put his views in these terms:

> "I believe the declaration [of Independence] that 'all men are created equal' is the great fundamental principle upon which our free institutions rest; that negro slavery is violative of that principle; but that, by our frame of government, that principle has not been made one of legal obligation; that by our frame of government, the States which have slavery are to retain it, or surrender it at their own pleasure; and that all others -- individuals, free-states, and national government -- are constitutionally bound to leave them alone about it."[62]

Lincoln argued that recognition of slavery was a necessity imposed by its *de facto* existence when the government "was framed."[63] But this was not the case with any newly acquired territories, and in these the principles of the Declaration should be respected.[64]

On October 22, 1858 Lincoln spoke in Carthage, Illinois, defending himself against a charge by Douglas that he was somehow corruptly beholden to the Central Railroad Company and that if elected he would relieve that company of its legal obligation to pay taxes to the state of Illinois.[65] It was the only speech Lincoln had made during the whole campaign which was not focused on the slavery question.

Unlike modern office-seekers and campaigners, Lincoln single-mindedly pursued the one great issue, moral and political, which always interested him. Such singlemindedness would, no doubt, disqualify him from seeking high office in the America of the 1990's, when lack of interest and knowledge about a variety of issues important to at least some voters would be taken as evidence of incompetence and unfitness. Lincoln not only did not raise other issues than slavery in his 1858 speeches (with the exception of the occasion mentioned above). He even refused to answer questions on other topics disclaiming knowledge of them.[66] It was one of the great coincidences of American and world history that Abraham Lincoln's most passionate interest also turned out to be, ultimately, the question of the age.

Lincoln's last speech of the campaign came on October 30, 1858 in Springfield. In it, he summed up the themes he had developed during the previous weeks:

> ..."I have neither assailed, nor wrestled with any part of the constitution. The legal right of the Southern people to reclaim their fugitives I have constantly admitted. The legal right of Congress to interfere with their institution in the states, I have constantly denied. In resisting the spread of slavery to new territory, and with that, what appears to me to be a tendency to subvert the first principle of free government itself my whole effort has consisted. To the best of my judgment I have labored *for*, and not *against* the Union. As I have not felt, so I have not expressed any harsh sentiment towards our Southern brethren. I have constantly declared, as I really believed, the only difference between them and us, is the difference of circumstances."[67]

And critically, Lincoln concluded:

> "I claim no insensibility to political honors; but today could the Missouri restriction be restored, and the whole slavery question replaced on the old ground of 'toleration' by necessity where it exists,

56

with unyielding hostility to the spread of it, on principle, I would, in consideration, gladly agree, that Judge Douglas should never be *out*, and I never *in*, an office, so long as we both or either, live."[68]

A letter written to Susan G. Henry, on November 19, shows this typical Lincoln reflection:

"I am glad I made the late race. It gave me a hearing on the great and durable question of the age, which I could have had in no other way; and though I now sink out of view, and shall be forgotten, I believe I have made some marks which will tell for the cause of liberty long after I am gone."[69]

That statement contained a number of vintage Lincoln themes -- focus on the great issues worth fighting for; a sense of despondency over being forgotten; and, above all, the reference to one's own mortality in the context of an immortal cause.[70]

Although Lincoln lost, he actually polled more votes than Douglas by a margin of about 50 percent for Lincoln and 48 percent for Douglas, but in terms of the electors voting to choose a senator, Lincoln lost by a margin of 54 to 46; this was largely on account of the uneven distribution of the population and votes in the districts selecting the legislature.[71]

What is of particular interest is that Lincoln never gave any indication after his 1858 loss that if perhaps he would alter his views somewhat in the direction suggested by various compromisers, including Douglas, he might be more successful at the polls. There is no evidence that Lincoln ever engaged in the kind of "learning" that might be suggested by the Downs electoral paradigm.[72] Instead, Lincoln left the perception that he would be rather right and lose than be rather wrong and win. In a March 1, 1859 Chicago speech, he had said:

..."perhaps the best way for [slavery] to come to an end peaceably is for it to exist for a length of time. But I say that the spread and strengthening and perpetuation of it is an entirely different proposition. There we should in every way resist it as a wrong, treating it as a wrong, with the fixed idea that it must and will come to an end."

...All you have to do is keep the faith, to remain steadfast to the right..."[73]

"Those who deny freedom to others, deserve it not for themselves; and, under a just God, can not long retain it."[74]

It is difficult to escape the conclusion that Lincoln was very much an inner-directed moralist, a man whose sense of purpose and mission, unlike that of most politicians, was not based on the flux of every day events and close soundings of popular whims.[75] At the same time, here was a leader profoundly sensitive to a great range of human experience and one both able and willing to make use of public opinion to advance his own goals.

In 1861 Lincoln said of the Civil War that

"On the side of the Union it is a struggle for maintaining in the world, that form, and substance of government, whose leading object is, to elevate the condition of man -- to lift artificial weights from all shoulders -- to clear the path of laudable pursuit for all -- to afford all, an unfettered start, and a fair chance, in the race of life."

G.S. Boritt perceptively observes that a majority of historians take Lincoln's "expressions about the Union as stating his fundamental war aim. If we focus on Lincoln's presidential years in isolation a fair case can indeed be made for such an approach. But if we scrutinize his life as a whole, and thus see those final, crowning years of conflict in the [larger] perspective...we should speak -- awkward as this is -- about Lincoln's War for the American Dream."[76]

In Lincoln's view, it was a struggle "against the bondage of labor."[77]   As Boritt notes, Lincoln's reply to Horace Greeley in August 1862 was "less an oath of allegiance to the Union" than it was a "stratagem addressed to people whose support was indispensable to ending slavery."[78]   The Union was for Lincoln itself a means to an end, "the prosperity and liberties of the people."[79]

Lincoln would not, and never did, compromise on his opposition to slavery, but as with all other great questions in his life, this opposition was always framed on his own terms. Lincoln separated himself from the abolitionists because he was unwilling to sacrifice three values indifferent to many other people, including many abolitionists. One of these was preservation of the Union. Another was concern for the due process of law. To be sure, Lincoln was not a legal "fetishist" by engaging in some form of blind worship of legalism and legal sanctions. But Lincoln exhibited great reverence for the law, both in its letter and in its spirit. He viewed the disregard or the non-observance of law justifiable only in the most dire and clearly temporary circumstances. John Brown's raid at Harper's Ferry was precisely the sort of social action that Lincoln hoped to avoid and that he regarded as reprehensible and destructive, even if motivated by high moral purpose.

Finally, there was the issue of legitimacy in an organic connection between himself and Washington and the Founding Fathers. Lincoln was unwilling to let the slaveholding states go their own way.   And he was unwilling to repudiate the constitutional compact of 1789. The Founding Fathers were open to the charge of gross hypocrisy in the very difference between the terms of the Declaration of Independence and the provisions regarding slavery embodied in the Constitution of the United States.[80]   But, in order to maintain legitimate continuity, Lincoln was never willing to acknowledge the enormous gap between these two documents or, indeed, between the professed ideals and the actual practices of the Founders. On the contrary, Lincoln always attempted to reconcile his own anti-slavery position within the framework of the Constitution. Since, manifestly, the Founders did not banish slavery throughout the states, Lincoln did not espouse that either. Whatever the Southerners had got under the terms of the Constitution, Lincoln promised to respect.

But Lincoln also relied upon opinions expressed by the Founders at various times, and *not* embodied in the Constitution itself, to the effect that slavery was an institution which should be somehow limited and ultimately terminated. He made use of the one constitutional reference to the power of Congress, not to be exercised before 1808, to prohibit the importation of slaves. He often spoke of accommodations to circumstances, as if to explain, and excuse, the Founders' conduct. One such accommodation was the continuing illegal importation of some quarter million slaves into the United States prior to the outbreak of the Civil War and despite Congressional prohibition of 1808.[81] Of course, Lincoln saw, or professed to see, in the Missouri Compromise of 1820, engineered by his hero, Henry Clay, and excluding slavery west of the Mississippi River and north of the 36 30' latitude, a policy in line with the Founders' intent. On the other hand, he considered the Kansas Nebraska Act of 1854, with its settler choice principle, a revolutionary departure from the Founders' course. He also regarded the 1857 Dred Scott decision of the Supreme Court in the same light.

In truth, Congress had admitted 5 new slave holding states into the Union prior to the Missouri Compromise. These were Kentucky in 1792; Tennessee in 1796; Louisiana in 1812; Mississippi in 1817 and Alabama in 1819. It also admitted 4 new slave holding states after the Compromise. These were Missouri in 1821; Arkansas in 1836; and Florida and Texas in 1845. The admission of 9 new slave states into the Union between 1792 and 1845, north, west, and south, was hardly a validation of an alleged policy of termination and limitation of the institution of slavery. In fact, it more than doubled the original number of slave states in the American Republic.[82]

Notwithstanding Lincoln's insistence on his own continuity of policy with the Founders, he began his tenure as President with a revolutionary innovation. He was the first President of the United States who had made his personal electoral platform, virtually his whole electoral platform, the public condemnation of slavery and the demand for its quarantine and ultimate extinction. Lincoln's position put slaveholders, and states dominated by the slaveholders, in an understandably very difficult position. Most of them, that is, states in which most of the economy was actually slave-supported, reacted by seceding from the Union, and the immediate issue of the Civil War was not slavery itself but secession.

While the President never budged from his positions enunciated in the Lincoln-Douglas debates and the electoral campaign of 1860, he was reproached for not rushing into immediate and general abolition of slavery once the War had got under way. His letter to Horace Greeley of August 22, 1862 is frequently cited as proof of his indifference on the slavery question, for here he was saying, among other things, that if he could save the Union by freeing no slaves at all he would do it. And when some of his generals, John C. Fremont and David Hunter, issued their own emancipation proclamations, Lincoln countermanded them. When suggestions were made to the President in the early stages of the War that he might use liberated or fugitive slaves as soldiers in the Union forces, the President rejected these proposals.

While worried about emancipation measures which might undermine the Union war effort, Lincoln gave a sense of his personal feelings in a response, recorded in the Fifth volume of the Basler collection, to a group of people urging him to act immediately on the issue of Africans' freedom. These are described as Lincoln's Remarks to a Delegation of Progressive Friends on June 20, 1862, on pp. 278-279 of volume V.

> "He agreed with the memorialists, that Slavery was wrong, but in regard to the ways and means of its removal, his views probably differed from theirs..."

... "he had sometimes thought that perhaps he might be an instrument in God's hands of accomplishing a great work and he certainly was not unwilling to be. Perhaps, however, God's way of accomplishing the end which the memorialists have in view may be different from theirs. It would be his earnest endeavor, with a firm reliance upon the Divine arm, and seeking light from above, to do his duty in the place to which he had been called."

Lincoln clearly realized, unlike some others, that the greatest blow which could possibly be struck against the Southern slave holders would be to defeat them in the war which they had started by firing on Fort Sumter. To achieve this victory, he needed popular support, partly in the so-called border states whose resources and manpower were a significant factor for both sides in the conflict, but, above all, in the North itself. Lincoln knew that pristine abolitionism did not command anything approaching a popular majority within the Northern states. Relatively few Americans in 1861 were willing to die or risk their lives for the liberation of the "Negro." Moral indifference, as is so often the case, was rampant. Racism was an important negative, too. On the other hand, patriotism, or nationalism, in terms of support for the preservation of the Union founded by Washington, was quite another matter.

Lincoln knew that no words, no proclamations, no manifestoes could possibly equal the force of a Union victory.[83] No less than Bismarck, Lincoln could tell the difference between words and deeds.[84] For this reason Lincoln needed to be prudent and cautious, especially until such time as the balance of Northern popular opinion might allow him greater opportunity for abolitionist initiatives. In early 1862, he tried to push a gradual emancipation bill through the Congress with compensation to slave owners and voluntary settlement of blacks in Africa. In fact, there is a record of measures and initiatives throughout the Lincoln presidency testifying to his continuing interest in the destruction of slavery. These ranged from his participation in the drafting of an 1861 plan for emancipation in Delaware, the July 1862 initiative calling on

Congress to legislate a compensation scheme for the emancipation of slaves throughout the U.S.; his schemes for the abolition of slavery in Louisiana and Arkansas in early 1863 and his support subsequently for the passage of the Thirteenth Amendment through the Congress.[85] All these were in addition to the Emancipation Proclamation of September 22, 1862 and January 1, 1863. Still, with admirable realism, Lincoln kept his principal focus on a Union victory over the slave-holding Confederacy.

⸺ After the issuance of Lincoln's Emancipation Proclamation in September of 1862, many Northerners accused Lincoln of falsely changing his war aims, from saving the Union to advancing the welfare of Africans. Many abolitionists, on the other hand, felt that the Emancipation represented empty rhetoric because it promised freedom to slaves who were still subject to the power of the Confederacy while denying freedom to those slaves who resided in states supporting the Union and under Union control.[86] Some believed that the Proclamation would stiffen Southern resistance by its blatant, wholesale and immediate threat to the South's most fundamental asset: i.e., by emancipation without compensation.[87]

In due course, Lincoln not only accepted former slaves as soldiers in the Union Army but argued to the whole nation that the help of these troops was indispensable to an ultimate Union victory. He praised their courage. He sponsored the passage of the thirteenth amendment through the Congress to give the abolition of slavery a firmly constitutional foundation. He moved to extend the suffrage to former slaves in the states of the defunct Confederacy. ⸺

Interestingly, all the questions about Lincoln's conduct concerning slavery after 1861 focus on how he moved forward, how quickly, how firmly, how consistently, how resolutely. But what was of critical importance was that Lincoln simply never moved back from the high ground he had staked out in the election of 1860. Neither publicly nor privately. The significance of that posture can be appreciated only in the context of Lincoln's war policy toward the Confederacy. Through all the carnage and suffering that the war had brought with it, Lincoln never once offered the South a compromise settlement either allowing it separation or concessions on the extent or permanency of slavery.

Here it is appropriate to recall Lincoln's letter to Horace Greeley of July 9, 1864 in which the President said:

"If you can find, any person anywhere professing to have any proposition of Jefferson Davis in writing, for peace, embracing the restoration of the Union and abandonment of slavery, what ever else it embraces, say to him he may come to me with you"...

This was Lincoln's reply to Greeley's letter in which the latter had said that

"our bleeding, bankrupt, almost dying country longs for peace -- shudders at the prospect of fresh conscriptions, of further wholesale devastations, and of new rivers of human blood...."

In a tone of despair, Greeley concluded:

"I fear you do not realize how intently the people desire any peace consistent with the national integrity and honor...it may save us from a northern insurrection."[88]

Lincoln would never even agree to a cease-fire, so that the parties to the dispute could just...talk. Granted, no one could tell what might have happened if Lincoln had died in, say, early 1862. Conceivably, war weariness in the North might have led to a cease-fire and then to some sort of compromise in a negotiated settlement with the Confederacy. But if the war were won by the North on Lincoln's terms, the likelihood of slavery's survival in the South would have been somewhat on the order of an all-Nazi government succeeding Hitler's regime in Germany after the Allied victory in 1945.

Beyond all the speculation, however, is the evidence of Lincoln's own words, and the recollections of those who knew him personally, indicating that for Lincoln the cause of African freedom in America was not a "political" cause; it was God's cause.[89]

We can conclude our discussion here most appropriately with these words from Lincoln's Second Inaugural Address in 1865:

> "Fondly do we hope -- fervently do we pray -- that this mighty scourge of war may speedily pass away. Yet if God wills that it continue, until all the wealth piled by the bondman's two hundred and fifty years of unrequited toil shall be sunk, and until every drop of blood drawn with the lash, shall be paid by another drawn with the sword, as was said three thousand years ago, so still it must be said 'the judgments of the Lord, are true and righteous altogether.'"[90]

REFERENCE

1. References to Lincoln speeches, papers, and correspondence are from Roy P. Basler, editor, Marion Dolores Pratt and Lloyd A. Dunlap, assistant editors, The Collected Works of Abraham Lincoln (New Brunswick, N.J.: Rutgers University Press) vols. I-VIII, 1953-1955, hereafter cited as Basler with appropriate volume and page citations.

2. See Lincoln's speech to the Temperance Society at Springfield, Illinois of February 22, 1842. "This is the one hundred and tenth anniversary of the birthday of Washington... Washington is the mightiest name of earth -- long since mightiest in the cause of civil liberty; still mightiest in moral reformation... to add brightness to the sun, or glory to the name of Washington is alike impossible." Basler, vol. I, p. 279. Note Cullom Davis, Charles B. Strozier, Rebecca M. Veach, and G.C. Ward (eds.), The Public and Private Lincoln, Contemporary Perspectives (Carbondale: Southern Illinois University Press, 1979). See Norman Graebner, Ch. 5, "The Apostle of Progress," pp. 71-85 on Lincoln's essentially optimistic outlook about American conditions... and especially Richard N. Current, Ch. 9, "Lincoln, the Civil War, and the American Mission," pp. 137-146... Lincoln believed that the U.S. "had a special calling to set an example for the rest of the world." P. 146.

3. Note Tyler Dennett (ed.), Lincoln and the Civil War in the Diaries and Letters of John Hay (New York: Dodd, Mead, 1939. On July 31, 1863, Hay made the following observation: "I had considerable talk with the President this evening on [Emancipation]... He considers it the greatest question ever presented to practical statesmanship. While the rest are grinding their little private organs for their own glorification the old man is working with the strength of a giant and the purity of an angel to do this great work." P. 73

4. Basler, vol. I, pp. 74-75.

5. See Address before Young Men's Lyceum in Springfield, Illinois on January 1837, Basler vol. I, pp. 108-115.

6. Basler, vol. I, p. 260.

7. Basler, vol. I, p. 278.

8. Basler, vol. I, p. 279.

9. Letter to Williamson Durley of October 3, 1845, Basler, vol. I, p. 348.

10. Basler, vol. II, p. 3.

11. Ibid, pp. 20-22.

12. Ibid, pp. 121-132. Six years later, in a speech in Carlinville, Illinois, on August 31, 1858 Lincoln said: "Clay always opposed the rightfulness of slavery -- Douglas always took the opposite, or kept mum. I can express all my views on the slavery question by quotations from Henry Clay. Doesn't this look like we are akin." Basler, vol. III, p. 79.

Lincoln defined the object of Republicanism as "the preventing the spread and nationalization of slavery." Note letter to Mark W. Delahay, May 14, 1859. Basler, vol. III, p. 379.

13. Basler, vol. II, p. 130.

14. Ibid, p. 132. Appropriately, toward the conclusion of the Civil War, in his Second Inaugural, Lincoln dramatically returned to this theme...

15. Basler, vol. IV, p. 5.

16. Note, however, the argument for an implicitly economic doctrine of liberty assumed by Lincoln -- for all men -- by G.S. Boritt, Lincoln and the Economics of the American Dream (Memphis: Memphis State University Press, 1978).

17. Basler, vol. II, p. 222.

18. Ibid, p. 223.

19. Ibid, p. 255.

20. Ibid.

21. Ibid.

22. Ibid.

23. Ibid, pp. 255-256.

24. Ibid, p. 256.

25. Ibid.

26. In a speech given in Cincinnati in 1859 Lincoln answered a hypothetical question: What would he do if the extension of slavery could be overcome? (..."when we...beat you, you perhaps want to know what we will do with you...")

This question he answered with the generosity of the Second Inaugural. "We mean to treat you as near as we possibly can, like Washington, Jefferson and Madison treated you. We mean to leave you alone; to abide by all and every compromise of the constitution...according to the example of those noble fathers -- Washington, Jefferson and Madison. We mean to remember that you are as good as we; that there is no difference between us other than the difference of circumstances. We mean to recognize and bear in mind always that you have as good hearts in your bosoms as other people, or as we claim to have, and treat you accordingly. We mean to marry your girls when we have a chance -- the white ones I mean." Basler, vol. III, p. 453. September 17, 1859.

Professor Richard Nelson Current mentions the impressions of Frederick Douglass, who had visited with Lincoln several times during his Presidency and was convinced of Lincoln's apparent lack of any racial prejudice toward him personally. P. 36. Note also the Current view that Lincoln was gradually evolving his views toward a more complete acceptance of black equality. See Current, p. 23, 24, 32-35, 37.

27. Richard Nelson Current notes that "as late as 1847 [Lincoln's] torment [over slavery] apparently was not troublesome enough to deter him from accepting a slaveholder as a law client and arguing against a slave's claim to freedom." See Richard Nelson Current, Speaking of Abraham Lincoln, The Man and His Meaning for Our Times (Urbana: University of Illinois Press, 1983) p. 20. Lincoln lost the case.

Lincoln wrote in December 1860: ..."I declare that the maintenance inviolate of the rights of the States, and especially the right of each state to order and control its own domestic institutions according to its own judgment exclusively, is essential to that balance of powers on which the perfection, and endurance of our political fabric depends -- and I denounce the lawless invasion, by armed force, of the soil of any State or Territory, no matter under what pretext, as the gravest of crimes." Basler, vol. IV, p. 162. These words Lincoln subsequently included in his First Inaugural Address of March 4, 1861. See ibid, p. 263. As Norman A. Graebner says: "Lincoln's reluctance to destroy slavery through war stemmed

68

partially from his constitutional and legal scruples. His oath, he insisted, forbade him from indulging his abstract judgement of the slavery question. He condemned all disrespect for property. Let every man remember, he warned early in his career, that 'to violate the law, is to trample on the blood of his father, and to tear the charter of his own, and his children's liberty. Let reverence for the laws...become the political religion of the nation.' In the midst of the Civil War, Lincoln reminded Congress, in December 1862, that the liberation of slaves was the destruction of property, acquired by purchase or inheritance as any other property. Nor was the South anymore responsible than the North for its original introduction into North America or for its continuance. Did not the North unhesitantly purchase and share the profits of cotton and sugar?" "Abraham Lincoln: Conservative Statesman" in a book he edited The Enduring Lincoln (Urbana: University of Illinois, 1959) p. 84.

28. Basler, vol. II, p. 449. May 18, 1858.

29. Ibid, p. 451.

30. Ibid.

31. Ibid, p. 452.

32. Ibid, p. 482.

33. Ibid, p. 492.

34. Ibid, pp. 496-497.

35. Ibid, p. 506.

36. Ibid.

37. Ibid, pp. 519-520.

38. Ibid, p. 532.

39. Ibid, p. 547.

40. Basler, vol. III, p. 276.

41. Ibid.

42. Ibid.

43. Ibid, p. 416.

44. Ibid, p. 276.

45. Ibid.

46. Ibid.

47. Ibid, p. 277.

48. Ibid, p. 278.

49. Ibid, p. 285.

50. Ibid, p. 286.

51. Ibid.

52. Ibid, p. 289.

53. Ibid.

54. Ibid, p. 290.

55. Ibid, p. 291.

56. Ibid, p. 296.

57. Ibid, p. 307.

58. Ibid, p. 313.

59. Ibid, p. 315.

60. Ibid, p. 324.

61. Ibid, p. 426.

62. Ibid, p. 327.

63. Ibid.

64. Ibid, pp. 327-328.

65. Ibid, pp. 330-331.

66. See Herbert Agar, The Price of Union (Boston: Houghton Mifflin, 1950) p. 389 on the narrow focus of the Lincoln Douglas debates. Following the Senate campaign, at Elwood, Kansas on December 1 or November 30th 1859 (the exact date is in doubt) Lincoln began a speech, according to a press report, by saying "that it was possible that we had local questions in regard to Railroads, Land Grants and internal improvements which were matters of deeper interest to us than the questions arising out of national politics, but of these local interests he knew nothing and should say nothing." According to the report of the Elwood Free Press, December 3, 1859, reported in Basler, vol. III, p. 495.

67. Ibid, p. 334.

68. Ibid. In a letter to Norman B. Judd on November 15, 1858, after the election, Lincoln wrote: "...let the past as nothing be... For the future my view is that the fight must go on. P. 336.

And on November 19, he wrote to one Henry Asbury, "the cause of civil liberty must not be surrendered at the end of one, or even, one hundred defeats..." P. 339.

69. Ibid.

70. See Richard Allen Heckman, Lincoln vs Douglas, The Great Debates Campaign (Washington, D.C.: Public Affairs Press, 1967) p. 141.

71. Ibid, pp. 136-137. This was Lincoln's appraisal of Douglas' victory (noting that some Republicans wanted to support Douglas as their own candidate): "True, Douglas is back in the Senate in spite of us; but we are *clear* of *him*, and *his* principles; and we are uncrippled and ready to fight both him and them straight along till they shall finally be "closed out." Basler, vol. III, p. 434.

"We want, and must have, a national policy as to slavery which deals with it as being a wrong. Whoever would prevent slavery becoming national and perpetual, yields all when he yields to a policy which treats it either as being right, or as being a matter of indifference." Basler, vol. III, p. 435.

"If we adopt a platform, falling short of our principle, or elect a man rejecting our principle, we not only take nothing affirmative by our success; but we draw upon us the positive embarrassment of seeing ourselves to abandon our principle." Basler, vol. III, p. 436.

72. See Anthony Downs, An Economic Theory of Democracy (New York: Harper and Row, 1957).

73. Basler, vol. III, p. 370.

74. Ibid, p. 376. On November 19, 1858, Lincoln wrote to Anson S. Miller: "I hope and believe seed has been sown that will yet produce fruit. The fight must go on." P. 340.

And on November 20th to M.M. Inman: "The fight must go on. We are right, and can not finally fail." P. 341.

And to H.D. Sharpe on December 8, 1858: "I think we have fairly entered upon a durable struggle as to whether this nation is to ultimately become all slave or all free, and though I fall early in the contest, it is nothing if I shall have contributed, in the least degree, to the final rightful result." P. 344.

In April 1865, among the last utterances of his life, Lincoln wrote: "Whenever I hear any one arguing for slavery I feel a strong impulse to see it tried on him personally." Basler, vol. VIII, p. 361.

75. See Roy P. Basler, The Lincoln Legend, A Study in Changing Conceptions (Boston: Houghton Mifflin, 1935) p. 23 on the inner-oriented man in Lincoln: "Throughout Lincoln's life in Illinois we see the evidence that inwardly he differed vastly from the ugly, humorous lawyer. Every accomplishment of his life seems to have come from an inward inspiration and for years there are lulls which are fraught with pathos in their descent into the depths of futility."

Above all, Basler's conclusion is especially relevant here, to wit: "He was the most individual man who ever lived. Singular and solitary he remains, as in his lifetime, at once familiar and remote, common but impressive, plain but mysterious, unmeasured and unsolved.... Admiration is still the common ground upon which we stand." P. 296. Note Francis Grierson, Abraham Lincoln, The Practical Mystic (New York: John Lane Company, 1919) "[Lincoln's] invincible trust in Providence held him aloof from the petty circumstances and daily routine of intrigue…while those around him flattered themselves that he was being influenced or led by their counsels and their interests." P. 69. And quoting Walt Whitman, Grierson concurs that "the foundations of his character more than any man's in history, were mystic and spiritual." P. 68. Also Jesse W. Weik, The Real Lincoln: A Portrait (Boston: Houghton Mifflin, 1922) "It can hardly be said that he had a confidant nor did he unbosom himself to others." P. 104. "To me he was imperturbable and mysterious." Ibid. On Lincoln's frequent "far away" look, see p. 105. See F.B. Carpenter, Six Months At the White House (New York: Hurd and Houghton, 1866) who says: "I have been repeatedly asked to what extent Mr. Lincoln read the newspapers…I recollect of but a single instance of newspaper reading on the part of the President, during the entire period of my intercourse with him." P. 153.

"The truth is…[that] Mr. Lincoln read *less* and thought *more* than any other man in his sphere in America." P. 331. See David Donald (ed.), Inside Lincoln's Cabinet, the Civil War Diaries of Salmon P. Chase (New York: Longman's, Green and Co., 1954). As late as July 4, 1864, Chase still thought that Lincoln and "his chief advisors" (?) might be willing to reconstitute the Union with Slavery (P. 230) but he also confessed, "I feel that I do not know him…" P. 254.

76. G.S. Boritt, Lincoln and the Economics of the American Dream (Memphis: Memphis State University Press, 1978) p. 275.

77. Ibid, p. 279.

78. Ibid.

79. Ibid, p. 280.

The famous statement was: "My paramount object in this struggle is to save the Union, and is *not* either to save or to destroy slavery. If I could save the Union without freeing *any* slave I would do it, and if I could save it by freeing *all* the slaves I would do it…" See Basler, vol. V, p. 388.

80. See Edmund S. Morgan, "Slavery and Freedom: The American Paradox," The Journal of American History, vol. 59, No. 1, June 1972, pp. 5-29. "The American Revolution only made the contradictions [apparent in Jefferson's Virginia] more glaring, as the slaveholding colonists proclaimed to a candid world the right not simply of Englishmen but of all men." P. 29.

81. Note Harral E. Landry, "Slavery and the Slave Trade in Atlantic Diplomacy, 1850-1861," The Journal of Southern History, vol. 27, No. 2, May 1961, pp. 184-207.

82. See William W. Freehling, "The Founding Fathers and Slavery" The American Historical Review, vol. 77, No. 1, February 1972, pp. 81-93. "Like reluctant revolutionaries before and since, Jefferson sought to have it both ways." P. 93. "In their own day, the Fathers left intact a strong Southern slave tradition." P. 92.

83. According to Mark E. Neely, Jr. this was the view of Secretary of State William Seward in that "the outbreak of war had sealed slavery's doom..." of course, as long as the Union could be victorious. The Last Best Hope of Earth, op. cit., pp. 109-110. See also Glyndon G. Van Duesen, William Henry Seward (New York: Oxford University Press, 1967) on the Secretary's view that a successful conclusion to the war would spell the end of slavery in the south and throughout the United States. P. 388.

84. Note here the conclusion of John S. Wright, Lincoln and the Politics of Slavery (Reno: University of Nevada Press, 1970) on the proposition that Lincoln saw the war itself as the ultimate and essential weapon in the destruction of slavery. P. 199. He quotes the President's July 1862 remarks to border states representatives: "If the war continues long, as it must, if the object be not sooner attained, the institution in your states will be extinguished by more friction and abrasion -- by the mere incidents of war." Ibid. What Lincoln attempted with respect to the removal of slavery during the war was ultimately designed to fit both political necessities and constitutional requirements. Pp. 199-202.

85. See Garry Wills, Lincoln at Gettysburg, the Words that Remade America (New York: Simon and Schuster, 1992) p. 287; cf. Lawanda Cox, "Lincoln and Black Freedom" in G.S. Boritt and N.A. Fornes (Urbana: University of Illinois Press, 1988) pp. 178-181.

86. See Stephen B. Oates, Abraham Lincoln, The Man Behind the Myths (New York: Harper and Row Publishers, 1984). Lincoln paid an enormous political price in the congressional elections of 1862 for his Proclamation as "northern voters dealt the Republicans a smashing blow." P. 108. "As the New Year approached, conservative Republicans begged Lincoln to abandon his 'reckless' emancipation scheme lest he shatter their demoralized party and wreck what remained of their country." P. 109.

87. See also James McCague, The Second Rebellion: The Story of the New York City Draft Riots of 1863 (New York: The Dial Press, 1968). Even in mid 1863, "the 'shame of Human Slavery' simply did not arouse men to any great pitch of crusading indignation..." "It was no longer easy to believe in victory, or even in the rightness of the course..." "Nobody could really claim to know the public mood this Fourth of July in 1863. But no one could deny, either, that it simmered in a murky mixture of doubt, disgust, impatience and brewing resentment." Pp. 4-5.

88. Basler, vol. VII, p. 435.

89. Note LaWanda Cox, Lincoln and Black Freedom, A Study in Presidential Leadership (Columbia, S.C.: University of South Carolina Press, 1981) p. 5. "On one crucial point...most Lincoln scholars agree -- [Lincoln] held a deeply felt conviction that slavery was morally wrong and should be placed on the road to extinction." To LaWanda Cox, we owe this important conclusion: "[Lincoln's] progression from prewar advocacy of restricting slavery's spread to foremost responsibility for slavery's total, immediate, uncompensated destruction by constitutional amendment...has often been viewed as a reluctant accommodation to pressures; it can be better understood as a ready response to opportunity." P. 6. L.E. Chittenden, Recollections of President Lincoln and His Administration (New York: Harper and Brothers, 1891) quotes Lincoln in early 1862 as saying ..."I have not the slightest fear of any result which shall fatally impair our military and naval strength.... I do not fear it, for this is God's fight, and he will win it in his own good time. He will take care that our enemies do not push us too far." P. 219. Abram J. Dittenhoefer, How We Elected Lincoln (New York: Harper and Brothers, 1916) who was a Lincoln elector in 1864, makes this very perceptive observation about Lincoln's stance on slavery during the great conflict: "[People] did not comprehend that [Lincoln] was at heart thoroughly imbued with the unrighteousness of property in human beings, but that he felt it was good policy to go gradually, step by step, hoping to unite the entire North and so bring about the ultimate abolishment of slavery; whereas, if the policy for the immediate extinction of slavery should be adopted it must inevitably have disrupted the Republican Party." P. 29. And the nation, we might add... On another occasion, he quotes Lincoln addressing Senator William P. Fessenden as his prospective Secretary of the Treasury, in June 1864, after Chase's resignation, in these words: "I believe that the suppression of the rebellion has been decreed by a higher power than any represented by us, and that the Almighty is using his own means to that end. You are one of them. It is as much your 'duty to accept as it is mine to appoint." P. 382.

90. James M. McPherson, <u>Abraham Lincoln and the Second American Revolution</u> (New York: Oxford University Press, 1990) p. 37. ..."The Civil War changed the United States as thoroughly as the French Revolution changed [France]." P. VII-VIII.

III

THE ELECTION OF 1860 AND LINCOLN'S POLICY CHOICES

Even though Lincoln had repeatedly assured the South that he would not interfere with slavery in the states where it already existed, his election constituted a damaging blow to the interests of the slave holders. Because he had publicly declared slavery to be morally wrong, and because he repeatedly called for it to be put on a course of ultimate extinction, his presidency was tantamount to a national delegitimization of the institution. It stood morally condemned by the Chief Executive of the United States, and, with his election, the federal government presumably stood pledged to its containment on the analogy of a plague.

Whatever means Lincoln might personally consider honorable, his opinions were likely to offer encouragement and justification to all manner of abolitionist sentiment, North and South, and, not the least, of course, among the African population. The great masses of the enslaved were bound to know that even the nation's Chief Executive thought that if slavery was not wrong, nothing was wrong. The Sixteenth President was the first to declare publicly that the nation could not, and would not, permanently remain half free and half slave, and this pronouncement had its ominously dynamic implications.[1]

Given Lincoln's own position, quite apart from any malicious vilification of him by political opponents, the slave holders' interest in secession was amply reasonable. And so was, presumably, the interest of all those Southerners who, on whatever grounds, identified with the cause of the slave holders.

Well aware of the tenor of the Southern press, and the pronouncements of various spokesmen of the slave holding interests, Lincoln faced a somber situation in November 1860. Unless he proceeded to somehow mollify and reassure the South, it was likely that at least some Southern states would effectuate secession; and if Lincoln and the federal government made any forcible attempt to prevent this from occurring, a civil war, with all manner of potentially catastrophic consequences was also very likely, even if not absolutely certain.

If Lincoln had been disposed to defuse the crisis facing him through the processes of conciliation, negotiation, and mutual agreement, he was certainly in a position to do so, and do so with a minimal "loss of face." Whatever personal views he may have expressed prior to the election, and whatever the language of the Republican platform of 1860, the electorate did not award Lincoln majority support. If ever there was a moment in history when the President might have been tempted to draw back, to invoke the spirit of caution, and to present some olive branches to his enemies, the election of 1860 certainly yielded such a moment. Moreover, Lincoln had himself, as a Congressman in the 1840's, enunciated a constitutional doctrine which would have amply justified throwing the burden of the crisis upon the Congress, or perhaps still other representative bodies or institutions (see infra).

To be sure, going into the 1860 election, the Republican platform boldly declared that "the new dogma that the Constitution, of its own force, carries Slavery into any and all of the Territories of the United States, is a dangerous political heresy...subversive of the peace and harmony of the country." It also declared that the Federal Union "must and shall be preserved."[2]

As for Lincoln's opponents, their views were much more conciliatory toward the South. John Bell's Constitutional Union platform sought to sidestep the issues of slavery and secession in the form of any kind of formalized program. The Party declared instead that "experience has demonstrated that Platforms adopted by the partisan Conventions of the country have had the effect to mislead and deceive the people, and at the same time to widen the political divisions of the country"...[3] Bell's followers pledged themselves, briefly, to the Constitution, the Union and the Enforcement of the

Laws, but also declared that through the appropriate observance of these verities, peace would be "restored" in the country, and the rights of the People and the States would be "reestablished."[4]

The implication was clearly that these values had been somehow lost and that the political system required a restoration. As a slave owner himself, Bell probably felt that he could reassure Southern opinion on the direction needed for these broad purposes. Among the remaining alternatives was the uninhibited extension of slavery into any and all territories supported by John C. Breckinridge and the Southern Democrats, and the so-called popular sovereignty position advocated by Stephen Douglas' Northern Democrats.[5]

When the ballots cast in the presidential election of 1860 were counted, the popular vote for Lincoln stood at 1,866,452, a figure which represented a mere 39.86 percent of the American electorate. Lincoln won the Presidency with 180 electoral votes as against 123 for all his opponents put together , but their share of the popular vote was 60.14 percent. Looked at in terms of policy positions, a large majority of American voters was far more favorable to the views of the South than to Lincoln's Republicans -- either because they actually supported slavery, states' rights and secession, or because they were seemingly willing to make greater concessions to slavery in order to avoid secession and war. Stephen Douglas received 1,376,957 votes; John Bell 588,879; John Breckinridge 849,781. Lincoln was a minority President supported by a plurality of the American voters.

Under these circumstances, one could certainly argue that for anyone seriously interested in political democracy, in government of the people, by the people, and for the people, the fact of such division of popular opinion, especially in the face of so ominous a crisis, would have to have the most far- reaching practical implications. Did not "democracy" demand that with all the risks and uncertainties involved, the "people" should be the ultimate judges of what they wished to do, or have done, for themselves? And was it not the democratic duty of elected officials to defer to the collective judgment of their popular masters? Listen to their voices?

Heed their call? In a study of the 1860 election, Reinhard Luthin concludes that "it is doubtful if the party which Lincoln headed represented what was in the minds of the American people. The conservative sense of the country stood arrayed against a northern and sectional minority -- but the Republicans were united for the duration of the contest, while their opponents were divided."[6]

Nevertheless, from the moment of his nomination for President, through his election and inauguration, Lincoln resolutely rejected all attempts at conciliation through compromise on the issue of slavery, and he also rejected the only other alternative that would have avoided war -- secession. In fact, from the very outset, Lincoln pursued a course of preserving the Union on the platform of the Republican minority at the very likely cost of civil war.

Already in the Lincoln - Douglas debates, the President had shown that his attachment to the ideals of "democracy" did not mean giving the people whatever they might ask. Lincoln believed in giving them only what was right to give by the tenets of his own conscience, including his reading of the Constitution and the Declaration of Independence. Stephen Douglas had espoused popular sovereignty; Lincoln, the great spokesman of democracy, opposed it if it connoted the extension of slavery. Now, on the brink of the Civil War, Lincoln was not about to appease popular opinion any more than he did when he contested the Senate seat from Illinois.

As Professor Harry Jaffa remarks, the definition of the issues Lincoln had provided in his 1858 debates with Douglas was profoundly disquieting to the South:

> "By creating the chasm between Douglas Democrats and Republicans [Lincoln] caused to be fastened upon the Republicans a character that would, to the existing mind and temper of the South, be indistinguishable from abolitionism, thus increasing beyond measure the likelihood of secession when such a party should carry a national election."[7]

Lincoln was bound to realize that his very nomination would arouse misgivings in the Southern states. If he had had any doubts on that score, certainly the perusal of Southern press from the period of early summer 1860 onwards would have clarified the matter for him. When the New Orleans *Crescent* greeted his election in November with an editorial declaring that the "Northern people, in electing Mr. Lincoln, have perpetrated a deliberate, cold blooded insult and outrage upon the people of the slave holding states,"[8] it was not exactly breaking new ground. Lincoln and the Republican Party had been anathema to much of the South for several years; they were often referred to as Black Republicans.

Notwithstanding Southern anxieties, Lincoln adopted a posture of studious silence as soon as he had received the Republican presidential nomination. As William Baringer observes:

> "Lincoln announced early that he would take no active part in the campaign. This decision followed the customary procedure of the time, but it suited his needs particularly well. Lincoln had no intention of committing himself further on any question before the nation. His debates with Douglas had already been printed in book form as a campaign document. Those who sought his views were referred to the speeches and to the Republican platform."[9]

As Baringer puts it: "This was not always a satisfactory response."[10] The debates with Douglas were about two years old, and whatever the Republican platform may have said, Lincoln would be the man to put its principles into practice, or perhaps moderate and restrain them, in case he were elected President. While Lincoln avidly followed the developments of the campaign waged by various surrogates on the Republican side, he carefully avoided any public declarations that might draw him into the battle.[11] He certainly did nothing to assuage Southern fears. By way of innovative contrast, Stephen Douglas, the Democratic candidate, personally undertook a major campaign effort, delivering speeches in various parts of the country and breaking with the heretofore observed traditions of passivity on the part of American presidential nominees.

Emerson David Fite wrote in his study of the 1860 campaign:

"Lincoln's reputation so far as it went, was consistent. He had never hedged. It was now recalled that he had expressed the 'irrepressible conflict' idea some months before [William H.] Seward.... He persistently endeavored to arouse moral sentiment against [slavery] and this position he never ceased to put forward....Lincoln ran from nothing; he sugar-coated nothing to propitiate enemies; neither did he try to fool the public by hair-splitting distinctions nor to coax and wheedle the Southerners by soft words...."[12]

Lincoln's silence between the election in November and the beginning of his train journey toward inauguration in March in Washington, D.C., clearly helped to further increase the tensions between North and South. The President-elect was careful not to make any statement that could be interpreted as a softening of his earlier position or as a qualification of the Republican Party platform of 1860. To the proponents of secession, and to those seriously worried by the prospects of secession, his silence perforce seemed ominous.[13]

In the winter of 1860, Senator John J. Crittenden of Kentucky had undertaken the task of finding a compromise plan in the Congress in order to save the Union without war and to avoid secession. Predictably, the key feature of the compromise he worked out was an extension of slavery south of the 36 -30 line. According to a number of sources, the plan had a reasonable chance of adoption by a committee of Senators if at least some Republicans had been willing to accept it. As Professor John D. Hicks says:

"Seward seems to have flirted with the idea, but before committing himself definitely he sent his friend, Thurlow Weed, to Springfield, Illinois, for a conference with the President-elect. Weed reported that Lincoln was willing to make almost unlimited concessions with regard to the enforcement of the Fugitive Slave Law and the repeal of the 'personal liberty laws' but that he was unalterably opposed to any yielding on the question of slavery expansion. Lincoln's opinion seems to have been conclusive, for the Republicans voted unanimously against the proposed dividing line, and the committee reported back to the Senate that it could not agree."[14]

Interestingly, Hicks also tells us that:

"Later Crittenden and his supporters argued that the compromise in which they were interested should be submitted to the people of the country for approval or rejection at the polls. But the machinery for obtaining such a referendum vote did not exist, and all efforts looking toward its creation failed, largely because of Republican opposition. Had there been such a possibility, however, there is some reason to suppose that during the winter of 1860-61 a popular majority for the compromise might have been obtained. The vote of November 1860 showed the extremists in the majority, both North and South, but at that time the actual specter of secession was not before the voters as they marked their ballots. Faced by the direct alternative of compromise or secession, many who had voted for Lincoln or Breckinridge a few weeks ago might well have changed their minds and voted for Crittenden's solution."[15]

During the winter of 1860 analogous initiatives toward some form of reconciliation were being carried on in the House of Representatives. A committee similar to the Senate's Crittenden group was formed and some of the politicians involved in it professed a sense of optimism that a compromise satisfactory to both South and North could be worked out. But, as William E. Baringer describes it, Lincoln would have none of that:

> "Lincoln, far from being swept along by the apparent easy acceptance by Congress of the idea that yet another compromise was in order, took steps to avoid that. He sent a private letter to [Lyman] Trumbull sketching the proper party line. 'Let there be no compromise on the question of extending slavery.... Have none of it. Stand firm. The tug has to come, and better now than any time hereafter.'"[16]

In a similar vein, Lincoln wrote a reply to Representative J. A. Gilmer of North Carolina who had asked him to clear up alleged misunderstandings in the hope that South-North differences could be bridged at the eleventh hour. Lincoln wrote:

> "Is it desired that I shall shift the ground upon which I have been elected? I cannot do it. You need only to acquaint yourself with that ground, and press it on the attention of the South. It is all in print and easy of access.... You think slavery is right and ought to be extended; we think it is wrong and ought to be restricted. For this neither has any just occasion to be angry with the other."[17]

Privately, Lincoln also expressed the view that the President ...."cannot entertain any proposition for dissolution or dismemberment. He was not elected for any such purpose. As a matter of theoretical speculation it is probably true, that if the people, with whom the whole question rests, should become tired of the present Government, they might change it in the manner prescribed by the Constitution."[18] As Baringer notes elsewhere, "Lincoln regarded the various compromise proposals as so many opening wedges for further expansion of slavery."[19]

Mark Neely, Jr., in his recent book, diagnoses the matter nicely when he observes that:

> "...it is difficult to imagine how war could have been avoided after Lincoln's election if he adhered to the Republican platform -- and he did."[20]

He also cites Lincoln's famous remarks to Senator Lyman Trumbull concerning any possible compromise with the Southern slave holders: "If there be [a compromise] all our labor is lost...." These remarks could be interpreted as indicating Lincoln's anticipation of war with the South, and perhaps even an eagerness to try the great issue by force of arms ("The tug has to come and better now than any time hereafter..."). Neely compounds this impression when he remarks that "Lincoln seemed tired of southern blackmail and took an intransigent position at first."[21] He refers to the language Lincoln proposed to use in his first Inaugural Address, to wit, "all the power at my disposal will be used to *reclaim* the public property and places which have fallen." This was eventually softened somewhat to "hold, possess and occupy property and places belonging to the government..."[22] He also reminds us that when Lincoln first raised the question of resupplying Fort Sumter, most of the Cabinet (all save for Montgomery Blair...) opposed the idea. And as he notes, "merely supplying the beleaguered fort with food risked war -- a risk Lincoln proved willing to take."[23]

History and tradition may have vindicated Lincoln's policy. The policy may have corresponded to the President's lofty moral impulse. But, whatever it was, it was scarcely a *democratic* policy in the sense of responding, or even attempting to respond, to the wishes of the people. In the case of Fort Sumter, Lincoln not only did not ask "What would a majority of American citizens want me to do?" He did not even follow the opinions of the great majority of the leaders of his own Republican Party.

The public and private positions of Lincoln may be seen as evidence of fidelity to his Party's platform. Nevertheless, for one professing such faith in the wisdom and rectitude of the people, it was hardly a very responsive decision, especially given the nature of the 1860 election results as well as the monumental risks of war and suffering clearly implicit in Lincoln's policy. With reasonable inference from the positions taken by the various contestants in the 1860 election, one could well ask, was it the case that 60.14 percent of the people were wrong and 39.86 right?

Lincoln himself appears to have understood the risks and the dangers confronting the country when he delivered a Farewell Address to his fellow citizens in Springfield, Illinois, before embarking on his journey toward inauguration in Washington, D.C. The date was February 11, 1861, and Lincoln said:

> "I go to assume a task more difficult than that which devolved upon George Washington."[24] [Although Basler reports three possible versions of what Lincoln said that day, all contain an equivalent passage. For example, version one includes the sentence:] "I now leave, not knowing when, or whether ever, I may return, with a task before me greater than that which rested upon Washington."[25] [In the second possible version, the sentence reads:] "A duty has devolved upon me which is, perhaps, greater than that which has devolved upon any other man since the days of Washington."[26]

In the version of the speech considered most authentic by Herndon and various other commentators, Lincoln added these words:

> "Unless the great God who assisted him, shall be with and aid me, I must fail. But if the same omniscient mind, and Almighty arm that directed and protected him, shall guide and support me, I shall not fail, I shall succeed."[27]

It may be noted parenthetically that the language which Lincoln used upon leaving Springfield for Washington indicated expectations of far more dramatic events than what he conveyed to various persons who talked with him specifically about the threat of war with the South shortly before and at the time of his inauguration.

In staking out his position of a mandate conferred upon him by electoral victory, Lincoln equated, and one could reasonably charge, confused traditional democratic rules concerning elections with the equally traditional rules concerning legislative and constitutional decisions. In the elections to the British House of Commons -- the ultimate institutional forerunner of American democracy -- going back as far as the thirteenth century, the person who won a plurality of the vote in a particular constituency was also the winner of the seat which represented that constituency in the House. Democratic practice around the world since that time, and well into the end of the present century, has continued to recognize the plurality principle with some frequency. In the United States, in most states most of the time, members of the House of Representatives and of the Senate have been elected on the basis of the plurality principle. British M.P.'s continue to be so elected. In the Federal Republic of Germany, half of the lower house of parliament is elected on the basis of the plurality principle with the rest chosen by proportional representation.

But in none of these countries, and hardly anywhere else, is the plurality principle extended to legislative and constitutional enactments by bodies representing the people, least of all in the United States of America, in Lincoln's time as in ours. In the U.S. Congress, all bills have always required majority support of those voting under conditions of a quorum. Resolutions expressing the "sense of the House," or the Senate, also have required majority support. In cases deemed of special importance to the nation, the requirement of a majority has been increased to that of two thirds. Congress requires the support of two thirds of the members of each house in order to submit constitutional amendments to the states. It requires an analogous majority to override a Presidential veto. The Constitution demands that the Senate produce a two thirds majority to convict a President of the United States on charges of impeachment. The same two thirds is required for the ratification of treaties submitted to it by the President. Analogous provisions characterize the public law of most modern democracies. Constitutional amendments, for example, generally require more substantial legislative majorities than do ordinary laws, whether three fifths, two thirds, or otherwise.

Lincoln, however, openly defended what may be termed a plurality doctrine of popular government. In effect, his view was that whoever was elected President was entitled, and even obligated, to put into effect those policies that he advocated in order to win the election, majority or no majority. This doctrine emerged as a theme of Lincoln's remarks on his way to Washington for the inauguration. It was elucidated most clearly in a speech Lincoln wrote for delivery in Kentucky c. February 12, 1861. Here he assessed the problem in these terms:

> "During the present winter it has been greatly pressed upon me by many patriotic citizens, Kentuckians among others, that I could in my position, by a word, restore peace to the country. But what word? I have many words already before the public; and my position was given to me on the faith of those words. Is the desired word confirmatory of these; or must it be contradictory to them? If the former, it is useless repetition; if the latter, it is dishonorable and treacherous. "[28]

In this particular document, Lincoln shifted and narrowed the ground of his argument somewhat by saying that his mere inauguration as President should not have to depend on his having to recant his views or compromise his principles. He asked:

> "Is there a Bell-man, a Breckinridge-man, or a Douglas-man, who would tolerate his own candidate to make such terms, had he been elected? ...Nor is this a matter of mere personal honor. No man can be elected President without some opponents, as well as supporters; and if when elected, he can not be

installed, till he first appeases his enemies, by breaking his pledges and betraying his friends, this government, and all popular government, is already at an end.   Demands for such surrender, once recognized, and yielded to, are without limit, as to nature, extent, or repetition.   They break the only bond of faith between public, and public servant; and they distinctly set the minority over the majority (sic).   Such demands acquiesced in, would not merely be the ruin of a man, or a party; but as a precedent they would ruin the government itself.

I do not deny the possibility that the people may err in an election; but if they do, the true remedy is in the next election, and not in the treachery of the person elected."

And, Lincoln continued even more pointedly on the question of mandate:

"During the winter just closed, I have been greatly urged, by many patriotic men, to lend the influence of my position to some compromise, by which I was, to some extent, to shift the ground upon which I had been elected.   This I steadily refused.   I so refused, not from any party wantonness, nor from any indifference to the troubles of the country.   I thought such refusal was demanded by the view that if, when a Chief Magistrate is constitutionally elected, he cannot be inaugurated till he betrays those who elected him, by breaking his pledges, and surrendering to those who tried and failed to defeat him at the polls, this government and all popular government is already at an end."[29]

The more genuine issue, however, was not whether Lincoln had a right to be inaugurated as President.   Only outright fanatics (and these, admittedly, were not lacking in 1861...) could have questioned that right. Lincoln had been elected "fair and square." A more serious problem was the nature of the policies that the new President might properly follow. Was it his obligation to fulfill the dictates of the Republican platform of 1860, or, given the divisions and problems facing the nation in 1861, should he have attempted to bring people together to avoid a potentially catastrophic conflict?

Clarence Macartney reports a grave change in the national mood following Lincoln's election. In retrospect, it seems quite natural that it occurred:

> "The triumph at the polls in November, 1860, was followed by a strange reaction. The vast enthusiasm with which the North had hailed the nomination of Lincoln began to subside. A chill swept over the people and men acted as if they were ashamed of their own handiwork, and as if a great mistake had been made in organizing the Republican Party and electing Lincoln. Those ringing words about a 'house divided against itself' and the 'irrepressible conflict' began to give way to the accents of compromise, conciliation, and dread of war. Even Horace Greeley practically told the South to go, if it wanted to, saying he hoped never to live in a republic where one section was 'pinned to the residue by bayonets.' Lincoln, who had delivered himself of a famous metaphor from the Gospels about the certain fall of a house divided against itself, now acted and spoke as if the house were not really divided and could not fall. Seward, who had thrilled the country with his prophecy of the 'irrepressible conflict' in his speech at Rochester in 1858, now acted as if there were no conflict at all, nor any danger of one. The Abolitionists, who had furnished the potent moral element in the long struggle with slavery, were now regarded as embarrassing excess baggage, and everywhere denounced. The desire for peace; the hope for

compromise; the persistent disbelief in the extreme purposes of the South; and, strangest of all, a certain national lethargy, utterly impossible to account for -- all seemed to mark a decadence in patriotic feeling. A palsy or stupor seemed to have come over the North, as if the people were exhausted by the tremendous moral enthusiasms of the struggle against slavery and the first victory of the Republican Party."[30]

Amidst this new atmosphere, on February 15th, Lincoln spoke in Pittsburgh, Pennsylvania, and -- oddly enough -- addressed the issue of future tariff legislation. What he said about this seemingly innocuous topic was clearly relevant to the great North - South crisis. The President-elect said:

> ..."here I may remark that the Chicago platform [of the Republican Party] contains a plank upon this subject which I think should be regarded as law for the incoming administration. In fact, this question, as well as all other subjects embodied in that platform, should not be varied from what we gave the people to understand would be our policy when we obtained their votes. Permit me, fellow citizens, to read the tariff plank of the Chicago platform...."[31]

Lincoln's insistence on a presidential policy mandate, with or without a majority in the country, was not without its serious difficulties. Like all ideas about a mandate, it presumably required adjustment to the effects of changing circumstances. The assumption that what Lincoln had said during his debates with Douglas three years earlier was necessarily to be regarded as immutable sometime in 1861 was hardly self-evident. For one thing, the threat of dissolution and civil war facing the nation was far more imminent in 1861 than in 1858. Ironically, Lincoln himself became one of the most articulate spokesmen on behalf of the proposition that even the

Constitution of the United States could not be interpreted in the same way in times of strife as in times of peace.

Moreover, the mandate idea has always had a major problem in the simple fact that elections generally record people's votes but not the reasons behind those votes. Given a multiplicity of positions, or planks, presented by a candidate or party, how would one know which of these, if any, were endorsed by the voters? Occasionally, the problem might be compounded by implicitly or explicitly contradictory positions presented by candidates; by misperception and, or, lack of information on the part of the voters; and by the likelihood that different members of the electorate would probably attach different degrees of importance to different policy positions presented by any given candidate. Occasionally, this might mean that a victorious candidate who had advocated positions X, Y and Z, won his victory *despite* the fact that most of his supporters disapproved of one or more of his policy stands but voted for him only because on some issue or issues, they preferred him to the other available choices.

As Franklin L. Burdette notes, the Republican platform of 1860 contained quite a few planks. The possible attractions and repulsions were many:

> "The platform, broader in constructive content than in 1856, proposed freedom in the territories, admission of Kansas to the union, homesteads in the public lands, internal improvements, including a Pacific railroad and a daily overland mail, tariff revision for 'development of the industrial interests of the whole country', liberal wages and agricultural prices, and guaranties against impairment of the rights of native or naturalized citizens. It contained also pledges to uphold the Union, principles of the Declaration of Independence, and the rights of states. With obvious reference to John Brown's raid at Harper's Ferry in 1859, it denounced the 'lawless invasion by armed force of the soil of any state or

territory'. It condemned the national administration as corrupt."[32]

This was obviously a diverse menu for voters to consider, and as Burdette points out, "of all the candidates, Lincoln alone made no major speeches."[33] Meantime, however, "Republican speakers and writers [had] placed greatest emphasis on change for improvement: homesteads, roads and waterways, railroad construction to the Pacific, and agricultural colleges. They [also] attacked the extension of slavery to the territories and the penchant of the administration to expand American slave territory to Cuba or elsewhere in the Caribbean. They elaborated charges of corruption and blundering against Democratic officialdom in Washington."[34]

Interpreting the Republican "mandate" in terms of what the voters really wanted when they cast their ballots for the Party's candidate in the 1860 election was hardly a simple and straightforward matter.

Lincoln himself had testified *against* the presidential mandate notion in a speech he had made as a Congressman in 1848. This is how he put the issue to his Democratic opponents then:

> "I understand your idea that if a presidential candidate avow his opinions ... and the people elect him, they thereby distinctly approve all those opinions. This, though plausible, is a most pernicious deception."[35]

Lincoln argued, sensibly enough, that given a few candidates with all sorts of views, some voters would have to accept what they actually opposed in a candidate simply because their available choices were limited. They might agree with a candidate on one or two issues while disagreeing on several others. He concluded:

> "We prefer a candidate, who, like General [Zachary] Taylor, will allow the people to have their own way, regardless of his private opinions.....He would force nothing on them which they don't want..."[36]

And further:

> "We, and our candidate, are in favor of making
> Presidential elections, and the legislation of the
> country, distinct matters; so that the people can
> elect whom they please, and afterwards, legislate just
> as they please, without any hindrance, save only so
> much as may guard against infractions of the
> constitution, undue haste, and want of
> consideration."

> "....That we are right we can not doubt. We hold
> the true republican position. In leaving the people's
> business in their hands, we can not be wrong."[37]

In 1848, Lincoln had rejected the presidential mandate idea in
part because he recognized the uncertainty of the alleged mandate,
but in part also because he was then clearly in favor of a more
congressional rather than presidential form of government.[38] In a
speech Lincoln had made on the floor of the House of
Representatives on July 27, 1848, he declared:

> "[The President] is elected by the [people] as well as
> congress is. But can he, in the nature of things,
> know the wants of the people as well as three
> hundred other men, coming from all the various
> localities of the nation? If so, where is the propriety
> of having a congress? ...The Constitution gives the
> President a negative on legislation ...[but] to take the
> whole of legislation into his own hands, is what we
> object to.... To thus transfer legislation is clearly to
> take it from those who understand, with minuteness,
> the interests of the people, and give it to one who
> does not, and cannot so well understand it."[39]

Now, however, that he had himself become President, and given
the depth of his personal convictions upon the right course for the
nation to follow, Lincoln was no longer willing to allow a (likely...)

fractious, contrary, and indecisive Congress to decide America's future. He was, no doubt, concerned with the likelihood of stalemate or compromise of principle.

But if compromise was to be ruled out, the main alternative to bloodshed was to allow the South to do what it seemed to want to do, namely secede from the Union. And here, Lincoln was prepared to defy the principle of self-determination, ironically, enunciated in his favorite American document, the Declaration of Independence.[40] It may be objected, of course, that the voting citizens of the South in 1860 and 1861 did not represent, and did not speak for several million enslaved Africans inhabiting their states. But this is substitution of twentieth century judgment on the reality, and above all, the law of 1860. By the federal constitution of 1789, and the respective state laws, the Southern slave owners voted and the slaves did not. Lincoln never challenged the franchise provisions of the Southern states; implicitly, he supported them by his assurances that the federal government would not interfere with slavery where it already existed, or with other internal state jurisdictions. To be sure, there were legitimate concerns about the representativeness of some of the Southern state conventions and resolutions opting out of the Union in 1861.[41] Nevertheless, the results of the 1860 election -- whose fairness Lincoln never disputed -- foreshadowed the verdict of preponderant Southern opinion in response to Lincoln's victory.

Within the total of 4,686,750 votes cast by Americans in 1860, 1,274,908 were cast in the slave states. Only 26,388 Southern voters, or about 2 percent, cast their ballots for Lincoln. Between them, Breckinridge and Bell drew almost 84 percent of the Southern vote, with the rest, some 14 percent, going to Stephen Douglas. There could be little doubt that the 1860 election signified a tremendous regional breach between North and South. In the 1856 election, Lincoln's predecessor, James Buchanan, had won 606,850 votes in the slave states and 1,226,105 votes in the free Northern states. This translated into a much more balanced 56.5 percent of the Southern vote and 41.3 percent of the Northern vote. The 1860 election, with its lopsided division of the national vote -- Lincoln receiving 54 percent of the Northern vote but only 2 percent of the Southern vote -- represented an unparalleled polarization of the American electorate along regional lines.[42]   As Philip S. Paludan observes in his recent history of Lincoln's Presidency, the nation's sixteenth chief executive obtained no electoral votes at all in the seven Deep South states, and "won only 2 of the 966 Southern counties.".[43]   A grave crisis was clearly approaching.

As Samuel Wylie Crawford wrote in a book published in 1887, the election of Lincoln was seen in South Carolina as an unambiguous signal to proceed with secession:

> "The result of the election for President was accepted by every class as decisive of the action of the state, and that action must be the separation from the Federal Union.... When, therefore, the election of Mr. Lincoln was announced to them [the people] saw in it the sure precursor of danger and ruin... Secession was seen as necessary for the welfare of the State."[44]

When at last Lincoln made his Inaugural Address in Washington on March 4th, he quoted from one of his own earlier speeches about slavery, and declared:

> "Those who nominated and elected me did so with full knowledge that I had made this, and many similar declarations, and had never recanted them."[45]

Clearly, the President meant to stand by his principles and the Republican platform. He said that "perpetuity is implied, if not expressed, in the fundamental law of all national governments. It is safe to assert that no government proper, ever had a provision in its organic law for its own termination...the Union will endure forever -- it being impossible to destroy it, except by some action not provided for in the instrument itself."[46]   Lincoln also put forward the idea that the Union could only be dissolved by the agreement of all parties to it, and advanced a somewhat troubling denial of what may be termed the right of self-definition.

Even though this notion may be seen as having some limits, it is still difficult to envision any political democracy in the modern sense in which what "we, the people" want or deserve is essentially defined for us by some outside power or authority. In Lincoln's case, the argument he made probably has gained some gratuitous credit from the mere fact that the particular people Lincoln opposed were, at least to a significant degree, slave owners. That anyone should have a claim or a "right" to be a slave owner seems to us intuitively wrong. It is wrong. But Lincoln cast a very wide net against self-definition. He said:

> "If by the mere force of numbers, a majority should deprive a minority of any clearly written constitutional right, it might, in a moral point of view, justify revolution -- certainly would, if such right were a vital one. But such is not our case. All the vital rights of minorities, and of individuals, are so plainly assured to them, by affirmations and negations, guaranties and prohibitions, in the Constitution, that controversies never arise concerning them."

Few Southerners in 1861 probably agreed with Lincoln that, basically, they "did not have a problem." If they were aggrieved, Lincoln seemed to be saying, they lacked true cause to complain. It was not their right to decide what was or was not being denied to them. The Constitution took care of everybody -- sufficiently.[47]

Lincoln also argued that since the South and the North could "not separate "geographically and physically, but would always face one another, it would always be easier for the entities thus involved to deal with each other as one nation-state rather than two -- or perhaps even several.[48] This proposition pushed to its limits would presumably deny independence to any contiguous nations seeking liberty from others, such as for example Poland or Ukraine from

Russia or Norway from Sweden or Pakistan from India. All that Lincoln was willing to concede was the right of amendment as provided under the Constitution itself.

What had the appearance of a concession, but really was not, was the President's expressed willingness to seek an amendment to the Constitution through Congress to forever prohibit the federal government from interfering with slavery within the states where it already existed.[49] Apart from the issue of the President's credibility -- or lack of it -- in the Southern states, this would not retreat from Lincoln's oft repeated principle that slavery needed to be limited by the federal power, not banished by it. The President also offered to deliver up fugitive slaves but simultaneously invoked his solemn oath to preserve, protect and defend the Constitution of the United States, promising to defend federal installations and throwing the onus of responsibility for conflict upon the Southern secessionists: "In your hands, my dissatisfied fellow countrymen, and not in mine, is the momentous issue of civil war. The government will not assail you..."

One of the major arguments advanced by Lincoln to rebut the claims of secession was that the states had no existence prior to the creation of the federal union. As states, they were created by the Constitution. Before the enactment of that document, Lincoln argued, they were merely colonies, and all state rights were, properly speaking, devolved upon them by the Constitution itself. Moreover, he held that since the Constitution prohibited the states from having any but a republican form of government (Article IV, section 4), it was also clear that the Constitution effectively prohibited secession, and that it envisioned the federal union as an irreversible arrangement.

These arguments, appealing as they were to an American, especially Northern sense of nationalism, were, nevertheless, open to serious objection. In very narrow legal terms, one might agree that prior to the Constitution of 1789 there were no states, only "colonies." But the states were more than artificial legal inventions created in the city of Philadelphia. They were societies and geocultural entities which clearly predated the machinery of the American federal system. Most of them had a longer continuous existence before the adoption of the Constitution than the United States had since 1789. The colonies possessed institutions of government in which the Governors were appointed by the Crown but they all had elective assemblies with substantial legislative powers subject to gubernatorial consent and intervention.[50] As John D. Hicks remarks:

> "The citizens of every colony...enjoyed the same personal rights as Englishmen...jury trial, freedom of speech, [and] freedom from arbitrary imprisonment... These were privileges, moreover, that were not enjoyed in like measure by the colonists of any other nation." According to Hicks, many Americans, long before 1776, came to "think of the colonies as practically separate and independent units of the British Empire..."[51]

The Declaration of Independence of 1776 could easily convince any innocent reader that the people of these societies, whatever one called them, did indeed possess certain prior rights which were being denied to them by the tyrannical and arbitrary government of King George III. Obviously, these rights, including the alleged right to "property", must have existed before the American federal union if they existed prior to the rule of George III. Moreover, it was historically clear that the Constitution itself was brought into being and ratified by the will of the representatives of each of these colonies, or if one preferred, colonies-turned-into-states. The creation of the Union required the consent of the several states, regardless of size or population, and no single state was bound to join the rest by the collective acts of people or states outside its own borders.

The argument about a republican form of government federally imposed upon the states was not especially convincing. Clearly, *if* there was going to be a federal union, the powers of the states would have to be in various ways circumscribed in relation to each other and to the federal entity. But this requirement was itself seemingly contingent on union. Illustratively, a person who is a judge might not be allowed to be a prosecutor or a defense attorney at the same time, but if he ceases to be a judge, he might be any number of things otherwise incompatible with judicial office.[52]

The Constitution of the United States in its original form, and in effect in Lincoln's time, said nothing about secession. It was neither allowed nor disallowed. The Preamble enumerated the purposes which the Constitution was to serve. The framers had hoped that it would promote "a more perfect Union, establish justice, insure domestic tranquility, provide for the common defense, promote the general welfare, and secure the blessings of liberty to ourselves and our posterity"... It could be legitimately argued in 1860 and 1861 that the Constitution was not serving all of these purposes very effectively, if at all, and most self-evidently so with respect to the goal of domestic tranquility.

To be sure, the Constitution provided in Article V for its own amendment on the basis of state majoritarianism. Amendments could be put forward by either two thirds of the members of each house of the Congress, or a convention called into being by Congress on the proposal of two thirds of the State legislatures. In either case, the ratification of any proposed amendment as part of the Constitution would require the consent of three fourths of the states through legislative or convention procedures. This process implied a subjection of the "minority" to the "majority" in that the Constitution could always be changed against the wishes of one quarter of the states. It also implied adherence to the *status quo* if a three fourths majority of states could not be brought together for the purpose of effecting a change.

If the idea of secession had been viewed as a form of "amendment" to the Constitution, then clearly the Southern states could be lawfully denied secession, or even the consideration of secession, since they could not possibly muster the necessary political support in the Congress or the state legislatures to put the proposal up for approval by all the states. But was it reasonable, and, above all, "democratic" of Lincoln, and others, to refuse to consider the lawfulness of secession in any form?

In ordinary legal usage, "amendment" and "secession" are not equivalent concepts. Secession denotes dissolution. Amendment denotes some form of internal change. A state seceding from the Union obviously wished to wholly dissolve its partnership and association with the Union which is hardly the same as wishing to change some of the terms of one's partnership. It is a remarkable fact of history that Abraham Lincoln, who had enjoyed a distinguished legal career in Illinois, put forward a singularly fallacious doctrine of contracts in order to oppose the claims of secession. The notion of unanimous consent as prerequisite to the dissolution of a contract was palpably controverted by, among others, the ancient institutions of marriage and employment.

While marriage might require the consent of two parties to the original contract, divorce generally would not. The hiring of labor would always involve the willingness of one party to offer employment and of another to accept it. But the right to quit, or fire, in the American experience and in other free market societies has been generally unilateral. The best explanation of Lincoln's argument, however he made it, is that he regarded the "contract" of 1789 as a sacred compact, not to be compared with the contracts of everyday life.

If the framers of the American Constitution did not mention "secession", that hardly proved that they disallowed it. Perhaps they did not mention it because they wished to discourage it. Perhaps they were excessively optimistic about the virtue of their own work, and did not think it a likely contingency to be anticipated in the foreseeable future. Quite likely, secession was viewed, or would have been viewed, by the framers as a species of revolution; and the ultimate right of revolution in the Lockean scheme of things was inherent in every polity, in every "people", as a corrective to tyranny when all other remedies have failed. It was so universally "residual" that perhaps it did not even need to be specifically mentioned. And then, perhaps the framers, or at least their immediate successors assembled in the first Congress in New York City on September 25th, 1789, provided for it in the text of the first ten amendments which became ratified as part of the Constitution on December 15, 1791. The Ninth Amendment declares that "the enumeration in the Constitution of certain rights shall not be construed to deny or disparage others retained by the people." The Tenth Amendment provides that "the powers not delegated to the United States by the Constitution, nor prohibited by it to the States, are reserved to the States respectively, or to the people."

This was the argument advanced by Alabama's William L. Yancey in a speech in New York City on October 10th, 1860:

> "The Constitution of my country tells me that certain powers were given to the general government, and that those which were not expressly given or were not necessary to carry out the powers granted, were reserved to the states and to the people of the states. My state has reserved powers and reserved rights, and I believe in the right of secession.... If any [state] dissented, there was no proposition [in 1787] to force them into the Union. Therefore, I believe in the right of a state to go out of the Union, if she thinks proper."[53]

And Yancey asked his New York audience rhetorically:

> "Who is there higher than the states? Who is there more sovereign than the parties to the compact who have the reserved rights guaranteed to them?"[54]

Indeed, could not the South take comfort in the words of Thomas Jefferson's Declaration of Independence of 1776 when it said that "whenever any form of Government becomes destructive of these Ends [Life, Liberty, and the Pursuit of Happiness....] it is the right of the People to alter or to abolish it, and to institute new Government, laying its Foundation on such Principles, and organizing its Powers in such Form, as to them shall seem most likely to effect their Safety and Happiness?"

The Constitution since its 1789 ratification was only 72 years old when Lincoln took office as President in 1861. Its Preamble and text did not use words such as "perpetual" or "indissoluble." As a lawyer, Lincoln might have known and expected that all human contracts, economic, social, political or personal, have a tendency to be overtaken by developments that are not foreseen at the time of their origin. He might have, but in this case he obviously did not believe that. Here, too, we find a great difference of opinion between an earlier Lincoln and a later Lincoln.

On January 12, 1848, Congressman Lincoln made a fairly lengthy speech on the floor of the House of Representatives opposing and condemning President Polk for allegedly dragging the nation into a war with Mexico. He argued that there was insufficient cause for war and that the President forced a conflict that was hardly an inevitable one.[55] In this speech, Lincoln employed an argument which could have been effectively used against him in 1861. He declared that:

> " Any people anywhere, being inclined and having the power, have the right to rise up, and shake off the existing government, and form a new one that suits them better. This is a most valuable -- a most sacred right -- a right which we hope and believe, is to liberate the world. Nor is this right confined to cases in which *the whole people of an existing government may choose to exercise it. Any portion of such people that can, may revolutionize, and make their own, of so much territory as they inhabit. More than this, a majority of any portion of such people may revolutionize putting down a minority, intermingled with, or near about them, who may oppose their movement.*"[56]

Lincoln's predecessor, President James Buchanan, in his last message to Congress on December 3, 1860, actually put forward this, not altogether unreasonable, interpretation of the Constitution:

> "The question fairly stated is, has the Constitution delegated to Congress the power to coerce a State into submission which is attempting to withdraw or has actually withdrawn from the Confederacy? If answered in the affirmative, it must be on the principle that the power has been conferred upon Congress to declare and to make war against a State. After much serious reflection I have arrived at the conclusion that no such power has been delegated to Congress or to any other department of the Federal Government.

> "The fact is that our Union rests upon public opinion, and can never be cemented by the blood of its citizens shed in civil war. If it can not live in the affections of the people, it must one day perish. Congress possesses many means of preserving it by conciliation, but the sword was not placed in their hand to preserve it by force...."[57]

Whatever the purely legal aspects of the conflict, it is clear that Lincoln viewed preponderant Southern sentiment for independence as an irrelevancy. South Carolina's decision to secede was the earliest on December 20, 1860, when it repealed its ratification of the United States Constitution effective December 24th. The other states, seceding in 1861, generally produced more lopsided majorities in convention meetings -- presumably dominated by a slave-owning elite -- than they did in instances where a popular vote was taken to ratify the decision. Illustratively, Mississippi's convention voted to secede by a margin of 84 to 15 on January 9, 1861. Florida voted 62 to 7 for secession the very next day. Georgia approved secession 208 to 89 on January 19th. Louisiana followed suit on January 26th by a margin of 113 to 17 and Texas by 166 to 7 on February 1st. In the three ratifying referenda, Texas voted for secession by a roughly three-to-one margin, 34,794 for secession and 11,325 against it. Virginia's decision to secede, taken after the attack on Fort Sumter, on April 17th was 88 to 55 in convention but actually 128,884 to only 32,134 against secession in the referendum. In Tennessee, the decision to secede was ratified by a popular vote of 104,019 for and 47,238 against secession.

If compromise over slavery, and secession, were both ruled out by Lincoln, all that remained by way of preserving the peace between the states in early 1861 was the hope that, somehow, the South would back down.[58] For those who harbored the hope that the South's "bite would not be as bad as its bark" even a policy of federal intransigence had its attractions. Since the North was by all indicators of population, wealth, resources and industrial development stronger than the South, it was an understandable proposition for many, including perhaps Lincoln himself, that a policy of "firmness" by the North against the South might best prevent war and secession alike. Of course, this policy option was fraught with a grave risk of bloody conflict. And, in the late 1850's, and 1860-1861, it was an interesting, highly speculative question of judgment among Americans whether the Southern states would, in fact, go beyond angry resolutions, words, and gestures, and actually resort to arms.

In the event, some 360,000 men died in the Civil War out of a population of about 22 millions in the North. The loss of some 260,000 lives in the South was even more appalling given a population of only 9.5 million c. 1860.[59] Taking the United States as a whole, the casualties of the Civil War projected onto the American population in mid 1990's would have been nearly five million in deaths alone.

Naturally, no one could have known this at Lincoln's inauguration in March of 1861. Many people on both sides of the conflict expected the war, if it did happen, to be short and relatively painless. Others were more pessimistic. It is not really clear what Lincoln's own anticipations were, though there is some evidence that he may have underestimated the actual impact of a North-South conflict.[60] As in most wars, the original anticipations were most often wrong.

REFERENCE

1. Note J.G. Randall, <u>Constitutional Problems Under Lincoln</u>, Revised Edition (Gloucester, Mass.: Peter Smith, 1963) p. 370. The slave holders of the South were always concerned -- understandably in view of their vulnerability -- to prevent the machinery of the federal government from aiding or encouraging abolitionism.

2. Horace Greeley and John F. Cleveland, <u>Political Textbook for 1860</u> (New York: The Tribune Association, 1860) p. 26.

3. <u>Ibid</u>, p. 29.

4. <u>Ibid</u>, pp. 29-30.

5. <u>Ibid</u>, p. 30-31.

6. Reinhard Luthin, <u>The First Lincoln Campaign</u> (Gloucester, Mass.: Peter Smith, 1964) p. 226.

7. Harry V. Jaffa, <u>Crisis of the House Divided, An Interpretation of the Issues in the Lincoln-Douglas Debates</u> (New York: Doubleday, 1959) p. 26.

8. William E. Baringer, "The Republican Triumph," in Norman A. Graebner (ed.), <u>Politics and the Crisis of 1860</u> (Urbana: University of Illinois Press, 1961) p. 116.

9. <u>Ibid</u>, p. 97.

10. <u>Ibid</u>.

11. <u>Ibid</u>, pp. 97-98. Note also Eileen Shields-West, <u>The World Almanac of Presidential Campaigns</u> (New York: World Almanac, 1992) p. 83.

12. Emerson David Fite, <u>The Presidential Campaign of 1860</u> (Port Washington, N.Y.: Kennikat Press, Inc., 1967) pp. 127, 129.

13. See Robert W. Johansen, <u>Lincoln, the South and Slavery, The Political Dimension</u> (Baton Rouge: Louisiana State University Press, 1991) pp. 112-118.

Philip S. Paludan offers a possible, different, interpretation of Lincoln's silence on policy questions between election and inauguration. "Lincoln listened to advice that counseled caution. He decided that not reacting would be the best reaction." Philip Shaw Paludan, The Presidency of Abraham Lincoln (Lawrence, Kansas: University Press of Kansas, 1994) p. 29. Naturally, Lincoln can be said to have been silent because, somehow, he thought that silence was the best course. How could one disagree? That this was a policy of caution however, is a far more problematic inference. Note also the Paludan discussion of this question on pp. 29-32. Against all the evidence to the contrary, Paludan affirms the claim that "the [American] people (!)...voted for the Republican ideas and platform." p. 30. Note also p. 49 on how Lincoln had refused to set foot in Washington substantially before the inauguration. Cautious or not, this was a political leader who was eager not to "wheel and deal" before taking office.

14. John D. Hicks, The Federal Union, A History of the United States to 1865 (Boston: Houghton Mifflin Company, 1937) p. 612.

15. Ibid, pp. 612-613. Note also McPherson, op. cit., p. 53 who agrees that if at the time of the Lincoln-Douglas debates of the late 1850's a national referendum had been held on the question as to whose interpretation of the Declaration of Independence was the correct one, Douglas would have prevailed.

16. William E. Baringer, A House Dividing: Lincoln as President Elect (Abraham Lincoln Association: Springfield, 1945) p. 194.

17. Ibid, p. 197.

18. Ibid, p. 198.

19. Ibid, p. 245.

20. Mark E. Neely, Jr., The Last Best Hope of Earth, Abraham Lincoln and the Promise of America (Cambridge: Harvard University Press, 1993) p. 62.

21. Ibid, p. 63.

22. Ibid.

23. Ibid, p. 64; see Allan Nevins, Ordeal of the Union, The Emergence of Lincoln, Prologue to the Civil War 1859-1861, Volume II (New York: Charles Scribner's Sons, 1950) on Buchanan's position of "national helplessness." P. 352. According to Nevins, President-elect Lincoln viewed "the situation at first with an excessive optimism believing...that the secession clamor was largely a bluff." P. 355.

Nevins concedes that the "Crittenden scheme had wide and enthusiastic public support." P. 392. He also notes, however, that Lincoln "without consulting others" opposed it because he believed that a "crisis must be reached and passed" and the country brought "to a completely new resolution respecting slavery." P. 395.

24. Basler, vol. IV, p. 190.

25. Ibid.

26. Ibid.

27. Ibid, p. 191.

28. Ibid, pp. 200-201.

29. Ibid.

30. Clarence Macartney, Lincoln and His Cabinet (New York: Charles Scribner's Sons, 1931) p. 8-9.

31. Basler, vol. IV, pp. 211-212.

32. Franklin L. Burdette, The Republican Party, A Short History (Princeton, N.J.: D. Van Nostrand Company, 1968) p. 28.

33. Ibid, p. 29.

34. Ibid.

35. Basler, vol. I, p. 504.

36. Ibid, p. 505.

37. Ibid, p. 506.

38. William H. Herndon and Jesse W. Weik, <u>Abraham Lincoln, The True Story of A Great Life</u>, Volume I (New York: D. Appleton, 1893) pp. 262-270 cover Lincoln's objections to the excessive use of presidential power in the Mexican War. At the time, Herndon appears to have warned Lincoln that his course implied political suicide. P. 270.

39. Basler, vol. I, p. 504.

40. Note Kenneth M. Stampp's essay "One Alone? The United States and National Self-determination," in Gabor S. Boritt (ed.), <u>Lincoln, The War President</u> (New York: Oxford University Press, 1992) pp. 123-144. He admits that Lincoln's legacy to posterity on the issue of self-determination is "ambiguous"... P. 143. This is quite an understatement. For reasons he deemed sufficient, Lincoln separated "self" and "determination" as far as the South was concerned.

41. Among modern scholars views differ. Ralph Korngold says: "It is now known that the majority of the people of the South did not want separation from the Union." He cites the view of James G. Randall ('there were evidences that secession as the answer to Lincoln's election by no means commanded the preponderant support of the southern people'). Lincoln himself questioned it, except in the case of South Carolina, in a message to Congress of July 4, 1861. See Ralph Korngold, <u>Thaddeus Stevens, A Being Darkly Wise and Rudely Great</u> (New York: Harcourt, Brace and Company, 1955) p. 161.

Interestingly, Roy Franklin Nichols in his <u>The Disruption of American Democracy</u> (New York: Macmillan, 1948) takes a different view of the matter. "The voters, the plain people, in large portions of the lower South were fearful and angry [about Lincoln's victory]. This sentiment seemed stronger among the poor than among the rich. It was deeply felt by the non-slaveholders ...The wealthy might flee insurrection and need not fear the competition of freed Negroes. Poor men, however, must stay...and dare...a degrading economic struggle with the erstwhile slaves." Pp. 415-416. In Mississippi, the bulk of pro-Union support, according to Nichols, was among the large plantation owners, as was the case in Florida. P.417. Despite all sorts of difficulty in estimating popular support for secession in 1861, Nichols sees the margin for rupture as relatively narrow.

Note Robin E. Baker and Dale Baum, " The Texas Voter and the Crisis of the Union, 1859-1860," <u>The Journal of Southern History</u>, vol. 53, No. 3, August 1987, pp. 395-420. This is one of several "micro" studies which demonstrate that the enthusiasm for secession was by no means confined to a few rich planters.

A "mass base" was mobilized, as the authors note. P. 419. Note also Fletcher M. Green. "Democracy in the Old South", The Journal of Southern History, vol. 12, No. 1, February 1946, pp. 3-23. Green concludes that "the interpretation of the southern states as 'political aristocracies of the sternest and most odious kind' had no basis in fact." P. 23. "One test of the effectiveness of democracy is the exercise of the suffrage by those qualified to vote. The southern states met this test to about the same degree that the northern states did." P.19. See also William S. Hitchcock, "The Limits of Southern Unionism: Virginia Conservatives and the Gubernatorial Election of 1859" The Journal of Southern History , vol. 47, No. 1, February 1981, pp. 57-72.

42. See William S. Gienapp, "Who Voted for Lincoln?" in John L. Thomas (ed.), Abraham Lincoln and the American Political Tradition (Amherst: University of Massachusetts Press, 1986) p. 77.

43. Paludan, op. cit., p. 5.

44. Samuel Wylie Crawford, The Genesis of the Civil War, The Story of Sumter, 1860-1861 (New York: Charles L. Webster and Company, 1887) p. 15. Cf. Thomas H. O'Connor, The Disunited States, The Era of Civil War and Reconstruction (New York: Dodd, Mead and Company, 1972) "Regarding the distinction Lincoln and the Republicans made between an attack upon slavery in the states themselves and attack upon the expansion of slavery into the territories as tricky semantics and utter hogwash, Southerners saw the Republican platform as merely the first step toward the destruction of the life, the society and the culture of the South." P. 111.

45. Basler, vol. IV, p. 263.

46. Ibid, pp. 264-265. See F. B. Carpenter, Six Months at the White House (New York: Hurd and Houghton, 1866). "On the morning of Mr. Lincoln's arrival in Washington, just before the inauguration, it will be remembered that the Peace Convention was in session. Among those who were earliest to call upon him was a gentleman from Pennsylvania, who had been in Congress with him, and who was a member of the Peace Convention. He at once commenced plying the President elect with urgent reasons for *compromising* matters in dispute, saying: 'It must be done sooner or later, and that this seemed a propitious month.' Listening attentively to all that was said, Mr. Lincoln finally replied: 'Perhaps your reasons for compromising the alleged difficulties are correct and that now is the favorable time to do it; still, if I remember correctly, *that* is not what *I* was elected for.' " Pp. 229-230.

47. Basler, vol. IV, p. 267.

48. Ibid, p. 269.

49. Ibid, p. 270.

50. Hicks, op. cit., p. 89. Note 1777 Articles of Confederation and 12 "State" constitutions adopted 1776-1780.

51. Ibid. See also Herman Belz, Reconstructing the Union, Theory and Policy During the Civil War (Ithaca, N.Y.: Cornell University Press, 1969) ..."in Lincoln's view the United States was a 'government proper' not an association of states in the nature of a contract merely. In a message to Congress of July 4, 1861, Lincoln declared that : "The States have their status in the Union, and they have no other legal status." Pp. 8-9.

52. See Garry Wills, Lincoln at Gettysburg, The Words That Remade America (New York: Simon and Schuster, 1992). The same contractual argument was made by Mr. Edward Everett at the dedication of the Gettysburg Cemetery on November 19th, 1863. Mr. Everett wanted to know how any state could possibly enter a Confederacy if the Constitution prohibits states from entering "into any alliance, treaty or confederation." P. 238. Naturally, a man or woman who was legally married could not enter into another marriage, but one who was already divorced could marry anyone he or she wanted. Mr. Everett also insisted that the tenth amendment could not have authorized states to secede because the powers reserved to the states and the people were only those that *could* have been delegated to the United States and secession as a federal power would have been absurd. Ibid. An amazing confusion of roles and denial of both Locke and Jefferson!

53. See Fite, op. cit., p. 324.

54. Ibid, p. 326. Note William L. Barney in his The Secessionist Impulse: Alabama and Mississippi in 1860 (Princeton: Princeton University Press, 1974). Barney sees racism and Southern white fears connected to racism as the most important weapons of the Secessionists' agitation. Pp. 229-230. He also says that the "exuberance and confidence with which the South seceded were unmistakable." P. 313. Ralph A. Wooster in his The Secession Conventions of the South (Princeton: Princeton University Press, 1962) shows in a detailed study not only of states but of counties within states that the proportion of slaves in the population varied directly with the support for secession among the departing states. E.g., pp. 202, 264, 266.

Voters in those areas were apparently most convinced that the maintenance of slavery was important to them and that it was threatened by the federal system.

55. Basler, vol. I, pp. 431-442.

56. Ibid, p. 438.

57. See James A. Rawley, op. cit., p.235. Bruce Catton in his Centennial History of the Civil War, The Coming Fury Volume I (Garden City, N.Y. : Doubleday and Company, Inc., 1961) describes President Buchanan's last message to Congress in these terms: "There was something here to irritate everyone and to encourage no one. Facing both ways, Buchanan had been able to see nothing but the difficulties." Pp. 128-129. Cf. Woodrow Wilson, Epochs of American History, Division and Reunion, 1829-1909 (New York: Longman's Green, and Co., 1909) P. 208. Wilson describes the South's perception of the Lincoln election as "countenancing and assisting servile insurrection." He also remarks that "The legal theory upon which [secession] was taken was one which hardly has been questioned in the early years of the government...It was for long found difficult to deny that a State could withdraw from the federal arrangement, as she might have decided to enter it. But constitutions are not mere legal documents...." P. 211.

58. See Kenneth M. Stampp, And the War Came: The North and The Secession Crisis, 1860-1861 (Baton Rouge: Louisiana State University Press, 1950) pp. 184-185. ..."Lincoln ruled out both compromise and peaceful disunion from the outset." See also p. 180 on Lincoln's "policy of silence" after the 1860 election. Whatever he may have said about Lincoln's "caution" and restraint, even Professor Paludan concedes that in 1860 "most Southerners and Northerners believed that slavery had to expand or die." Op. cit., p. 35. On this issue, Lincoln offered no "give"...

59. Hicks, op. cit., p. 657.

60. William Barney, The Road to Secession: A New Perspective on the Old South (New York: Praeger Publishers, 1972) ..."The secessionists did not expect the fighting to be either prolonged or socially destructive." P. 197. This was a more prevalent view in the lower South than in the border states because of its greater, and presumably safer, distance from the North. Note also Richard Nelson Current, Lincoln and the First Shot (Philadelphia: J.B. Lippincott Company, 1963) ..."it appears that Lincoln, when he decided to send the Sumter expedition, considered hostilities to be *probable*, although

he may have believed that a peaceful provisioning of the fort was barely possible." P. 193.

Cf. Charles W. Ramsdell, "Lincoln and Fort Sumter," The Journal of Southern History, vol. 3, No. 3, August 1937, pp. 259-288. The author concludes that Lincoln engineered the outbreak of hostilities at Fort Sumter by very capably, and very discreetly, provoking the Confederate response on April 12, 1861. "Some, perhaps, will be reminded of the famous incident of the Ems telegram of which the cynical Bismarck boasted in his memoirs." P. 288. See also Kenneth M. Stampp, "Lincoln and the Strategy of Defense in the Crisis of 1861," The Journal of Southern History, vol. 11, No. 3, August 1945, pp. 297-323. Lincoln's strategy was such, the author maintains, that "the burden of aggression" would always be upon the secessionists. P. 315.

Appropriately, the author begins his essay with this quotation from Herndon: "Lincoln never poured out his soul to any mortal creature at any time... He was the most secretive -- reticent -- shut-mouthed man that ever existed." P. 287. Oates, op. cit., in his biography of Lincoln presents the more conventional view that Lincoln, far from seeking to provoke the Southerners into a war, desperately sought to avoid it. Nevertheless, as Oates sees it, "there was no conceivable way that Lincoln could avoid an armed collision with Southern rebels; if he did not hold Sumter, he would have to stand somewhere else or see the government collapse." P. 84.

According to Oates, the outbreak of the war plunged Lincoln "into a depression that would plague him throughout his embattled presidency." He saw himself as one who abhorred violence but was forced to suffer it, and was also a cause of it..." P. 86. Herndon recalled that following his election, Lincoln "apprehended no such grave danger to the Union as the mass of the people supposed would result from Southern threats, and said he could not in his heart believe that the South designed the overthrow of the Government." William H. Herndon and Jesse Weik, Abraham Lincoln: The True Story of a Great Life, vol. II (New York: D. Appleton, 1893) p. 183.

Whether Lincoln really believed this is highly problematic. It certainly suited Lincoln's purposes of not engaging in any negotiations over policy questions prior to taking office. It helped him in maintaining a basic intransigence toward the South. Horatio King recalls that when he first met Lincoln in February, 1861, when the President elect called upon the President, "I did not observe in him the least sign of nervousness or deep concern." P. 283. King explains this by the supposition that Lincoln was expecting "to gain the good will of the Southern malcontents and of soon bringing the seceding states back to their proper relations in the Federal

Government." <u>Ibid.</u> But there was still greater likelihood that Lincoln was already resolved to defeat the secession by force, and his mind was serene precisely because he had settled upon his course beyond any vacillations.

IV

METHODS OF RULE

Inaugurated March 4th, Lincoln faced secession by seven states in the Deep South led by South Carolina, the likelihood of several additional defections, and a great deal of unrest in the border region among such states as Kentucky, Virginia, and Maryland. Under the circumstances, the President might have been expected to call the newly elected Congress into session to help him formulate appropriate policies and responses to the unfolding crisis. Indeed, based on Lincoln's own views, as expressed when he was himself a Congressman, one would have thought that he would do no less. But Lincoln did not call Congress into session until July 4th, 1861, giving himself fully four months of executive rule without the advice and consent of the national legislature.

This was hardly accidental, nor was it somehow forced upon the President. In the age of railroads, Congress could have been easily convened within a matter of several days, perhaps a comfortable fortnight at most. While representatives from the Southern states, or at least some of them, might not have responded to the call, there were no really significant impediments to a gathering of the nation's legislators in virtually any of the Northern states. There may have been plots aimed at Lincoln's life in Baltimore, or elsewhere on his train journey from Springfield to Washington, but there was no guerrilla warfare, and no noticeable disruption in most of the states of the Union in March of 1861, not in Massachusetts, or New York, or Michigan, or many other states and localities outside the South and the border states. Many of the people who would have attended an early meeting of Congress, if Lincoln had called one, were probably in Washington already to attend the President's inauguration. Some were "old Washingtonians" and at least part time District of Columbia residents as hold-over incumbents from the Congress elected in 1858.

On the other hand, it is a reasonable inference that Lincoln realized what the Congress' political complexion -- all labels notwithstanding -- was likely to be. He did not want legislative advice and action which he feared or of which he disapproved. Nor did he welcome the prospect of a policy stalemate in the face of the impending crisis. He had had some inkling as to just what the Congress might do from the Crittenden initiative of the previous Fall, and he certainly realized how politically divided the new House and Senate would be. The experience of what Congress was like, and what its potential for action, or inaction, was, had been amply demonstrated during the previous decade. Apparently, in Lincoln's mind, the spring of 1861 was a time for resolute action but it was not a time for democracy in its usual sense: dialogue among the people's representatives.[1]

Judging by past conduct, by the nature of the election results, and by future events, that is, the behavior of Congress after it was convened on July 4th, Lincoln was almost certainly right. What is beyond dispute, however, is that he was not prepared to take a chance on the collective wisdom of the people's freely elected representatives in the spring of 1861. The stakes seemed too high. He acted first, and in effect, presented the Congress with a *fait accompli* in the series of measures appropriating men and money for the pursuit of war against the Southern states: a war which, practically speaking, was undertaken by the President and not by the Congress.

Admittedly, it was not Lincoln, or the Union forces, which fired the first shot. That distinction belonged to the Confederates, and, arguably, they did so in the reasonably clear knowledge of what Lincoln's response would be. Nevertheless, Lincoln's reaction to the threat to Fort Sumter, five weeks after his inauguration as President, owed nothing to Congressional advice or consent, not even to the advice and consent of Congressional leaders of Lincoln's own party let alone the opposition. By the time Congress did convene, the war between the states was a full blown affair.

What is of special interest in this sequence of events -- quite apart from inconclusive speculations about Lincoln wishing to provoke the Confederates into firing the first salvo of the war -- is the element of forethought and planning. The war began when the Southerners fired upon Union forces attempting to provision the garrison of the Federal fort in Charleston Harbor. But the decision to resupply the Fort, in the face of obvious risks, and the initial opposition even of Lincoln's own Cabinet, was itself a Presidential initiative, a deliberate act carried out over a period of time.

Even if we grant, retrospectively, that the relief of Fort Sumter was the precisely proper policy response, it was hardly the only possible response. The garrison might have been withdrawn, for example. There might have been formal or informal negotiations with the authorities in South Carolina concerning the disposition of the Fort and its garrison. In any case, the single most important decision of the war was very much the President's decision.[2]

On April 15, 1861, Lincoln issued the Proclamation Calling forth the Militia and Convening the Congress....on July 4th. The Proclamation declared that in South Carolina, Georgia, Alabama, Florida, Mississippi, Louisiana and Texas, the laws of the United States had been opposed and obstructed by "combinations" too powerful to be suppressed by "ordinary judicial proceedings."

> "Now, therefore, I, Abraham Lincoln, President of the United States, in virtue of the power in me vested by the Constitution, and the laws, have thought fit to call forth and hereby do call forth, the militia of the several states of the Union, to the aggregate number of seventy-five thousand, in order to suppress said combinations, and to cause the laws to be duly executed.... The details for this object will be immediately communicated to the State authorities through the War Department....[3]

> "I appeal to all loyal citizens to favor, facilitate and aid this effort to maintain the honor, the integrity,

and the existence of our National Union, and the perpetuity of popular government and to redress wrongs already long enough endured"...[to] repossess the forts, places and property which have been seized from the Union; and in every event, the utmost care will be observed, consistently with the objects aforesaid, to avoid any devastation, any destruction of, or interference with, property, or any disturbance of peaceful citizens in any part of the country.

And I hereby command the persons composing the combinations aforesaid to disperse, and retire peaceably to their respective abodes within twenty days from this date...."[4]

In a letter written on April 24th, Lincoln wrote:

"I have no purpose to invade Virginia or any other State, but I do not mean to let them invade us without striking back."[5]

On April 25th, Lincoln informed General Winfield Scott that if the Maryland legislature should vote to arm the people of the State against the Union, the General may bombard the cities in the State and suspend the writ of habeas corpus.[6]

Thus it appeared that in the spring of 1861, Lincoln was not about to adhere to the constitutional doctrines which he had espoused -- seemingly ages ago -- as a young Congressman from Illinois. It may be recalled that both publicly and privately Lincoln had criticized President Polk for unilaterally taking the nation into war with Mexico and usurping the powers constitutionally vested in the Congress. He did so in a speech in the House of Representatives[7] on January 2, 1848, and emphatically also in a letter to his then law partner, William Herndon, on February 15, 1848. In the letter, Lincoln had accused Polk of placing himself in the role of a king and destroying the constitutional scheme of things which placed the power to declare war in the Congress.[8]

But now, apparently, it was Lincoln's turn to be King. Professor James G. Randall, one of the great Lincoln scholars of modern times, notes that while:

> "Lincoln's course was undoubtedly patriotic, capable, and forceful, for which reasons it has been generally applauded..." [yet] it presented Congress with "an accomplished fact for its subsequent sanction...." something jurists would have to agree was "bad practice..."[9]

Even Lincoln referred to his own measures in somewhat troubling terms:

> ..."Whether strictly legal or not, [as] ventured upon, under what appeared to be a popular demand and a public necessity; trusting...that Congress would ratify them...." of course, post facto.[10]

As Randall remarks:

> "The conflict began during a recess of Congress and...for nearly three months all the necessary measures of resistance were executive acts, performed in the absence of legislative authorization. To that extent it was a presidential war.[11] ...certainly the enlargement of the army and navy and the suspension of the habeas corpus privilege were open to grave doubts [as to their constitutionality] while the proclamations of a blockade were widely regarded as unwarranted. In referring to his proclamation of May 4, 1861, calling for enlistments in the regular army far beyond the existing legal limits, Lincoln himself frankly admitted that he had overstepped his

authority. It was such acts as these that gave rise to
the charge of 'military dictatorship' and this charge
seemed to gain weight from the President's
deliberate postponement of the special session of
Congress until July 4, though the call for such
session was issued April 15."[12]

To be sure, Lincoln never openly challenged the constitutional
powers of the Congress, never threatened to shut it down, or suspend
it, or nullify its measures. He acted astutely, but he nevertheless
acted to hold Congress very much at arm's length, out of harm's
way, treating it as a lesser, subordinate-to-the-executive, branch of
government. On issues of central concern to him, Lincoln sought to
have Congress ratify his initiatives or stay out of his way. He was
willing to let it talk and legislate on matters of peripheral interest to
his presidency. Lincoln's doctrine of congressional powers, when
he was in office as President, was a virtual 180 degree reversal of
the views he had espoused so forcefully as a Whig congressman in
1848.[13]

When at last the Congress convened in July, Lincoln sent it a
message which, indirectly, but nevertheless quite clearly, explained
his underlying conception of the crisis. Lincoln's subject here was
the military, not the political leadership of the nation, but the
principle was readily apparent, relevant and applicable:

"It has been said that one bad general is better than
two good ones; and the saying is true, if taken to
mean no more than that an army is better directed by
a single mind, though inferior, than by two superior
ones, at variance, and cross-purposes with each
other.

...In a storm at sea, no one on board *can* wish the
ship to sink ; and yet, not infrequently, all go down
together, because too many will direct, and no single
mind can be allowed to control."[14]

Lincoln's "congressional management" was aided by some fortuitous circumstances, including the absence of twenty two Senators from the 11 seceding states and 66 House members. This weakened the Democrats and indirectly strengthened the Republicans. To the extent that the Democrats were identified and to a degree compromised by their past association with the Southern secessionists and slave-holders, their popularity and support in some of the Northern states was undermined. This, in turn, produced defections among the remaining Democrats in the national legislature, who, in many cases, began to identify themselves with the Republican majority in both houses.

The Republican Party itself, nominally supportive of Lincoln, was split into factions, the most influential of which, and not always supportive of the President, was led by Representative Thaddeus Stevens of Pennsylvania. The latter was also chairman of the powerful House Appropriations Committee and later of the Joint Committee on the Conduct of the War which consisted of three Senators and four Representatives. The Radical Republicans, led by Stevens, were much more abolitionist in their views than Lincoln. As long as the principal issue before the federal government was fighting the Southern secessionists, their differences with Lincoln were fairly muted. When, however, issues of post-war reconstruction and the treatment of slavery became increasingly important, Lincoln encountered mounting opposition from within the ranks of his own Party.[15]

If the President was able to do as much as he did in relative independence of the Congress, it was, in part, at least, because Congress as a body was not easily capable of producing its own expeditious policy alternatives. The Congress was, party labels notwithstanding, a body deeply divided over policy questions, and uncertain, if not actually confused, about what needed to be done in the face of the great constitutional crisis.[16] Quite importantly also, the organization and the powers of the Congress in Lincoln's time had not yet nearly approached the formidable dimensions of the modern era.

In his study of the evolution of Congress, Randall Ripley defines the differences between that institution in Lincoln's time (and, of course, earlier...) and the more recent period in terms of several basic criteria. The pre-modern Congress, as Ripley calls it, was characterized by high turnover in its membership and many contested elections. Its sessions were relatively short and the work load was light. Floor proceedings tended to be chaotic. There was high turnover in committee personnel and numerous, poorly specified criteria for the appointment of committee chairs; the political party organizations within the Congress were not well developed. The modern Congress, as he calls it, has tended to have low membership turnover; few contested elections; orderly floor proceedings; stable membership of legislative committees; seniority as the dominant criterion of appointment for committee leaders; and well developed party organizations.

Moreover, the Congress of Lincoln's day lacked the formidable staff resources which are so characteristic of the modern institution.[17] The literally thousands of research and clerical staffers and assistants supporting Congress in its investigative and legislative roles were simply not there. Congress lacked the powerful bureaucratic "muscle" with which it could confront and assail its executive opponents as it would in modern times.[18] Oddly enough, Lincoln also benefited by the crisis-inspired decline in the expertise of the post 1860 Congress. As Harold Hyman says:

> "Many Republicans who were elected with Lincoln in 1860 possessed neither parliamentary deftness nor expertness in Congress' internal machinery.... Seceders included many of Congress' experienced parliamentarians and constitutionally minded men. Each of the twenty two southern senators who went with their states had served in Congress more than ten years, fourteen had extensive legal training, six had been judges."[19]

It is, nevertheless, Hyman's view, and that of many other commentators, including Woodrow Wilson in his *Congressional*

Government: A Study in American Politics, that Congress actually tended to become *more* powerful and active after the outbreak of the Civil War than before it. Hyman places great emphasis on the development of more standing, specialized committees, Congressional investigations, and the increased powers of the Speaker of the House of Representatives.[20] Hyman sees the Republicans in Congress of the early 1860's as "pushing" the President to do more rather than trying to restrain him.[21] Democrats were, admittedly, a different matter, and the author duly records that they even planned a veritable congressional *coup* against Lincoln but the attempt never materialized due to the opposition's and Lincoln's own vigilance. Thus:

> "In 1863, Democrats angry with the Emancipation Proclamation toyed with a plan to seize control of the House by excluding Republican representatives. Their notion was to have the sympathetic Clerk of the House, Emerson Etheridge, leave key Republicans off his roll at the convening of the 38th Congress in December. Democrats would exploit the confusion and northern whitelash, reverse the administration's emancipation policy, and restore [General] McClellan to top command and thence to the White House. Then the war could end on southern terms with respect to slavery. Lincoln sniffed out the plot, however, and let slip the news of his knowledge. Fearful, the schemers gave up the project."[22]

Even among Republicans, where Lincoln's support was greater, there were pockets of dissension and dissatisfaction, and occasional talk of impeaching Lincoln or "dumping" him at the next election. The movement to nominate Salmon P. Chase was illustrative of this tendency, though it, too, failed at the 1864 convention. Notwithstanding all the divisions, Lincoln capitalized on the obvious "central tendency" of the Republican majority in both houses of Congress: the disposition to preserve the Union and see slavery eliminated as well as general hostility toward the Southern secessionists.

Various writers have explored the paradox of Lincoln's Presidency in terms of his use of executive power. Lincoln was a great "activist" as a Presidential leader on some questions -- those he considered central to his historic mission. He largely neglected many other areas of policy, administration, and legislation, allowing Congress and the Cabinet, or, more properly speaking, individual Cabinet officers, to do as they would. Thus, according to some views, Lincoln could be said to have simultaneously strengthened and also weakened the Presidency, and correspondingly strengthened or weakened the Congress.[23]

Professor David H. Donald attributes Lincoln's ambivalent conduct to his Whig background. He says:

> "On key policies...especially those involving the use of the war power, Lincoln, like Harrison and Taylor before him, departed from the Whig theory of cabinet responsibility, but he could not rid himself of the political ideas with which he had been raised."[24]

In the words of another distinguished scholar, Professor Edward S. Corwin:

> "Lincoln came to regard Congress as a more or less necessary nuisance and the Cabinet as a usually unnecessary one."[25]

One effect of this was to provide the precedent that when the country is engulfed in a "widespread condition of violence," the President may be entitled to ignore all "constitutional and statutory restraints in favor of personal liberty" [for the Executive to act as he may consider appropriate].[26] Lincoln, according to Corwin, "left the task of processing necessary legislation to his Cabinet secretaries, and especially to Chase and Stanton, theirs being the departments most concerned."[27]   The net result of the interactions between Lincoln and Congress, despite a certain undeniable amount of give-and-take on both sides, was to increase the preponderance of the executive over the legislature with respect to virtually all war-making functions. But inasmuch as the Lincoln administration sank almost all its energies into the conduct of the war, a good deal of ground was left open for legislative cultivation and development, even in the shadow of the most powerful Presidency of the nineteenth century. Paradoxically, Congressional activism grew even as the Executive branch tilted the balance of power in one sense more than ever before against the national legislature. And thus Lincoln at once managed to be faithful and also unfaithful to the Whig theory of government. Conduct of the war and questions relating to slavery engaged his passionate interest, and here he was no Whig. He exhibited "extraordinary vigor" in these areas of policy. In over-all terms, one might say that Lincoln struck an implicit -- though admittedly imperfect -- bargain with Congress. As G. S. Boritt puts it: ... "giving Congress a free rein on the one hand [in some areas] probably gave the President a firmer grasp on the other [in other areas] where for the moment the more substantial issues were."[28]

In George Galloway's view:

> "Under stress of the war crisis and impelled by his overriding determination to preserve the Union at all costs, Lincoln ignored the constitutional position of Congress and asserted and exercised powers that were unprecedented in American history and that brought him repeatedly in conflict with his fellow partisans in Congress. During his administration legislative-executive relations were embittered by controversies over the conduct of the war, the expansion of the Armed Forces, the expenditure of public funds, the emancipation of slaves, and over plans for post-war reconstruction. In each of these areas Lincoln took steps that challenged the Republican theory of congressional dominance in the government."[29]

Another distinguished scholar of the subject, Wilfred E. Binkley, provides this interpretation in his *President And Congress*:

"Unquestionably the high-water mark of the exercise of executive power in the United States is found in the administration of Abraham Lincoln. No President before or since has pushed the boundaries of executive power so far over into the legislative sphere. No one can know just what Lincoln conceived to be the limits of his powers.... Nor was any of this done innocently. Lincoln understood his Constitution. He knew, in many cases, just how he was transgressing and his infractions were consequently deliberate. It is all the more astonishing that this audacity was the work of a minority President who performed in the presence of a bitter congressional opposition even in his own party."[30]

Analogously, the Cabinet, too, was gravely diminished. Lincoln cultivated an aloofness from the work of the several Cabinet departments which allowed for Congressional criticism of the Administration to be directed not at him personally but at his several secretaries. He also studiously avoided giving the Cabinet any collective policy-making significance.

A number of successive recollections by Gideon Welles, Lincoln's Secretary of the Navy, taken almost at random, illustrate the relative disuse of the collective mechanism of the Cabinet, or, indeed, any "team concept" by Lincoln as Chief Executive. Thus, on Tuesday, April 12, 1864:

"It is curious that the President...should have consulted the Secretary of War and Assistant Secretary of State without advising me, or consulting me on the subject.... When some of the difficulties which I had suggested began to arise, the President preferred not to see me..."[31]

On Friday, April 22nd:

"Neither Seward nor Chase nor Stanton was at the Cabinet meeting today. For some time Chase has been disinclined to be present and evidently for a purpose. When sometimes with him, he takes occasion to allude to the Administration as departmental -- as not having council, not acting in concert. There is much truth in it and his example and conduct contribute to it."[32]

On Tuesday, April 26th, Welles notes:

"Neither Chase nor Blair were at the Cabinet today, nor was Stanton. The course of these men is reprehensible, and yet the President, I am sorry to say, does not reprove but rather encourages it by bringing forward no important measure connected with either."[33]

On Friday, December 9th:

"At the Cabinet little as usual was done. Fessenden and Stanton were not present. Seward came late. No measure of any importance was introduced."[34]

On Tuesday, December 27th:

"At Cabinet today Seward, Fessenden and Stanton were absent. The three most important of all who should be at these meetings. The President was very pleasant over a bit of news in the Richmond papers, stating the fleet appeared off Fort Fisher, one gunboat got aground and was blown up..."[35]

On Tuesday January 17th, 1865:

"At the Cabinet meeting there was a very pleasant feeling. Seward thought there was little now for the Navy to do. Dennison thought he would like a few fast steamers for mail service. The President was happy. Says he is amused with the manners and views of some who address him, who tell him that he is now reelected and can do just as he has a mind to, which means that he can do some unworthy thing that the person who addresses him has a mind to. There is very much of this."[36]

On Tuesday, February 7th:

"Very little before the Cabinet. The President, when I entered the room, was reading with much enjoyment certain portions of Petroleum V. Nasby to Dennison and Speed. The book is a broad burlesque on modern Democratic party men. Fessenden, who came in just after me, evidently thought it hardly a proper subject for the occasion and the President hastily dropped it."[37]

A few examples cited by Edward Corwin may be added to the list:

"There is really very little of a government here at this time, so far as most of the Cabinet are concerned; certainly but little consultation in this important period..."

...."All this has been done without Cabinet consultation, or advice with any one, except Seward and the President..."

"Cabinet meetings which should at that exciting and interesting time, have been daily, were infrequent, irregular and without system..... A majority of the members of the Cabinet are not permitted to know what is doing...."[38]

In December of 1862, thirty-one of the thirty-two Republican Senators held meetings at which they agreed that Lincoln's operation of the executive branch of government did not correspond to "important constitutional principles." Senator Jacob Collamer of Vermont specifically criticized Lincoln for not consulting the Cabinet and for allowing each member of it to run his own department at will. There was a widespread perception that Lincoln was under the excessive influence of the relatively conservative Seward. Lincoln's meeting, later that month, with a Republican Senate delegation and simultaneously his own Cabinet, was an eminently successful effort by the President to maintain intact the personnel and the heretofore followed procedures of this controversial Cabinet collectivity.

Among the individual members of the Cabinet, few pleased their master as much and exercised as much authority as the pugnacious Secretary of War, Edwin Stanton. His devotion to the cause of the Union and grim determination in pursuit of his duties made him a fit civilian leader for the likes of Grant, Sherman and Sheridan. The account presented by Clarence Edward Macartney in his *Lincoln and His Cabinet* (New York: Scribner's Sons, 1931) helps explain Lincoln's fondness for the man.

> "His one purpose was to throttle the rebellion, and for this he labored day and night. No scruples as to the Constitution or the etiquette of military arrest troubled him in the least. When men argued with him about violating the Constitution, he would say in a soft voice ...'When the country is gone, it will be a comfort to know that the Constitution is saved.'" (Pp. 319-320). Stanton "was given a free hand in discharging the somewhat loosely defined duties of his great office"... (P. 321).

When a lower ranking general once remonstrated with Stanton to remove U.S. Grant from his command because he drank whiskey,

130

Stanton told him: "You are mistaken, Sir, it is blood, rebel blood, that the general drinks." Stanton obviously would not even consider removing Grant from his post...[39]

Lincoln himself gave Stanton "wide berth" and there was the famous episode in which, when someone told Lincoln that Stanton had called the President a damned fool, Lincoln replied "If Stanton said I was a damned fool, then I must be one, for he is nearly always right, and generally says what he means."[40]

It was hardly accidental that in making his historically most acclaimed decision of the War -- the issuance of the Emancipation Proclamation -- Lincoln did not consult either Cabinet or Congress, or even Congressional leaders, for that matter, on the substance of the question. So far as the Cabinet was concerned, Lincoln "read them what he had been composing" on July 22, 1862. As Mark Neely, Jr. says: "He did not offer it for approval or disapproval -- his mind was made up to issue it -- but he did want advice on timing and composition."[41] The final draft issued on September 22, 1862, the so called Preliminary Emancipation Proclamation, was a "much longer" document than what Lincoln had unveiled before the Cabinet in July.[42] It had not been cleared with Congress in any sense of the word, and its introductory portion was all in the name of the Chief Executive, "I, Abraham Lincoln, President of the United States of America, and Commander in Chief of the Army and Navy...etc."[43]

By the time of the 1862 Congressional elections, Lincoln had incurred the wrath of much of his original constituency. There were no significant military victories with which to placate the electorate. Casualties were mounting. Economic hardships in the shape of lost trade with the South and the discomfort of families deprived of their breadwinners took their toll. All hope of a quick and cheap war was gone. Those who had suspected Lincoln of waging the war not to save the Union but to destroy slavery were ever more resentful toward the policies of the administration.

The President, as it were, "fell between two stools." Lincoln's Emancipation Proclamation was unpopular in the North because it was seen by abolitionists as limited in extent and giving the South a chance to reclaim its slaves if it only gave up the war before January 1, 1863. Since Lincoln did not control the Southern states, emancipation there seemed to be just a gesture, a possible promise for the future. On the other hand, no slaves in the so-called loyal states were being set free by Lincoln. The Peace Democrats, in turn, saw Emancipation as proof that Lincoln was waging war against the South for "wrong reasons." They also believed that the Proclamation would actually strengthen the Southern resolve to resist. Many pictured Lincoln as fighting the war solely for the benefit of the "Negroes."[44]

Herbert Agar describes the outcome of the 1862 Congressional elections in these terms:

> "Ohio and Indiana and Pennsylvania held Congressional elections in October. The Democrats won heavily in the first two states, and in the last they elected half the Congressmen. In November, therefore, troops were sent home from the field to vote Republican in the critical states; but still the Democrats won Illinois and Wisconsin. They might have won control of Congress, they might even have compelled a negotiated peace, had not the border states, soothed by Lincoln and patrolled by troops, and diligently combed of anti-war voters under Lincoln's suspension of the Habeas Corpus Act, returned enough Republicans to ensure a small majority."[45]

Given the 1862 electoral results, Lincoln might have reasonably considered the outcome as a mandate of sorts: a mandate for negotiated peace. He might have reasonably inferred from it that the People were dissatisfied with the thrust of his policies.[46] But he resisted this temptation. Far from backing down, Lincoln actually intensified the Union's war effort in 1863, intensified military controls over civilians and proceeded to step up all these efforts even in the face of new forms of popular opposition to his policies, opposition which was now physical and violent, not merely symbolic and legal as in the Fall of 1862.

On the war fronts, Lincoln pursued victory with utmost determination. Grant, Sherman and Sheridan pushed ahead and gave no quarter. Lincoln accepted disproportionate Northern losses in dead and wounded in the knowledge and expectation that the South could not afford to lose as many soldiers as the North. He allowed his generals to lay waste to the civilian hinterland of the Confederacy. He always encouraged his commanders to fight but he never reproached them for excessive losses or for excessive severity toward the enemy. This is certainly the case so far as the President's authenticated orders, public declarations, and statements are concerned -- as opposed to various forms of "hearsay" evidence. Note Basler, Nos. IV-VIII.

The perusal of Lincoln's White House correspondence reveals a very telling dichotomy. The President evidenced great compassion toward personal appeals for mercy and toward all manner of individual human suffering. It is quite understandable that the President was actually reproached by some of his associates for being too lenient.[47] On the other hand, Lincoln combined this merciful sympathy for the sufferings of individuals with an all but inflexible commitment to unconditional victory on the battlefield. Lincoln dreaded the notion of a ceasefire because he feared that, once concluded, a war-weary nation might acquiesce in the Southern possession of its separate and politically independent domains rather than resume the fighting -- and killing.

In his book, *Merchant of Terror, General Sherman and Total War*, John Bennett Walters observes that William Tecumseh Sherman conducted war upon the South's civilian population which in its brutality exceeded at least some World War II cases, with all manner of "burning, sacking and pillaging of towns."[48] He acknowledges that this was, in fact, an effective method of waging war. "By paralyzing the economy, Sherman destroyed the Confederacy's ability to supply its armies; and by despoiling and scattering the families of the soldiers in the opposing armies, he undermined the morale of their military forces."[49] But, above all, he notes, that "it is...evident that [Sherman] would not have dared do so without the tacit approval of Abraham Lincoln and General Grant."[50] Walters describes the "keystone of Sherman's harsh theory of war: strike with vengeance; unleash a horde of destroyers to prowl over the country; offer no restraints to their cruelty, thievery and practice of arson; encourage by silence or studied oversight their utter lack of regard for law and order and the rights of private property."[51]

Walters quotes one of General Sherman's reports to U.S. Grant on the work his army had done upon occupying the town of Meridian, Mississippi, in February of 1864:

> "For five days, ten thousand of our men worked hard and with a will, in that work of destruction, with axes, sledges, crowbars, clawbars, and with fire, and I have no hesitation in pronouncing the work well done. Meridian with its Depots, Storehouses, Arsenals, Offices, Hospitals, Hotels, and Cantonments, no longer exists." (P. 116). In addition, Sherman's troops destroyed "the only remaining railroads in the state" and "subsisted [the] army and animals" on locally found provisions.[52]

As the war dragged on through the summer of 1863 without a decisive Union victory, Lincoln turned to a new source of manpower for the federal armies. The Administration proposed, and the Congress approved, a Draft law to be imposed uniformly upon all the states. It called for the compulsory induction of men between ages of 20 and 45, to be chosen by lot from among the registered eligibles. The law provided for some exemptions, the most controversial of which allowed people to donate 300 dollars to the federal government in lieu of their own persons. Heretofore, Lincoln had relied upon the strength of federalized militia units and upon volunteers. But with the great volume of losses and desertions, a fresh source of manpower was needed.

The new Draft measure was without precedent in American history, and it was seen by many as a violation of state rights. Moreover, its imposition coincided with all sorts of popular discontent linked to the War -- the elusiveness of victory, casualties, economic privations, Southern sympathies, the perception that the President's Emancipation Proclamation diverted the purpose of the war from saving the Union to the cause of Abolition, and hence, some thought, made the resolution of the war more difficult; latent and overt racism in the form of resentment about fighting to help the "colored race."[53]   In July 1863 these elements of popular disaffection ignited in the great Draft riots in New York City with the consequent killing of at least one hundred persons and the wounding of several hundreds in the course of successive days of violence, burning, and looting in the nation's largest urban center.

This was a more serious outbreak of diffuse "anti-war" sentiment than any event that had taken place during the Johnson or Nixon administrations in relation to the Vietnam War, a century later. To be sure, the opposition to Lincoln and his war policies, on this occasion as on all the others, did not speak with one voice. But to anyone interested in, or sensitive to, the direction of public opinion, there could be no doubt that the American people were greatly distressed and upset by the course of national policy. A weaker or lesser -- or perhaps more democratic leader -- than Lincoln might have given up or relented. But Lincoln did neither. There was no roll-back in federal policies in consequence of the New York riots, not on Emancipation, not on the Draft, and not on the seemingly attractive proposal of a ceasefire to be followed by a "negotiated peace." Lincoln held firm in a veritable storm of popular disapproval. He was not about to become, as modern-day democratic ideologues would say, "responsive."

Lincoln's attitude may be reasonably inferred from the text and tenor of his communications concerning military and military-political matters. Thus, at one juncture, we see a fairly exasperated President writing to his timid General, George McClellan, in October of 1862:

> "Will you pardon me for asking what the horses of
> your army have done since the battle of Antietam
> that fatigue anything?"[54]

On the other hand, to the grimly determined, Ulysses S. Grant, in August of 1864, with victory now more clearly in sight, Lincoln writes:

> "I have seen your despatch expressing your unwillingness to break your hold where you are. Neither am I willing. Hold on with a bull-dog gripe, and chew and choke, as much as possible."[55]

Contemporaneously, Lincoln writes to Major General Butler:

> "Nothing justifies the suspending of the civil by the military authority, but military necessity, and of the existence of that necessity the military commander, and not a popular vote, is to decide."[56]

On September 3, 1864, yet closer to victory but in the wake of enormous casualties, Lincoln issues an Order of Thanks to General William Tecumseh Sherman, expressing the nation's appreciation for his "distinguished ability...capture of Atlanta...famous in the annals of war" and reiterates that Sherman has the "applause and thanks" of a grateful nation.[57]

As late as November 6, 1864, Lincoln directs the following communication to Major General Edward R. Canby at New Orleans:

> "Do not, on any account, or on any showing of authority whatever, from whomsoever purporting to come, allow the blockade to be violated."[58]

At last, with victory virtually assured, Lincoln characteristically communicates with his commanding General through the Secretary of War:

> "To Ulysses S. Grant,
>   message of March 3, 1865
> Lieut. Gen. Grant

The President directs me to say that he wishes you to have no conference with General Lee unless it be for the capitulation of General Lee's army, or on some minor, purely military matter. He instructs me to say that you are not to decide, discuss, or confer upon any political question. Such questions the President holds in his own hands; and will submit them to no military conferences or conventions. Meantime you are to press to the utmost your military advantage."

Edwin M. Stanton
Secretary of War"[59]

Indeed, Professor James G. Randall aptly summarizes Lincoln's inflexible will to victory in the conflict with the secessionists when he observes that:

"On those occasions during the war when the question of negotiating for terms of peace with the Southern Government presented itself, President Lincoln, while manifesting generosity on collateral points, carefully avoided any recognition of the Confederacy and invariably imposed a condition which amounted to surrender -- i.e., the complete reunion of the warring states with the North. It was for this reason that these attempted negotiations, notably the Hampton Roads Conference, ended in failure."[60]

With but days to go in the War, on April 7, 1865, Lincoln sends a message to General Grant, this time quoting General Philip Sheridan:

"Gen. Sheridan says 'if the thing is pressed I think that Lee will surrender.' Let the *thing* be pressed. Abraham Lincoln."[61]

Chided for his allegedly tyrannical ways by some opponents earlier in the War, Lincoln met the criticisms head on. One question addressed to him by certain critics in 1862 was:

"Does your Excellency wish to have it understood that you hold, that the rights of every man throughout this vast country are subject to be annulled whenever you may say that you consider the public safety requires it in time of insurrection or invasion? The undersigned are unable to agree with you in the opinion you have expressed that the constitution is different in time of insurrection or invasion from what it is in time of peace and public security."[62]

To this reproach Lincoln answered:

"You ask, in substance, whether I really claim that I may override all the guaranteed rights of individuals on the plea of conserving the public safety -- when I may choose to say the public safety requires it. This question, divested of the phraseology calculated to represent me as struggling for an arbitrary personal prerogative, is either simply a question of *who* shall decide, or an affirmation that *nobody* shall decide, what the public safety does require, in cases of Rebellion or Invasion. The constitution contemplates the question as likely to occur for decision, but it does not expressly declare who is to decide it. By necessary implication, when Rebellion or Invasion comes, the decision is to be made, from time to time; and I think the man whom, for the time, the people have, under the constitution, made the commander-in-chief of their Army and Navy, is the man who holds the power, and bears the responsibility of making it. If he uses the power justly, the same people will probably justify him; if

138

he abuses it, he is in their hands, to be dealt with by all the modes they have reserved to themselves in the constitution."[63]

Lincoln's firmness gave rise to oft-repeated charges of tyranny and dictatorship leveled against the Chief Executive from all sorts of sources, including his own party.[64]   Indeed, when John Wilkes Booth shot Lincoln at the Ford Theater on the night of April 14th, 1865, he invoked the justification of "Thus Always to Tyrants." The terms "dictatorship" and "tyranny" have historically, and especially in modern times, revolved around three interrelated themes. The first is the scope of political power, with the notion of dictatorship implying unlimited scope, not subject to any restraint or jurisdictional check. The second theme is in the matter of duration. Dictatorial power is generally perceived as not limited in time beyond the natural life span of the dictator. The latter rules as long as he wants to rule and as long as he possibly can rule. This notion is at variance, of course, with the Roman concept of dictatorship as office or power limited to a specific term or emergency to be surrendered at its conclusion and subject to a post-facto accounting. The third theme concerns the uses made of power, with a tyrant or dictator being usually someone whose use of power is thought of as arbitrary, cruel, reckless, self-serving, and heedless of the true welfare of the community over which it may be applied.

In virtually all these respects, Lincoln did not readily fit the tyrannical or dictatorial model of power. Lincoln used the powers of his office broadly but he used them toward relatively specific and limited aims -- to save the Union by suppressing the rebellion waged against it. Lincoln's government could not be described as one of gross interference by the President in all spheres of social activity or government operations.   Lincoln did not care very much what people, including legislators, judges, bureaucrats, and politicians, did or said about matters unrelated in his own mind to the singular task of prosecuting the war against the Confederacy.   On economic, social, cultural, and political questions not connected to his all consuming passion, Lincoln had no interest whatever in "maintaining control".   Unlike most dictators, or tyrants, Lincoln did not care whether he was being criticized or not. No one was ever forced to sing his praises.

The focus of his administration was always narrowly kept on what may be termed the fundamental issue of his political career, saving the Union without concessions to slavery. If people gave aid and comfort to the rebels, they were liable to be arrested and incarcerated by Lincoln's soldiers. If they chose to "sing off key," that is, if they differed with the President on such issues as finance, internal improvements, immigration, homesteads, foreign policy (apart from questions bearing on the Confederacy at least in some instances...)or any number of other possible concerns, it simply did not matter to the President. They could do as they liked, and they could call him a tyrant if they liked, too.[65]

As for the second theme, Lincoln did subject himself to the judgment of the American electorate. He was no leader-for-life. Admittedly, however, it was a somewhat pressured judgment that the President offered to the American voters. Both 1862 and 1864 were significantly tainted elections. To be sure, people within and outside the Republican Party were free to challenge Lincoln. The Democratic standard bearer of 1864, General George McClellan, had ample opportunity to campaign against the incumbent, and for some time before the election Lincoln actually thought that he would lose the race to McClellan. Still, the elections left something to be desired. No questionable fraudulent acts are directly traceable to the President, though he may have known, or realized perhaps, what some of them were. There are all sorts of clues on this question.

In pursuit of renomination in 1864, Lincoln was no self-effacing wallflower though judgments require an appreciation of the context of the time. Generous distributions of federal patronage and strategic uses of office holders constituted a potent weapon on the road to the President's renomination in Baltimore on June 7, 1864. Even after the convention, Lincoln was still threatened by the enmity of various radical elements within his own Party which hoped to cause the President to withdraw from the race. Disappointed followers of

Salmon P. Chase and, in lesser measure, William H. Seward, were prominent among these.

The initiative for "dumping the President" was associated with Congressional elements supportive of the Wade - Davis bill, demanding that Congress take over the responsibility for a reconstruction policy in the South.[66] The sponsors of the measure attacked Lincoln for his allegedly dictatorial usurpation of congressional prerogatives. Lincoln did not hesitate to use the power of patronage to buttress his own political position. Through the office of his campaign manager, Henry J. Raymond, Lincoln effectively assessed his federal appointees for substantial contributions of money to his campaign.

> ..."Raymond directed the collection of a campaign fund by assessing federal government employees in all departments. When in some cases office holders refused to pay or obstructed the collection, Raymond requested and even insisted upon their removal. Pressure was brought upon Lincoln, who seems to have had full knowledge of this expedient and at least did nothing that served to discourage it."[67]

The total amount of money thus collected and spent on the President's behalf was "exceptionally large" according to the Carman-Luthin study. And the Administration's use of patronage powers in the 1864 presidential contest as a whole was nothing short of all out:

> "Patronage was withheld and contracts were awarded as might affect the November poll in the interests of Republican victory. Even promotions in the army appear to have been in some instances contingent upon correct party allegiance."[68]

In addition there were certain substantial "broadly structuring factors." A great deal of information about Civil War censorship and governmental repression is presented in the work of Robert S.

Harper.[69] Even if not very uniform or systematic in nature, and even if not explicitly guided by narrow partisanship, the broad brush of Republican-sponsored controls obviously hurt most forms of political opposition to Lincoln's government. This could hardly be helped in view of the obvious issues. Apart from those who thought Lincoln too timid, it was difficult for anyone to oppose the government's policies with respect to the war or abolition and not appear to be a disloyal Southern sympathizer. Denunciations of the war as unjustified, unnecessary, doomed to failure, excessively costly, or grossly mismanaged, were all bound to be interpreted by some federal officials, including the military, as round-about attempts to interfere with the draft and to undermine popular or military morale in war operations. The line between dissent and treason was not very clearly drawn. Under the circumstances, such clarity would have been all but impossible.

People could be, and often were, imprisoned on mere suspicion of aiding the enemy in one way or another. Newspapers were sometimes closed, or attacked by mobs, for just such reasons. The story of the Ohio newspapers which reprinted the speeches of the notorious peace-activist of his day, Congressman Clement Vallandingham, was amply illustrative. In a speech given in the House of Representatives on January 14, 1863, Vallandingham made these critical, though hardly self-evidently treasonous, comments:

> "A war for the Union!... History will record that after nearly six thousand years of folly and wickedness...it was reserved to American statesmanship of the 19th century of the Christian era to try the grand experiment...of creating love by force, and developing fraternal affection by war; and history will record, too, on the same page, the utter, disastrous, and most bloody failure of the experiment."[70]

When the 37th Congress adjourned in March of 1863, Vallandingham returned to his home state of Ohio and began a speaking tour up and down the state presenting his anti-war views to the public. As Harper explains :

> "The editors of Ohio's Democratic press who followed in Vallandingham's footsteps took their papers down the road to ruin. More than a score of antiwar newspapers felt either the fury of mob violence or the hand of the Federal government. Although arrests were made frequently, they did not keep pace with public opinion (!) and in instances where the government failed to act, the people (?!) took matters into their own hands. Nowhere in the North was the purpose of the people (!) to kill off that segment of the press injurious to the Union cause more prominently displayed than in Ohio."[71]

Clearly, in this case "the people" manifested itself as riotous mobs. They certainly were not a universal popular category. Presumably, persons who could be described as Peace Democrats, not to mention outright Southern sympathizers, were not a part of this "people." It is hard to imagine that twenty Democratic newspapers in Ohio had had no popular following whatever. It is also apparent that local authorities, and certainly the federal military, tolerated and condoned the activities of the various mobs and did not attempt to interfere with their manifestly illegal and violent behavior. Such activities fit into a pattern of Northern, civilian and military, controls over the population. Quite tellingly, there are no reports by Harper -- or anyone else -- of analogous attacks by "the people" on Republican newspapers.

Coercion, and the credible threat of coercion, were bound to have some strongly inhibiting consequences for transactions occurring in the political market place. Oppositionists were likely to be restrained by fear of reprisals. People who may have had private doubts about policies and policy makers were more likely to keep such doubts to themselves when there was reasonable likelihood that acting out one's preferences and suspicions could result in arrest and imprisonment or perhaps in mob violence. To the extent that it was

143

often difficult for various subordinate officials, civilian and military, to distinguish between loyalty to the Union and loyalty to Lincoln, the President was the beneficiary of an almost natural linkage between the two. To an unknown, but probably quite significant, degree this linkage was working in Lincoln's favor in the elections of 1862 and 1864. In the first case, it helped to minimize Republican losses. In the second, it may have insured the margin of victory.

The official results of the Presidential contest of 1864 indicated a roughly 55-45 split in the popular vote between Lincoln and McClellan. If only five percent of the American electorate of 1864 had been intimidated into a combination of actions involving either simply not voting for McClellan, or voting for Lincoln instead of McClellan, the result of the election would have been a toss-up. Given the intricacies of the electoral college vote, a switch of even two or three percent of the popular vote would probably have had the same effect.[72]

Writing about the Presidential election of 1864, Herbert Agar says:

> ..."as late as September, the Republicans feared that if the army were not sent home to vote where needed, and if fraud were not practiced where all else failed, McClellan might win."

> "In retrospect, we can see that the frauds and intimidations practiced by the Union Party in 1864 were unnecessary. Lincoln would have won anyway, even if no 'steps' had been taken. Yet it is interesting that Lincoln did not choose to run the risk. He allowed the small frauds, as he had allowed the steady unconstitutional pressure on the border states throughout the war, not because he felt superior to the people, but because he felt that he knew their needs and must safeguard their future. This is a perilous decision for the head of a free

state. Lincoln made it in silence and on his own responsibility, as he made all the basic decisions of the war: to reinforce Sumter; to suspend habeas corpus and pay no heed to the protests of the Chief Justice; to ask for troops without authority; to start the fighting before he called Congress in 1861, so that he could present that body with a war which was already under way and which must be won; to build for the first time in American history a national army serving the national state, instead of depending on local forces which had long been thought the safeguard of republican freedom. ...When Lincoln decided to fight, he decided to win."[73]

Apart from overt acts of fraud, whether in the process of casting votes or in counting them, intimidation appears to have been a very important factor in the 1864 election. The combination of Martial Law and Federal troops, in the context of Republican portrayals of the Democrats as the "Party of Treason," was designed to discourage potential McClellan voters. The 1864 electorate, only 3.39 percent larger than the 1860 in the same states, was anomalously low for all presidential elections of the nineteenth century. It is noteworthy, of course, that U.S. population had risen by 22.63 percent during the 1860's, mostly in the North, Civil War notwithstanding.

Agar argues that Lincoln would have got a majority of the popular vote in the Union as a whole anyway, but probably would have *lost* the election to McClellan in the archaic electoral college. This, according to Agar, Lincoln was not willing to risk. He concludes:

"We have no record of what Lincoln thought, only of what he did. He built a temporary dictatorship,

brushing the Constitution aside when he thought
necessary, and custom and legality as well."[74]

Another recent scholar, Mark E. Neely Jr., substantially
corroborates the story of a blemished 1864 election. He notes, for
example, that "tarring the Democrats with treason did help the
Republican cause, and it fit with what can only be called a pattern or
strategy of making the Democrats appear to be opposed to the
Union."[75] (The Democratic Party's platform called for an armistice
to be followed by negotiations to restore the Union. The war was
described in it as a "failure". McClellan personally insisted that it
was not a failure but supported the desirability of moving toward
negotiated peace...). As for the polling itself, Neely says that:
"government control of certain disputed areas in the border states
may have brought the Republicans unnaturally high [vote] totals
there -- through outright intimidation in some cases. Likewise, the
soldier vote, where recorded separately from the civilian...was given
under unusually controlled circumstances."[76] Neely does not offer
a judgment of the net effect of these practices on the outcome of the
election.

Whatever else could be said of General George McClellan, he
had been a very popular man with his troops, partly because he was
seen as careful, may be even timid, about sacrificing soldiers' lives
in bloody engagements with the enemy. Even his harsh detractors
grant McClellan significant popularity among the ranks. When he
was relieved of his command by Lincoln, seasoned troopers were
reported to have wept like children. But when it came to the 1864
election, admittedly many months later, a seeming miracle had
occurred. As Stephen W. Sears says:

> "The most surprising of the election statistics, and
> for McClellan surely the most shocking, was the
> soldier vote. It was always supposed that if he ran
> he would capture the soldier vote, and in theory, had
> he received an overwhelming share of the votes of
> the men in the field and on leave and of the ex-
> soldiers at home, it is possible that he would have

146

won the election. In fact, however, in every instance where the soldier vote was recorded, it was overwhelmingly in favor of his opponent."[77]

According to Sears, 78 percent of the 154,000 military ballots cast in the field went to Lincoln. "The men in Sherman's army from states where statistics are complete voted against McClellan by an extraordinary 86 to 14 percent." Even in the case of such a suspect margin, Sears refuses to believe that fraud, or coercion, may have played a part in these results, at least not "appreciably," according to him.[78]

Even though there were no public opinion polls in the 1860's, the known expectations of the two sides just prior to the election, based on informal soundings, strengthen the circumstantial case for substantial fraud. In late October, McClellan's managers believed that he would win the contest with the support of New York and Pennsylvania, the border states and the far western states, and a combination of at least one New England and one midwestern state. "Only a week earlier, President Lincoln had drawn up a strikingly similar tally of the electoral vote. He too gave New York and Pennsylvania and the border states, along with Illinois and Missouri, to McClellan."

There is no evidence that Abraham Lincoln authorized or knew about any specific acts of fraud or coercion designed to influence the outcome of the election. That such acts, however, were perpetrated, with some significant degree of success, by others on his behalf, is reasonably certain.

McClellan himself in two letters written after the election gave the impression that he viewed the result as a "fair and square" test of American public opinion. On November 10, 1864 in a letter to Samuel L.M. Barlow, e.g. he wrote: "For my country's sake I deplore the result -- but the people have decided with their eyes wide open and I feel that a great weight is removed from my mind." And on November 11th in a letter to his mother, he wrote : "The smoke has cleared and we are beaten! All we can do is to accept it as the will of God..."[79]

Nevertheless, at least one letter published in the Sears' collection suggests that McClellan may have thought otherwise. This is implicit in the message of November 16th to Robert C. Winthrop in which the General says: ..."it is possible, perhaps probable, that no course could have resulted otherwise than that actually pursued -- so great was the power wielded by the Administration."[80] So does a letter received by McClellan from one of his political associates, Manton Marble, who wrote: "I never despaired of a constitutional restoration of things in the South. The election shows that we had more reason to despair of constitutional restoration of things at the North."[81]

Finally, there are some more general considerations about the conduct of government with respect to the Lincoln administration where candor requires some accommodation of Lincoln's critics. In pursuit of the obligations of his oath, as Lincoln saw it, he was willing to go to great lengths, defying hostile public opinion, bending the law if not breaking it, and showing great ruthlessness in policy where he saw it as warranted by wartime necessity. It is notable, for example, that Lincoln wholeheartedly supported the burn-and-slash policies of his ablest generals, Grant, Sherman and Sheridan, even when those policies meant brutal treatment of people who, by Lincoln's own definition, were fellow Americans. In the North, Lincoln allowed and encouraged his military to narrow down the sphere of American civil liberties as never before.[82]

To be sure, the number of civilians arrested and detained in military custody for various periods of time during the Civil War is not easily ascertainable. Mark E. Neely, Jr., in his recent and most far reaching study of the issue, estimates the total to be in excess of 14,000.[83] Even if the actual number were twice or three times this figure, that would still be a fairly modest total for a Northern population of over 20 million, should anyone wish to compare Lincoln's rule with the likes of Hitler, Stalin or Mao. Moreover, most of these people were held for very short periods of time.

148

According to Neely, the largest number of civilian prisoners at any one time during the Civil War was only 2006 in November 1864.[84]

In some cases, nevertheless, people were arrested and jailed not for any easily defined activities but for apparent expressions of opinion which were viewed by the authorities as somehow dangerous or injurious to the cause of the Union. As Neely remarks:

> "'Treasonable language,' 'Southern sympathizer', 'secessionist' and 'disloyalty' were standard notations next to prisoners' names on the State Department record books. Even more serious sounding terms were vague and sometimes denoted offensive words rather then deeds: 'aiding and abetting the enemy,' 'threatening Unionists' or 'inducing desertion'...."[85]

Military judgments differed in place and time. The General who commanded the military district in Baltimore, for example, would not tolerate the public display of pictures of Confederate generals, while his New York counterpart would not arrest people for such displays. At least some newspaper editors and writers suffered imprisonment.[86] Many Unionists apparently came to believe that the state of Maryland was saved for "the cause" precisely because of the harsh, and quick, measures taken against disloyal elements in the state administration.[87]

In some cases, at least, there is evidence that civilians -- suspected of desertion from the army -- were subjected to torture by military authorities. Neely describes the so-called "violent cold shower baths " administered to some prisoners.[88] On the other hand, Neely makes the case for widespread observance of the principles of international law in combat operations conducted by the Union armies.[89] But whether Grant's, and especially Sherman's, operations against civilians in the South can be fully reconciled with such principles is, frankly, doubtful.

What is, nevertheless quite clear, is that Lincoln in applying his policies was remarkably free of any personal malice, meanness, or wantonness. He was never interested in "settling private scores." There were no mass executions of civilians under the Lincoln administration. There was no systematic application of torture and violence toward detainees. Even the military were required to give suspected individuals the benefit of some form of due process in terms of trials and avenues of appeal in the more substantial, serious cases.[90]

Lincoln never invoked Nazi or Soviet-style notions of collective responsibility, holding relatives or friends of law-breakers or suspects equally culpable with the actual perpetrators of hostile acts. Lincoln was a high minded authoritarian. In monarchical analogy, he might be described as a compassionate and just Prince, one who sought the public good, not his own private advantage, and one who treated his subjects, insofar as this was possible within the larger framework of his policy, with sympathy and consideration.

Certainly, Lincoln was no ordinary Chief Executive, measured by the experience of his predecessors, Washington included. No one before him ever "stretched" the law as much as he did, granting that no predecessor confronted the circumstances that confronted Lincoln. His administration did not fit the model of a modern dictatorship, largely because of Lincoln's admirable sense of self-restraint. What it did reflect was Lincoln's mission as a political prophet to the American people, dedicated to the sublime cause of saving the Union and banishing slavery from America's horizon. For this purpose, Lincoln was prepared to make whatever sacrifice was necessary, including that of his own existence. No statute, or doctrine, or opinion, however widely shared, was going to stand in his way. Lincoln was no less resolved in support of the integrity of the Union than Moses was in support of the ten commandments. A popular majority for the Golden Calf was irrelevant. Lincoln was prepared to fight the enemies of Right with whatever it took to prevail. General William Tecumseh Sherman may have marched through Georgia, but it was Lincoln who sent him.

Lincoln sympathized with people who were suffering and he felt anguish for those who died in battle or bore wounds. He felt compassion toward orphans and widows. But he did not shrink from the fight, and he did not let casualties determine his policies. Simultaneously, Lincoln as other prophetic leaders before him, saw his power as based not on force but on moral appeal to the hearts and minds of a "target audience." For Lincoln that audience was the American people in a historically enduring, transcendent existence, the future as well as the present.

Lincoln was a statesman who did not fit the "broker-facilitator" model implicit in the democratic ideal as it has evolved into modern times. He was not one who asked: "What do the people want? Let's give it to them." Nor was he one who asked: "How can we bring everybody under one big umbrella?" Lincoln had a moral political program which was not based on public opinion polls, or anything which, remotely, in his own time might have substituted for such polls. It was not a response to newspaper editorials. It was never the subject of a political auction. It was, practically speaking, ahistorical, a moral given, beyond the judgment of any majority or plurality to validate.

Lincoln's mind and character were marked by a certain principled inflexibility which is implicitly contrary to the bargaining model of a no-holds-barred democracy. In retrospect, most Americans have come to associate Lincoln's conduct with fidelity to a great cause, the cause of Right, the cause of Liberty, and the cause of Union. In his own time, there was much less agreement among Americans on such characterizations of the Sixteenth President. He was widely denounced and reviled. Ultimately, Lincoln was vindicated, partly by victory, partly by martyrdom, and, most fundamentally in a way he would have appreciated best, by the judgment of posterity.[91]

REFERENCE

1. Note Paludan, op. cit., p. 58 on Lincoln's opportunities to convoke Congress much earlier than he, in fact, did.

2. According to Paludan, "When Lincoln asked cabinet members for written opinions on Fort Sumter, five of the seven men advised against trying to supply it." Ibid, p. 61. Still, on p. 65 Paludan also maintains that the Republican Party was "almost unanimous" in insisting that standing up to the secessionist threats was imperative....

3. Basler, vol. IV, pp. 331-332.

4. Ibid, p. 332. See George Fort Milton, The Eve of Conflict, Stephen A. Douglas and the Needless War (Boston: Houghton Mifflin Company, 1934) pp. 553-559 on the initiation of hostilities at Fort Sumter. Milton implies that Lincoln consciously opted for war in his final decision on provisioning the Fort. "Dr. Charles W. Ramsdell, of the University of Texas, [in a] letter to [the] author of June 18, 1934, suggests his strong suspicion that Lincoln's course as to Sumter was from the outset aimed at getting the Confederates to fire the first gun." P. 554. Fn. 8. See also Edgar Lee Masters, Lincoln: The Man (London: Cassell and Company, Ltd., 1931) who embraces the view of a Union provocation engineered by Lincoln through the relief of Fort Sumter. Pp. 401-402. "If the United States sent a relief squadron to Southampton, carrying food to Americans there, whom England did not want to be succored, for State reasons of her own, the question could never be raised that England began the hostilities by repelling the relief squadron with her guns." P. 402.

At any rate, Lincoln's decision to resupply the Fort was taken against the advice of most of his Cabinet. See infra.

5. Ibid, p. 343.

6. Ibid, p. 344.

7. Basler, vol. I, pp. 431-442.

8. Basler, vol. I, pp. 451-452.

9. James G. Randall, Constitutional Problems Under Lincoln, Revised Edition, (Glocester, Mass.: Peter Smith, 1963) pp. 58-59.

10. <u>Ibid</u>, fn. 1, p. 58.

11. <u>Ibid</u>, p. 51.

12. <u>Ibid</u>, p. 52.

13. See Christopher H. Pyle and Richard M. Pious (eds.), <u>The President, Congress and The Constitution, Power and Legitimacy in American Politics</u> (New York: The Free Press, 1984) pp. 67-68 on Lincoln's suspension of the writ of Habeas Corpus and his famous query: ..."are all the laws, but one, to go unexecuted, and the government itself go to pieces, lest that one be violated?" P. 67. Lincoln denied, however, that any laws were being violated by military suspension of the writ, since the Constitution authorized such suspensions in cases of rebellion or invasion when public safety might require them. See pp. 298-299 on the inconsistency between Lincoln's opposition to President Polk' use of war powers in the conflict with Mexico in 1846 and his own use of such powers in 1861. That the circumstances were really analogous was arguable.... Note also Louis Fisher, <u>Constitutional Conflicts Between Congress and the President</u>, Third Edition, (Lawrence: University of Kansas Press, 1991) pp. 248-249 on Lincoln's post facto requests to Congress to legalize the actions which he had undertaken between March 5, 1861 and July 4, 1861. As Fisher puts it, "under these extraordinary circumstances, Lincoln believed it was more important to preserve than to observe the Constitution". P. 248.

14. Basler, vol. V, p. 51.

15. Among many examples, see Herman Belz, <u>Reconstructing the Union : Theory and Policy During the Civil War</u>, (Ithaca: Cornell University Press, 1969)." Was reconstruction a subject for legislative or executive action? ...Lincoln considered it fundamentally an executive function...at his last Cabinet meeting Lincoln said that he was glad the war had ended when it did, so that he could deal with reconstruction without interference from Congress...." Pp. 300-301. Radical Republicans in Congress, on the other hand, "regarded his death as a providential means of saving the country." P. 305. Note the observation by Burton J. Hendrick, <u>Lincoln's Cabinet</u> (Boston: Little, Brown, 1946) that among radical Republicans in Congress "political considerations governed everything." P. 281. Congressional oversight of military affairs focused much more on an Abolitionist "correctness" than on professional military prowess of Union commanders. Pp. 280-283. See H.L. Trefousse, <u>Benjamin Franklin Wade, Radical Republican from Ohio</u> (New York: Twayne Publishers, 1963). Although there has been some effort in recent years to "paper over" the differences between Lincoln and Republican radicals, the biographer's

comment is telling when he writes about Senator Wade as follows: "...the more he saw of Lincoln, the more he became convinced that 'Old Abe' was a 'fool,' wholly under the influence of Seward...'by nature a coward and a sneak.'" P. 154.

16. See Willard L. King, Lincoln's Manager, David Davis (Cambridge: Harvard University Press, 1960) for this incisive observation: "As soon as Congress met, in July 1861, Lincoln laid the whole matter [of the suspension of habeas corpus] before it. The provision in the Constitution for suspension of the writ, he said, had plainly been made for a dangerous emergency. He did not believe that the danger should be allowed to run its course until Congress could be called together, but he was now submitting the question to their consideration. For almost two years Congress took no action, and Lincoln regarded this failure to act as a confirmation of his power to suspend the writ." P. 247.

17. Robert A. Diamond (ed.), Origins and Development of Congress (Washington, D.C.: Congressional Quarterly Inc., 1976) p. 100.

18. Ibid, p. 198. Note also James T. Currie, The United States House of Representatives (Malabar, Fla.: Robert Krieger Publishing Company, 1988). "Until about 1880, more than half the members elected to each new Congress were first termers... By 1891, the first year for which we have good data, there were 103 persons working full time for committees of the House and the Senate. By 1985...3300 persons [were so employed], "Personal staffs for members did not exist until the end of the last century, but in 1985 there were over 11,600 personal staff members, 7,500 of whom worked on the House side." Pp. 1-2. Cf. Randall B. Ripley, Congress, Process and Policy, Third Edition (New York: W.W. Norton, 1983) pp. 52-53.

19. See Harold M. Hyman, A More Perfect Union, The Impact of the Civil War and Reconstruction on the Constitution (New York: A.A. Knopf, 1973) p. 180.

20. Ibid, pp. 180-187.

21. Ibid, p. 187.

22. Ibid, p. 174.

23. Note David H. Donald, "Abraham Lincoln: Whig in the White House" in Norman A. Graebner, The Enduring Lincoln (Urbana: University of Illinois Press, 1959) p. 60.

24. Ibid.

25. See Edward S. Corwin, "The Scope of Presidential Power," pp. 245-258, in Robert S. Hirschfield (ed.), The Power of The Presidency: Concepts and Controversy, Second Edition (Chicago: Aldine Publishing Company, 1973) p. 250.

26. Ibid.

27. Ibid, p. 251.

28. G.S. Boritt, op. cit., p. 227.

29. George B. Galloway, The Legislative Process in Congress (New York: Crowell, 1953) p. 309.

30. Wilfred E. Binkley, President and Congress, Third Revised Edition, (New York: Vintage Books, 1962) p. 126. See also the encyclopedic study by John Y. Simon, Congress Under Lincoln, 1861-1863 unpublished 1960 Ph.D. dissertation, Harvard University. Note Simon's conclusion: "It is doubtful that a representative legislative body is qualified to conduct a war. The American experience in 1861-1863 confirms this." P. 758. See also pp. 594-595 on the role of federal "repression and control" in the outcome of the 1862 congressional elections.

31. Howard K. Beale (ed.), Diary of Gideon Welles, Vol. II (New York: W.W. Norton, 1960) pp. 9-10.

32. Ibid, p. 16.

33. Ibid, p. 17.

34. Ibid, p. 194.

35. Ibid, p. 210.

36. Ibid, p. 227.

37. Ibid, p. 238.

38. Edward S. Corwin, The President, Office and Powers, 1787-1984, Fifth Revised Edition (New York: New York University Press, 1984) p. 369. See also David H. Donald, Inside Lincoln's Cabinet, The Civil War Diaries of Salmon P. Chase (New York: Longmans, Green and Company, 1954). In the words of the author, "Chase's efforts to introduce some administrative system among the President's advisors were unsuccessful, and soon he, like Bates and Welles, was wondering whether he should bother to attend the 'Cabinet' (so-called)'" P. 17. Cf. Frederick J. Blue, Salmon P. Chase, A Life in Politics (Kent, Ohio: The Kent State University Press, 1987) pp. 173-174. "Cabinet members often found out what the administration was up to by reading newspapers -- for example, when Lincoln suspended *habeas corpus* throughout the North." Paludan, op. cit., p. 169.

39. See Erwin S. Bradley, Simon Cameron, Lincoln's Secretary of War, A Political Biography (Philadelphia: University of Pennsylvania Press, 1966). Lincoln's first Secretary of War was one of those favorably inclined to the Crittenden compromise effort. P. 158. Note also his opposition to resupplying Fort Sumter, along with a majority of the Cabinet, in mid March 1861. P. 182.

40. Clarence Macartney, op. cit., p. 341. Note also G.S. Boritt, Lincoln and the Economics of the American Dream (Memphis: Memphis State University Press, 1978) who says that Lincoln kept himself "at arm's length from his Cabinet." P. 227. And John M. Taylor, William Henry Seward, Lincoln's Right Hand (New York: Harper Collins Publishers, 1991) on the substantial subordination of the "star of the Cabinet" to Lincoln during the President's administration, both with respect to foreign affairs and to general policy matters. Pp. 211-212. Cf. Burton J. Hendrick, Lincoln's War Cabinet (Boston: Little, Brown and Company, 1946) which abounds with descriptions documenting the Cabinet's disuse as a collective entity. Note especially pp. 189-193.

His account of the protests of Attorney General Edward Bates to the President is singularly illustrative. "The administration, he declared, was not a unit; it was departmentalized, each Secretary keeping monastic-like in his own office, knowing little of what was going on in the others, not participating in the general concerns of the nation."

"Why," he asked Lincoln, "could not the cabinet come together on stated days, and on such special occasions as the national emergency might make desirable?" P. 191. According to Hendrick, Secretary of State, Seward, regarded the rest of the Cabinet with contempt, while Lincoln never hesitated to overrule him when it seemed useful. P. 192. Note also Jeffrey E. Cohen, The Politics of the U.S. Cabinet, Representation in the

156

Executive Branch, 1789-1984 (Pittsburgh: University of Pittsburgh Press, 1988) p. 28.

41. See Mark E. Neely, Jr., The Last Best Hope of Earth (Cambridge: Harvard University Press, 1993) p. 109.

42. Ibid, p. 113. Note Philip S. Paludan on Lincoln's statement to the Cabinet with respect to the Emancipation Proclamation: "I do not wish your advice about the main matter -- for that I have determined for myself." Op. cit., p. 179.

43. Ibid. See also John G. Nicolay and John Hay, Abraham Lincoln, A History, Volume Six (New York: The Century Company, 1890) ..."on the...policy of emancipation the President had reached a decision which appears to have been in advance of the views of the entire Cabinet.... P. 125. "Every member of the council was, we may infer, bewildered by the magnitude and boldness of the proposal".... "Only two [members] gave the measure their unreserved concurrence, even after discussion." P. 127.

44. See John Hope Franklin, From Slavery to Freedom: A History of American Negros, Second Revised Edition (New York: A.A. Knopf, 1963) p. 278.

45. Herbert Agar, The Price of Union (Boston: Houghton Mifflin Company, 1950) p. 426.

46. See William B. Hesseltine, Lincoln and the War Governors (New York: A.A. Knopf, 1955) p. 265. He observes that the 1862 elections showed "that the people of the North were opposed to the Emancipation Proclamation, opposed to governmental encroachment on individual rights and opposed to conscription."

47. Gideon Welles' view of Lincoln's character is reflected in this passage: "Called on the President to commute the punishment of a person condemned to be hung. He at once assented. [Lincoln] is always disposed to mitigate punishment and to grant favors. Sometimes this is a weakness..." Op. cit. p. 207. Entry of December 24th, 1864. On the basis of a more complete compendium of cases, Mark Neely shows that Lincoln tended to follow the advice of his Judge Advocate General, Joseph Holt. When he disregarded Holt's advice, it was more often than not "to indulge mercy." See Mark E. Neely, Jr., The Fate of Liberty: Abraham Lincoln and Civil Liberties (New York: Oxford University Press, 1991) pp. 165-166.

48. J.B. Walters, Merchant of Terror, General Sherman and Total War (Indianapolis: The Bobbs Merrill Company, Inc., 1973) p. XIII.

49. Ibid, pp. XII-XIII. Note also Archer Jones, Civil War Command and Strategy, The Process of Victory and Defeat (New York: The Free Press, 1992) p.230. "Although Grant's logistic raiding strategy has never received much recognition because it failed to win the war, it would have, had the war lasted long enough. And its political byproduct, the intimidation engendered by his raids and their psychological effect as symbols of defeat, made a powerful contribution to inducing the South to give up its quest for independence...."

Cf. Stephen Oates, op. cit., p. 136: "It cannot be stressed enough that Lincoln...fully endorsed Sherman's scorched earth policy. If Sherman was a 'total warrior,' so was his Commander-in -Chief." The author quotes a Confederate officer who observed that Sherman moved like a "fully-developed cyclone, leaving behind him a track of desolation and ashes fifty miles wide. In front of [him] was terror and dismay." P. 159.

See James M. McPherson, "Lincoln and the Strategy of Unconditional Surrender" in Gabor S. Boritt (ed.) Lincoln, The War President (New York: Oxford University Press, 1992) pp. 29-62. McPherson says that Lincoln's "role in shaping a national strategy of unconditional surrender by the Confederacy was more important to the war's outcome than his endless hours at the War Department sending telegrams to generals and devising strategic combinations to defeat Confederate armies." Pp. 40-41.

50. Walters, loc. cit., p. XIII.

51. Ibid, p. 119.

52. Ibid, p. 117. See also Walters' account offered in his "General William T. Sherman and Total War", The Journal of Southern History, vol. 14, No. 4, November 1948, pp. 447-480. Sherman's methods, while brutal, were also effective, according to the author. Cf. John G. Barrett, Sherman's March Through The Carolinas (Chapel Hill: The University of North Carolina Press, 1956). "The use of a military force against the civilian population and economic resources unquestionably helped to undermine the morale of the South producing a 'defeatist psychology' both on the home front and on the battlefield. Lee's ranks were thinned daily by the desertion of soldiers going home to protect their families in the line of Sherman's march.... In applying total war to the people of the South, Sherman inflicted wounds which would remain open for generations to come. The hatred for the North instilled in the hearts of many Southerners

by Sherman's operations lengthened the South's road to reunion...." Pp. 280-281.

53. According to Stephen Oates, op. cit., Lincoln "was the most unpopular President the Republic had known up to that time. His hate mail from the public was voluminous and grotesque." P.89. Among the more important causes of the New York City riots was white racism -- the perception that the war was fought, primarily or exclusively, to benefit African-Americans at the expense of whites, and resentment of blacks who took over jobs left behind by white soldiers. Note Iver Bernstein, The New York City Draft Riots, (New York: Oxford University Press, 1990) pp. 119-124. See also Adrian Cook, The New York City Draft Riots of 1863 (Lexington: The University Press of Kentucky, 1974) pp. 194-195. It is of some relevance that for most of American history since 1863, it had been a settled notion that at least 1000 persons and perhaps even more were killed in the New York Draft riots. Cf. Ernest A. McKay, The Civil War and New York City (Syracuse: Syracuse University Press, 1990) p. 131: "The critical voices that fed the prevalent despair came from many directions, and their ideas, theories, and convictions were often vastly different. Some were Peace Democrats, some were War Democrats, some were Republicans, and some were simply disloyal, but they all agreed that the war was poorly led and worthless to pursue." In the nation's "premier city"...a solid phalanx of presidential support was missing." Ibid.

See also Eugene C. Murdock, "New York Civil War Bounty Brokers," The Journal of American History, vol. 53, No. 2, September 1966, pp. 259-278. "Toward the close of the war it was not uncommon for recruiting committees to abandon all efforts to meet their quotas and contract with brokers to do the job for them." P. 261. Note also Peter Levine, "Draft Evasion in the North during the Civil War, 1863-1865," The Journal of American History, vol. 67, no. 4, March 1981, pp. 816-834. As the author says, "most men who were drafted [776,829] avoided military service by legal means. Over 160,000...were illegal draft evaders." P. 817. This was obviously a very high figure and one related to the war's unpopularity.

A contemporary author, J.T. Headley, put the matter as follows: "The ostensible cause of the riots of 1863 was hostility to the draft because it was a tyrannical, despotic, unjust measure -- an act which distinguished tyrants the world over, and should never be tolerated by a free people...." The Great Riots of New York (New York: E.B. Treat, 1873) p. 136. Adrian Cook in his The Armies of the Streets : The New York City Draft Riots of 1863 (Louisville: University Press of Kentucky, 1974) says: "Arrests without trial, the suspension of habeas corpus, the suppression of newspapers and the horror of 'abolition Bastilles' was drummed across the

159

country, and Lincoln was denounced as 'a weak imitation of the besotted tyrant Nero.'" P.50.

54. Basler, vol. V, p. 474. Letter of October 24th, 1862.

55. Basler, vol. VII, p. 499. Letter of August 17th, 1864.

56. Ibid, p. 488. Letter of August 9th, 1864.

57. Ibid, p. 533.

58. Basler, vol. VII, p. 93.

59. Ibid, pp. 330-331.

60. James G. Randall, Constitutional Problems, op. cit., p. 64.

61. Basler, vol. VII, p. 392.

62. Basler, vol. VI, p. 301.

63. Ibid, p. 303. Lincoln neglected the fact that the Constitutional provisions concerning insurrections and invasions, Article 1, Section 8, Par. 15, were specifically designated as the powers of Congress, not the President.

64. "Not surprisingly, the severity of Lincoln's war measures prompted charges of 'military dictatorship' even from some Republicans." Sidney M. Milkis and Michael Nelson, The American Presidency, Origins and Development, 1776--1990 (Washington, D.C.: CQ Press, 1990) p. 149.

65. See Paludan, e.g., op. cit., pp. 113-117 on legislation passed by Congress in the Civil War period -- legislation in which presidential interest and influence were not very significant. As for the administration, Lincoln... "found men he would trust with ongoing operations and let them do their jobs." p. 123.

66. Note William Safire, Freedom (Garden City, N.Y.: Doubleday, 1987) pp. 897-898, on the differences between Lincoln and Senators Wade and Davis as both constitutionally and politically very fundamental, contrary to the views of some scholars.... According to Oates, op. cit., Lincoln and congressional Republicans, despite some differences of views, "retained a close and mutually respectful relationship, so much so that many

contemporaries thought they could remain as united in working out reconstruction problems as they had in prosecuting the war." P.141. This is hardly reflected in the Wade-Davis controversy, among many examples....

67. See Harry J. Carman and Reinhard H. Luthin, Lincoln and the Patronage (New York: Columbia University Press, 1943) pp. 228-260. Quotation on p. 288.

68. Ibid, pp. 294 and 299.

69. Robert S. Harper, Lincoln and the Press (New York: McGraw Hill, 1951) p. 197.

70. Ibid. Notably, he was jailed and exiled with Lincoln's explicit sanction.

71. When Vallandingham ran for Governor of Ohio in 1863, some of his supporters addressed a letter to Lincoln accusing him of unconstitutional behavior. Finding the charge very one sided, Lincoln replied to them as follows: "You...reserve to yourselves to decide what are constitutional means...and you...omit to state, or intimate, that in your opinion, an army is a constitutional means of saving the Union against a rebellion; or even to intimate that you are conscious of an existing rebellion being in progress with the avowed object of destroying that very Union. At the same time your nominee for Governor, in whose behalf you appeal, is known to you, and to the whole world, to declare against the use of an army to suppress the rebellion. Your own attitude, therefore, encourages desertion, resistance to the draft and the like, because it teaches those who incline to desert, and to escape the draft, to believe it is your purpose to protect them, and to hope that you will become strong enough to do so." June 29, 1863 Basler, vol. VI, p. 305.

Discussing the 1863 and 1864 elections, Professor Philip Paludan makes the following observation, worth citing here at some length:
"State political organizations attacked with charges of treason and conspiracy, asserting that opposition to the president equaled disloyalty and was probably spawned in Richmond or some other Confederate locale. Almost any charge was legitimate, and conspiracy theories were staples of the campaigns. The president could not directly control or shape the arguments that the leagues used to defeat the Democrats in the election, but their speeches and actions were not beyond his knowledge or his influence. A word of disapproval from him and tactics would have been moderated, rhetoric

restrained. Yet with so much on the line and with war critics challenging his party, ... Lincoln looked the other way." Paludan, op. cit., p. 225. Note also pp. 285-286.

72. See James G. Randall and Richard Nelson Current, Lincoln the President, Last Full Measure (New York: Dodd, Mead and Company, 1955) pp. 260-264 on Lincoln's reelection. The authors report that Lincoln's victory margin over McClellan in New York, the most populous state in the Union, was less than 7000 votes. P. 261. They do not report, however, any "irregularities" beyond some charges by Democrats on very selective furlough policies followed by the War Department toward Union soldiers.... P. 262. See also Frank L. Klement, The Limits of Dissent (Louisville: The University Press of Kentucky, 1970) on Clement Vallandingham's failed campaign for the governorship of Ohio in 1863. ..."never in American history was a Democratic gubernatorial candidate more scorned, more misrepresented and misquoted, more vilified than Vallandingham." P. 229. Among a variety of "dirty tricks," Federal postmasters used their facilities to promote John Brough, Vallandingham's Republican opponent. P. 235.

In a speech given three years after the end of the Civil War, William Seward maintained that had President Lincoln lost his fight for reelection in 1864, the result would have been "a speedy, if not an immediate, dissolution of the Union." Undoubtedly, many officials in 1864, and throughout the war, acted on this premise in managing the electoral process. See George E. Baker (ed.), The Works of William H. Seward, The Diplomatic History of the War for the Union, vol. V (Boston: Houghton Mifflin and Company, 1890) p. 543.

73. Agar, op. cit., pp. 433-434.

74. Ibid, p. 434.

75. Mark E. Neely, Jr., The Last Best Hope of Earth, op. cit., p. 175.

76. Ibid, p. 177. Note that the secret ballot was not generally adopted in the United states until 1904. See Christopher Hewitt, "The Effect of Political Democracy and Social Democracy on Equality in Industrial Societies: A Cross-National Comparison," American Sociological Review, Vol. 47, No. 3, June 1977, p. 457.

77. Stephen W. Sears, George B. McClellan, The Young Napoleon (New York: Ticknor and Fields, 1988) pp. 341-343. See also Stephen W. Sears

(ed.), <u>The Civil War Papers of George B. McClellan</u> (New York: Ticknor and Fields, 1989) p. 589.

78. <u>Ibid</u>, p. 385.

79. <u>Ibid</u>, pp. 618-619.

80. <u>Ibid</u>, p. 621.

81. <u>Ibid</u>, p. 625. Note Joel H. Silbey, <u>A Respectable Minority, The Democratic Party in the Civil War Era, 1860-1868</u> (New York: W.W. Norton, 1977) who puts the question into the following perspective: "There is no doubt that the way the soldiers' vote distributed itself gave the Republicans a number of crucial states. Whether the result was *entirely* (sic!) the result of intimidation and fraud is not clear." P. 161. Italics are mine. Note also Frank L. Klement, "Civil War Politics, Nationalism, and Postwar Myths," <u>The Historian</u>, vol. 38, No. 3, May 1976, pp. 419-438. He deals at length with the issue of Republican propaganda of the 1860's falsely designed to discredit the Democrats and other opposition forces as "treasonous." He also surveys various "dirty tricks" perpetrated by the opposition. Although the author implicitly condemns the subsequent glorification of Lincoln, notably, he does not make any personal connections between the President and the assorted "lies" and "tricks." On the 1864 election more generally, see William F. Zornow, <u>Lincoln and The Party Divided</u> (Norman: University of Oklahoma Press, 1954).

Note the discussion of measures taken by the Army to quell possible "secessionist demonstrations" (during the voting) in the principal states of the North by John G. Nicolay and John Hay, <u>Abraham Lincoln, A History</u>, Volume Nine (New York: The Century Company, 1917) pp. 373-375. They deny any wrongdoing, but admit some division of opinion among the supporters of the Administration with respect to the deployment of troops in New York. P. 374.

Although Philip Paludan in his recent work discusses the deployment of federal troops during the presidential election of 1864 in various places, including New York City and Baltimore, e.g., he makes no mention of fraud and intimidation with respect to the conduct or results of the election. On the contrary, he hails the result as a victory for the democratic process. <u>Op. cit.</u>, pp. 290-291.

82. See Robert S. Harper, <u>Lincoln and the Press</u> (New York: McGraw Hill, 1951) "...the Constitution was stretched until it threatened to crack." P. II. As Professor James G. Randall has observed: "It is indeed a striking fact

that Lincoln, who stands forth in popular conception as a great democrat, the exponent of liberty and of government by the people, was driven by circumstances to the use of more arbitrary power than perhaps any other President has seized...." Constitutional Problems, op. cit., p. 513. ..."It would not be easy to state what Lincoln conceived to be the limit of his powers...freeing the slaves by proclamation, setting up a whole scheme of statemaking for the purpose of reconstruction, suspending the *habeas corpus* privilege, proclaiming martial law, enlarging the army and navy beyond the limits fixed by existing law, and spending public money without congressional appropriation...the national legislature was merely permitted to ratify these measures, or else to adopt the futile alternative of refusing consent to an accomplished fact. [Lincoln] while greatly enlarging his executive powers, seized also legislative and judicial functions as well." Pp. 514-515.

To be sure, there are some representations by Lincoln himself as to what he viewed to be the limits of his power. In a letter written to Secretary of State Seward on June 28th, 1862, Lincoln expressed himself as follows: "I expect to maintain this contest until successful, or till I die, or am conquered, or my term expires, or Congress or the country forsakes me." Basler, vol. V, p. 292.

On October 19th, 1864, Lincoln publicly declared: "I am struggling to maintain the government, not to overthrow it. I am struggling especially to prevent others from overthrowing it. I therefore say, that if I shall live, I shall remain President until the fourth of next March; and that whoever shall be constitutionally elected...in November...shall be installed as President on the fourth of next March; and that in the interval I shall do my utmost that whoever is to hold the helm for the next voyage, shall start with the best possible chance to save the ship.... If [the people] should deliberately resolve to have immediate peace even at the loss of their country, and their liberty, I know not the power or right to resist them. It is their own business, and they must do as they please with their own." Basler, vol. VIII, p. 52.

83. Mark E. Neely, Jr., The Fate of Liberty, Abraham Lincoln and Civil Liberties (New York: Oxford University Press, 1991) p. 234. Note also the estimate of 38,000 incarcerations referred to on p. 113.

84. Ibid, p. 134.

85. Ibid, p. 27.

86. Ibid.

87. Ibid, p. 28.

88. Ibid, p. 30.

89. Ibid, pp. 109-112.

90. Ibid, pp. 139-159. "Though war may have been at least as savage in the New World as in the Old, American generals and statesmen usually sought to live up to the standards of international law." P. 159.

Note, however the following Order of Retaliation signed by Lincoln on July 30, 1863, in response to rumors of the Confederacy's incipient measures against the Union's black soldiers: "The government of the United States will give the same protection to all its soldiers, and if the enemy shall sell or enslave anyone because of his color, the offense shall be punished by retaliation upon the enemy's prisoners in our possession.

It is therefore ordered that for every soldier of the United States killed in violation of the laws of war, a rebel soldier shall be executed; and for every one enslaved by the enemy or sold into slavery, a rebel soldier shall be placed at hard labor on the public works and continued at such labor until the other shall be released...." Basler, vol. VI, p. 357.

91. See Elbert J. Benton, The Movement for Peace Without Victory During the Civil War (New York: Da Capo Press, 1971) p. 53: "A judicious student of history may find it difficult to endorse formally acts of questionable constitutionality; a grateful nation will in its judgments cleave through strict legalism, and endorse the acts of an agent whose, like Lincoln's, were so tempered with justice, and served no selfish purpose. May it not be true that the use of such powers in an emergency which a people cannot foresee is the supreme test of statesmanship?"

V

SANCTIFICATION OF THE PRESIDENTIAL ROLE

In order to succeed in the great enterprise of saving the Union on a foundation of freedom, Lincoln needed important personal resources, resources which he proved uniquely capable of supplying. There is no doubt that Lincoln's position toward the secessionists implied not only the possibility but even the likelihood of fratricidal civil war. To be sure, Lincoln's 1861 Inaugural Address employed some conciliatory language. The President would not invade the South. He would not disturb the South's peculiar domestic institution where it already existed. He was willing to enforce the fugitive slave laws. He appealed to the Southerners' lingering Union loyalties. He did not use the rhetoric of threats and intimidation.

But he would not back down on the propositions on which he was elected. The specific and immediate issue before the country was the matter of holding federal forts in Union hands. Lincoln was ready to use force to defend remaining installations belonging to the national government, and specifically to resupply Fort Sumter even if such action should be opposed by force by the Confederates.

Under the circumstances, great sacrifices might be required of the federal forces. Indeed, great sacrifices were required. Blood flowed throughout the land before the issue of the War was finally settled. In order to fight such a war, Lincoln needed great moral capital, the confidence, loyalty, and support of millions of people, not necessarily something called "majorities", but certainly millions. Lincoln's moral assets were in his conduct and his reputation. For the great task at hand, the public Lincoln was substantially supported by the private Lincoln.

To the extent that the United States -- even in 1861 -- was a pluralistic society with a significant tradition of free speech, free press, and far ranging rights of association, Lincoln needed to sanctify his mission to soldiers and civilians alike in order to make and win the fight. In this respect, reputation for integrity and regard for the public interest were critically important. It was necessary for Lincoln to conduct himself in a fashion that would maintain and bolster his moral authority as President in the midst of the unprecedented crisis. And Lincoln brought a lifetime of preparation to his mission. In that respect, he was a figure rare in history.

Although the evidence may be described as circumstantial, it seems reasonably clear that Lincoln, unlike most mortals, set out from the very beginnings of his life to fulfill a heroic destiny. The aspiration to heroism may be distinguished from mere "ambition." Ambition may be defined as desire for riches, for power, for status, or for fame, and as such it is obviously common in history. But Lincoln was someone who desired to achieve renown and recognition in subordinate furtherance of a great cause: the cause of America as bequeathed to his and all future generations by America's Founding Fathers. Lincoln, even as he occasionally despaired of the chances of success, wanted to be a President who would advance the achievements of Washington and Jefferson, and if he could not be President, he would still seek to promote, with all his means, the ideals which he associated with these leaders.

Since heroism involves a noble willingness to subordinate one's own welfare and even life for what is conceived a higher good, and, concomitantly, the willingness to bear pain and suffering for the sake of that higher good, heroism and ambition are not synonymous. Each could exist without the other, and ambition is clearly the more common of the two. In Lincoln, the attributes of heroism and ambition were joined together.[1] Lincoln strove consciously, and probably to a degree subconsciously, to live a life worthy of the men who were his heroes, and one that would be appropriate to the solemn mission that he envisioned for himself. Endowed with extraordinary qualities of character, temperament, and intellect, Lincoln succeeded as few mortals have, in living a life of exceptional moral achievement as well as political attainment. His historical reputation, quite understandably, is based only in part on what he believed and what he did; it is greatly influenced by who he was, by the sheer force of his extraordinary character and example.

To employ a useful metaphor, Lincoln can only be understood if we grant the proposition that his mind was always focused on a far shore, to which various lesser objectives and events in the here-and-now of life, including his own legal career and everyday matters, were always almost palpably subordinated. Paradoxically, Lincoln's ability was such that it obscures his sense of life-for-a-higher-and-nobler purpose. Lincoln was an excellent and highly successful lawyer, and he got on so well with so many different kinds of people in his routine, social, professional and political pursuits, that one cannot think of him as some sort of single-minded zealot or fanatic.[2] Clearly, he was neither. But he was a man driven, all but inexorably and inexplicably, by an immanent purpose. His life until March 1861 was but a preparation for the role of the savior of the Republic. It was all prologue.

It is of interest to recall Lincoln's first public statement concerning his aspirations. On March 9th, 1832, Lincoln addressed a message to his fellow citizens in Sangamon County in connection with his candidacy for a place in the State legislature. The message was contained in a handbill. He was then only 23 years of age and it was his debut as a politician. Young Lincoln told the voters that:

> "Every man is said to have his peculiar ambition. Whether it be true or not, I can say for one that I have no other so great as that of being truly esteemed of my fellow men, by rendering myself worthy of their esteem. How far I shall succeed in gratifying this ambition, is yet to be developed. I am young and unknown to many of you. I was born and have ever remained in the most humble walks of life. I have no wealthy or popular relations to recommend me. My case is thrown exclusively upon the independent voters of this county, and if elected they will have conferred a favor upon me, for which I shall be unremitting in my labors to

compensate. But if the good people in their wisdom shall see fit to keep me in the background, I have been too familiar with disappointments to be very much chagrined. Your friend and fellow citizen, A. Lincoln."[3]

In the event, Lincoln was defeated; he placed eighth among thirteen candidates. Characteristically, however, among the people who knew him best, in New Salem, he polled 277 out of 300 votes. There was something compelling about Lincoln's character and personality and it endured a lifetime.

Charles Carlton Coffin, who had travelled to Springfield in June of 1860 as one of the men who notified Lincoln of his nomination for President by the Republican Party, recalled that there was a sincerity about the man that won his instant admiration:

> "A stranger meeting him on a country road, ignorant
> of his history, would have said, 'He is no ordinary
> man.'"[4]

Among those who saw Lincoln and were greatly impressed by his natural dignity and impressive bearing was one Robert Brewster Stanton, son of a friend of the President. As a young man, he had lived in Washington when Lincoln was inaugurated in 1861 and observed him on a number of both public and private occasions. He characterized Lincoln's speech as "gentle, loving, yet earnest, unafraid, determined, ready to take up any burden or any task and carry it through as God gave him the strength....Simplicity... firmness...self-possession...naturalness...sincerity...dignity...these were Stanton's descriptions of Lincoln in communication and demeanor.[5]

Another young interlocutor, Waller R. Bullock, who sought and obtained from Lincoln the release of his captured brother (a Confederate officer) described the President somewhat differently:

"He was not a handsome man. Neither was he a
graceful one. His appearance when in repose was
rather dull and listless. Indeed, I was struck with
his awkwardness while receiving the guests at his
levee, walking upstairs, and sitting in the chair. His
hair was cut unevenly on the back of his head, his
features were rugged, and he had evidently paid but
little regard to his tailor. And...he had that far-way
look in his eyes so often spoken by those who knew
him intimately during those awful years of blood and
carnage, when his great soul was wrung with the
anguish of a nation at war with itself."[6]

Though only fifteen years old then, Bullock reported that in his
brief conversation with the President at the White House "I was as
much at ease with President Lincoln as if talking to my own
father.... No sooner had he laid his hand upon my shoulder, and
said 'My son' than I felt drawn to him...I saw before me the
countenance of a man I could trust, one which invited confidence."[7]

E.W. Andrews, a Democrat and an officer in the Union Army
during the War, was present at Gettysburg when Lincoln delivered
his famous speech there. On the one hand, he recalled that Lincoln
was "so put together physically that...gracefulness of movement was
an impossibility" but on the other hand, he remembered that:

"In his whole appearance as well as in his wonderful
utterances, there was such evidence of wisdom and
purity and benevolence and moral grandeur, higher
and beyond the reach of ordinary men, that the great
assembly listened almost awe-struck as to a voice
from the divine oracle."[8]

In the recollection of Francis Fisher-Browne, Lincoln was, at
once, "about the ugliest man I had ever seen" yet "his very
awkwardness was an asset in public life in that it attracted attention
to him" and, more importantly, no doubt, "he seemed like some
grand Hebrew prophet" and when he spoke...he directed his thoughts

to the ends of justice, freedom and humanity. He *seemed* to be a man who cared more for his cause than for his personal advancement, even if ambitious."[9]

Lincoln was, in many ways, a mysterious and paradoxical personality. In one sense, he was folksy, given to telling western stories, jokes and anecdotes. He was friendly and easily approachable. He was a man without any airs about him. He was in this sense a very democratic personality, the very opposite of, say, a Charles de Gaulle. But he was also given to alternating moods of sadness and introspection. At times, he could cry as easily as he could laugh, and, above all, he was a very private person. His innermost thoughts, his private aspirations, his visceral reactions to persons and events, all these things Lincoln tended to keep to himself.[10] People always had to satisfy themselves with guesswork in interpreting the President's state of mind.

Indeed, Lincoln was quite self-consciously a very controlled personality. He liked to measure his words carefully and to take his time in preparing important decisions. It is reasonable to infer that he exerted enormous will power to overcome the common appetites of humanity in order to lead a life so personally exemplary. He was a man all but devoid of personal malice. And he was, despite his western informality and predilection for stories some people thought too earthy, very high minded.[11] Lincoln's conversation rarely, if ever, focused on gossip. It did not feature cursing or profanities. Lincoln never boasted about his life or career and never busied himself in condemning or investigating the private lives of others. For all these reasons, his demeanor was unusual and unusually impressive. Moreover, it was bolstered by a prophet-like indifference to the material world all around him.

It is a truism that all personalities are different and that every human being may be described as unique. But Abraham Lincoln was more different from ordinary mortals, either of his time or ours, than most people. His mental and spiritual qualities put him into the category of a holy man or a prophet, that is, someone who has a sense of his own redeeming mission in behalf of humanity; someone who has a very strong sense of moral values largely independent of the judgment of others; someone who is apparently prepared to, and somehow expects to sacrifice his life for the purpose of realizing this mission; and someone who exhibits a certain other-worldly detachment, or spirituality, that is, a remarkable indifference or disassociation from the kinds of gratifications that are characteristic of most ordinary people, including ordinary politicians.

Although he had been one of the most successful lawyers in the state of Illinois for nearly twenty five years prior to his election to the Presidency, Lincoln did not amass a huge fortune.[12] He was not a speculator or avid investor.[13] His photographs, pictures and contemporaneous accounts of his appearance and deportment, all testify to a remarkable indifference to those things which most mortals prize so highly. No President dressed more plainly than Lincoln. None was more indifferent to appearance and ornaments. Lincoln was not interested in liquor, sumptuous food, gaudy furnishings, sexual conquests of women (or men) or in the conspicuous company of the rich and the powerful. Sprung from dire poverty, he remained throughout his life personally immune to all the blandishments of modern day materialism.[14] To be sure, Lincoln loved and indulged his wife, but Lincoln was never a "yuppie."[15]

According to John J. Duff, Lincoln was in the 1850's "looked up to by his contemporaries as virtually the leader of the Illinois bar, which was noted for its lawyers of genuine stature." Yet, after 25 years of practice -- and before the income tax -- he had only amassed $15,000 dollars net worth by the time of his election to the Presidency.[16] At his death, Lincoln's estate amounted to $85,000 "nearly all of it [saved from his] White House salary" which had amounted to $25,000 a year.[17]

An old Springfield physician and former mayor, Dr. William Jayne, recalled Lincoln almost forty years after his death:

> "There was not a particle of avarice in our subject's mental make-up. Greediness of wealth was

absolutely foreign to his nature. He wanted money sufficient to pay living expenses for his household, but he cared not for gold just to possess and handle."

Jayne illustrated the point reminiscing about how Lincoln was once asked to give a lecture in order to raise money for the Illinois College library. Seeing that the audience was rather small, Lincoln offered to waive his fee, telling the sponsor that he would settle for a railroad ticket home and fifty cents for supper.[18] A fitting summary of some of the most striking aspects of Lincoln's character is put forward by the eminent student of his life, Richard Nelson Current:

"...there are [Lincoln's] inner qualities -- the humor and the sadness, the essential humanity, the basic integrity and incorruptibility that resist all debunking, all scholarly prying, and that generation after generation cause those who know him best to admire him most.[19]

Never did Lincoln show any hankering for the perquisites or trappings of exalted power. If absolute power corrupts absolutely, he was absolutely safe from corruption.[20]

Whatever the secret of his leadership, he seems to have had in full measure at least one quality that all the others lacked in some degree. This was not humility or even modesty but a kind of ego perspective...It kept him well away from illusions of grandeur."[21]

There is also another sense in which Lincoln, the prophet, showed detachment from ordinary human concerns. His focus on what he saw as the great issues of his time, the goals to be advanced, was so intense, that it largely precluded him from involvement in a wider range of political and social questions, more typical of ordinary politicians.

Already at the time of the Lincoln-Douglas debates, a certain narrowness of focus was evident with respect to Lincoln's political interests. As Herbert Agar notes:

> "Perhaps the most remarkable feature of the debates was the number of problems which were ignored. The nation had just suffered a severe economic depression. Yet...there was not a word about unemployment, the condition of factory workers, the tariff, immigration, rail roads and federal land grants, homesteads and the protection of public lands against greedy plunder, agriculture, or banking or any of the agrarian grievances which were soon to rend the nation."[22]

Agar places the onus for the narrow scope of the debates on Lincoln. He attributes some very political motivations to Lincoln, suggesting that Lincoln did no address other issues simply because he realized that his Republican following was not yet agreed upon them. It was a matter of clever electoral tactics presumably. But the explanation misses out on Lincoln's obvious interests. The debates were not an isolated incident in Lincoln's career. To be sure, Lincoln was cautious and deliberate in his actions and he was politically astute, but his energies were, nevertheless, focused on what he viewed as the great moral and historical question of his time.

Finally, in the true prophet -- in this case Abraham Lincoln -- one finds the remarkable confluence of skill and of purpose, not only a vision, but the ability to make great impact among one's fellows in articulating, defending, and advancing such a vision.

Lincoln differed from Max Weber's "charismatic leader" because he enjoyed a perfectly ordinary family life with a wife and four children, and also because he was strongly integrated into a conventional structure of professional and social associations, as a lawyer and as a member and participant in such entities as the Illinois Bar, the Illinois State Militia and, of course, the Whig and Republican parties.

Part of what Lincoln was, perceptible to any observant eye around him, was simply an unusually good man in the conventional sense of the term. He was remarkably lacking in vices. He did not drink. He did not smoke. He was not a womanizer. He was not much of a gambler. He was not only scrupulously law abiding in his life, but had a well established reputation for honesty and truthfulness among those who knew him personally.[23]

A life-long seeker of high public office, he was simultaneously tolerant of slights and slurs which would make most lesser mortals blanch and probably vow eternal vengeance. The well known Stanton and Seward episodes are illustrative.

In the case of Edwin Stanton, we have the singular spectacle of a man who had publicly called Lincoln a "long-armed baboon" and a "giraffe" in 1855. In 1861, Lincoln appointed him Secretary of War. In the case of William Seward, great Republican leader and Senator from New York, a leading candidate for the Presidency in 1860, a political prima donna par excellence, we have someone who had treated Lincoln with conspicuous contempt and condescension during the 1860 campaign. Lincoln appointed him Secretary of State.[24]

Emerson David Fite in his book originally published in 1911 describes Seward's campaign trip on behalf of the Republican ticket in the fall of 1860:

> "Lincoln, the orator [that is, Seward] scarcely mentioned, and when he did condescend to refer to the candidate, it was done curtly. Returning homeward Seward's party reached Springfield, Illinois, where the proud, haughty, domineering New Yorker never left the railroad car. Far from it. But Abraham Lincoln, humble American, one in a

large crowd, came to the depot and nudged his way through the crowd to Seward's car and into it: Seward rose, shook hands with the visitor, introduced him to the members of the little party, then again sat down! There was no conversation. Finally, to relieve the situation, Seward made a short speech to the people and Lincoln found his way out of the car as best he could."[25]

Lincoln's high minded indifference to these kinds of personal slights may seem unusual. It invites the justified commendation of his own character and modesty, or as some would have it, his extraordinary "ego perspective."[26] But there is clearly another, additional explanation. Lincoln's focus, the great concentration of his life energies, was different from that of most mortals, and it was exceptional in his time as it would have been in ours.

If many men may be said to pursue "glory" in some sense, and if Lincoln, too, was one of those pursuers, his glory was to be realized in the vindication of a great, transcendent cause through the agency of his person, and that was American Union in Freedom with universal implications for all mankind.

The best and most reliable source on Lincoln is, naturally enough, Lincoln himself. The Basler edition of eight volumes of Lincoln's authenticated utterances is a powerful witness to the extraordinary life and character of the sixteenth President. To read it is to appreciate the organic link between Lincoln the American myth, and Lincoln the human being.

Given the period of Lincoln's life, the collected papers include items which would nowadays be only available in telephone tapes and would probably not be parts of equivalent modern day documentary collections. Here, for example, one finds not only speeches and proclamations, but also Presidential messages that include at times just a few words, such as "Will Mr. Smith please call on me tomorrow afternoon," or perhaps "Send the Jones file."

What is extraordinary in all this material is both the things that are to be found in it and also some things not found. It is, for example, astonishing that in a period of approximately four years and one month which Lincoln spent in the White House, from his inauguration on March 4, 1861 to his assassination on April 14, 1865, there are only two references to his own and his family's finances. These are expressed -- literally -- in only three sentences, two of these are part of a brief note to his wife in which Lincoln tells her that he invested some money in a way she would probably like. The other is part of a brief note to his erstwhile law partner, William Herndon, in which Lincoln tells the latter to do as he, Herndon, suggests in his own earlier letter to Lincoln. The details are not explained, and Lincoln tells Herndon that he doesn't have time for lengthy letters anymore.[27]

Most of the correspondence and messages in Lincoln's White House years are concerned with two subjects. He writes notes relating to federal job appointments, usually directed to officials, recommending particular persons to them or inquiring about various cases. A subject of approximately equal attention for him is correspondence concerning appeals. Lincoln was clearly the chief military justiciar of the Civil War. As Commander in Chief and as President he received a seemingly endless stream of requests for clemency. Although the correspondence does not indicate the ratio of Lincoln's responses to requests made of him, it is extremely one sided so far as it goes. Lincoln issued hundreds of stays-of-execution, commutations of sentences, and out right pardons and releases from imprisonment.

What is remarkable in this record is literally the total absence of personal meanness or vengefulness on Lincoln's part. In only one instance during Lincoln's tenure as President do we find a case in which Lincoln merely insists that the verdict of a military court be carried out. In all other cases, in 1861, 1862, 1863, 1864, and 1865, Lincoln's interventions are uniformly on the side of mercy. His actions are all but invariably directed to lessening the punishment of individuals, or as he had put it in another context, to lifting burdens. There is not a single note in the entire body of his correspondence whose focus is, either directly or by implication, to add to or hasten the punishment which may have been meted out or perhaps even contemplated by some subordinate or some subordinate agencies. Given the context of a murderous civil war and the high stakes involved, this is all the more remarkable. Very few statesmen in world history could possibly have exceeded Lincoln's qualities of mercy and human compassion.

What is also extraordinary about the whole collection is the tone and temper of Lincoln's utterances. There is never any hint of loss of self-control, of anger, pique, frustration, envy or spite: not even during the most trying times of struggle in the early months and years of the Civil War.[28] Not a single curse is to be found in the whole collection of Lincoln papers. In fact, there are no intemperate messages addressed to anyone. With Lincoln, there is no gloating and there is no whining. Lincoln never complains á la Hitler, about the incompetence and disloyalty of his generals or his political assistants -- much as he might. Even his outright political opponents, from Jefferson Davis on down, receive scarcely any mention. They seem to be passing shadows in the great fabric of his life and career. Lincoln expresses sympathy, humor, grief and compassion. He is resolute in his principles. But he never expresses feelings of hate or contempt for anyone. In the parlance of our time, he "bends over backwards" to indicate the appreciation of the human condition, in which other people, perfectly good people perhaps, see things differently than he might see them.

Lincoln is religious and fatalistic; he believes in God's immanent will and judgment working out their way in the lives of men. He believes in a great American destiny which he identifies with universal human well being, improvement, progress, and, above all, freedom and self-government. He appears to see himself as an instrument of that destiny.[29]

Given his own testimony and the impressions of those who knew him, many great imponderables attach to this unique figure. Why did Lincoln seek historical immortality alongside of Washington and Jefferson? Why did he care so much about the judgment of just human beings, and, above all, the judgment of posterity? The answers will forever remain part of the great mystery of politics and history. For while it is possible to infer a pattern of action and a purpose or purposes from Lincoln's words and conduct, the underlying reasons are elusive.[30] A rare moral and political genius, he was sprung from unlikely circumstances of poverty and hardship, and possibly even from difficult or troublesome family relationships in his youth. But in all those respects, Lincoln was not much different from thousands, if not millions, of other human beings across the millennia. Yet, he was the Hope Diamond of the American national experience. He can be "explained" just as easily as Mozart and Moses and Michelangelo can be "explained...."

Lincoln's performance in the office of President had a mysteriously providential quality about it. After all, how had Lincoln prepared himself for the task of America's chief executive? The likelihood of Lincoln providing the leadership for the United States which, in fact, he did provide, was in 1860, roughly equivalent to the chance of becoming a millionaire on a national lottery ticket.

Considering both political and administrative experience, Abraham Lincoln was, without a doubt, the least qualified person to serve as President in the history of that office both before and after 1861. Lincoln had served four 2-year terms in the Illinois state legislature without any apparent distinction. He was never Speaker, Majority Leader, Minority Leader, nor did he serve in any other capacity which would give him at least some prima facie institutional claim to being something more than a run-of-the-mill state legislator.[31] He subsequently served a single, undistinguished term in the United States House of Representatives from 1847 to 1849.

An article appearing in the *Philadelphia Evening Journal* of May 24, 1860, summed up some, not altogether unreasonable opposition perspectives:

> "It is very evident that the Republican newspapers
> are hard put to it for something to say in favor of

Mr. Lincoln. His record as a statesman is a blank. He has done nothing whatever in any executive, judicial, or legislative capacity, that should entitle him to public respect.... When in Congress from 1847 to 1849, he was not only not distinguished by any display of parliamentary talent, or by any special service, but those who sat in the same Congress find it difficult to remember that any such person as Abraham Lincoln occupied a seat on the floor."[32]

On the other hand, a defence of Lincoln's qualifications published on May 23, 1860 in the *Chicago Tribune* devoted most of its coverage to Lincoln's honesty and to the simplicity and moderation of his habits. The best that could be said about him was that he was a wise and honest man. In truth, Lincoln had never managed or administered any organizations, however small, either of government or of private enterprise. He never attended college or even high school, being essentially a self-taught lawyer.

In contrast, his first illustrious predecessor, George Washington, had been the Commander in Chief of the Revolutionary Army. John Adams was a Harvard graduate, a signer of the Declaration of Independence, and one who had held a multitude of impressive offices before succeeding to the Presidency, including some diplomatic posts and the Vice Presidency. Thomas Jefferson, among many distinctions, served as Secretary of State and as Governor of Virginia before becoming President in 1801. He had attended the College of William and Mary. James Madison graduated from Princeton and served as Secretary of State in Jefferson's administration among his many other impressive achievements. James Monroe had been a United States Senator, Minister to France, Governor of Virginia, and Secretary of State under Madison. He was also a graduate of William and Mary. John Quincy Adams served as a diplomat and U.S. Senator before becoming President. He had graduated from Harvard.

Andrew Jackson was no scholar but he had served twice in the United States Senate and commanded large federal military forces before ascending to the office of Chief Executive. Martin van Buren served as both U.S. Senator and Governor of New York before winning the Presidency in 1836. William Henry Harrison had had the experience of military command and served as the first governor of Indiana Territory in 1800. John Tyler had served in Congress, in the Virginia legislature, in the United States Senate, as Governor of his state and finally as Vice President. James K. Polk not only spent fourteen years in the Congress but was Speaker of the House of Representatives from 1835 to 1839. He had also served as Governor of Tennessee before assuming the Presidency.

Zachary Taylor, the Whig President from 1849 to 1850, had had no experience in political office of any kind but as a general he had commanded large American forces and in 1848 was considered a national hero for his military role in the war against Mexico. Even the otherwise undistinguished Millard Fillmore had served in the Congress three times as long as Lincoln and was first elected to the Vice Presidency in 1848. Franklin Pierce had been both a Congressman and U.S. Senator, as well as a general, before succeeding to the Oval Office. James Buchanan, Lincoln's hapless predecessor, was a man hardly lacking for political credentials. A graduate of Dickinson College, he had served in the Pennsylvania state legislature and eleven years in the U.S. House of Representatives. He was the American Ambassador to Russia from 1831 to 1833, and then served ten years in the United States Senate.

Interestingly, it is also true that all American Presidents subsequent to Lincoln have had more impressive credentials in terms of education, service in public office, and/or administrative experience than did Lincoln himself. Andrew Johnson had served in Congress, in the Senate, and as Governor of Tennessee before becoming Lincoln's Vice President in 1865. U.S. Grant, no politician, was, nevertheless, the nation's incomparable and victorious Commander of the Union Armies. Rutherford Hayes achieved a general's rank and had served in Congress and also three terms as Governor of Ohio. James Garfield was also a general in the

Civil War, served in Congress, and was elected to the Senate before becoming President. Chester Arthur, who never received a presidential nomination, was a Union College graduate who had served as Collector of the Port of New York from 1871 to 1879 before securing the Vice Presidential nomination in 1880. He succeeded to the Presidency on the death of Garfield in 1881. Grover Cleveland had served as district attorney, sheriff, and mayor of the city of Buffalo, before becoming Governor of the state of New York, and then President. Benjamin Harrison was a college graduate and a general during the Civil War, and served seven years in the United States Senate prior to his election as President in 1888. William McKinley put in many years of service both in the House of Representatives and the Senate before winning the Presidency. Theodore Roosevelt, who had succeeded to the office on McKinley's death, had been Governor of New York, among other credentials, when he was nominated for Vice President in 1900.

Woodrow Wilson had been a University president and a Governor of New Jersey. Warren Harding, though little esteemed as President, was, nevertheless, a state senator and a Lieutenant Governor of Ohio before serving in the U.S. Senate from 1915 to 1920. Calvin Coolidge served as mayor of Northampton, Massachusetts, and then as state senator, lieutenant governor and governor, before winning the Vice Presidential nomination in 1920. Herbert Hoover was Secretary of Commerce from 1921 to 1928 in addition to holding various other impressive executive responsibilities before his 1928 Presidential nomination. Franklin Roosevelt served as Governor of the nation's then largest state, New York, before assuming the Presidency. Harry Truman spent ten years in the U.S. Senate before getting the Vice Presidential nomination in 1944. Dwight Eisenhower had been Supreme Commander of Allied Forces in Europe. John Kennedy had been both a Congressman and a Senator before securing the nomination in 1960. Lyndon Johnson's experience and background, in both houses of Congress, were well nigh legendary when he was chosen as Kennedy's running mate. Richard Nixon had been a Congressman, U.S. Senator and Vice President before his election as Chief Executive in 1968.

Even Gerald Ford, with his modest presidential reputation, was a man who had a college degree from Michigan, a law degree from Yale, and had spent twenty five years in the House of Representatives, with eight of those years as Republican leader. Jimmy Carter was a one-term Governor of Georgia when nominated to the Presidency in 1976. Reagan, though a career actor, was also twice elected Governor of the state of California before achieving the Presidency in 1981. George Bush served two terms in the House of Representatives and lost a Senate race but he had held a number of important executive branch positions and the Vice Presidency before his election in 1988. Bill Clinton had had the benefit of multiple terms as Governor of Arkansas before 1992.

It is hardly surprising that the man generally considered America's greatest President was, upon taking office,[33] viewed with a combination of curiosity and contempt by people who would nowadays be called "Washington insiders." Such people tended to underestimate Lincoln because of his apparent inexperience, his genial, seemingly guileless manner, his proclivity for telling homespun stories, and his backwoods, lackluster background. This attitude toward Lincoln was characteristic of long-time politicians, legislators, journalists, career military, and the social set. It was not difficult, after all, for people who had had quite a bit of formal education -- often at the very best of places -- and a good deal of experience in high political office, as well as the assets of long-time family connections, wealth, and what used to be termed "breeding" to look down upon this man, Lincoln, so clearly lacking in all of these. These were the typical attitudes of the men of Lincoln's Cabinet, although undoubtedly much more so at the beginning of Lincoln's administration than at its conclusion. To such people as they, the sixteenth President seemed to be just an accident of the democratic aspect of American politics, especially in 1860 and in 1861.[34]

But, fundamentally, Lincoln was far more subtle, discerning, and intuitive than virtually all those around him realized. And, contrary to what one might have anticipated, he was also amazingly resolute.

In his recent book, *Icons of Democracy*, Bruce Miroff concludes his chapter on Lincoln with these words:

> "He does not answer all the questions that need to be raised about democratic leadership in America. But of all those figures who have labored and risen to positions of power within the American political mainstream, Lincoln remains the best model Americans have of democratic leadership."[35]

This view corresponds to the classic interpretation of Lincoln. And it has its reasons. Part of the great democratic mystique of Lincoln was simply his origin. He was a poor lad, born in dire circumstances, without formal education, who had worked his way up the ladder of economic and political success to be the leader of the nation. That in itself seemed to be a testimonial to American democracy, and Lincoln himself greatly emphasized his organic connection to the common people of the nation. There was also the matter of his aspirations. Clearly, the President saw himself as a champion of the democratic ideals of freedom, equality, and self-government. One could also say that Lincoln was a "born democrat" in terms of his political style or how he interacted with most people most of the time. The President was folksy, easily approachable, capable of engaging in discourse with most anybody, outwardly friendly, sympathetic and patient as well as modest. He was in interpersonal relations what moderns would call a low-key sort of leader. He possessed a democratic demeanor. There is also something to be said for Lincoln's concern about and sense of public opinion. In retrospect, he is often given credit for excellent timing of some of his major political initiatives, for sensing the pulse of national feeling.

But where Miroff's characterization of Lincoln breaks down is on the substantive issue of the President as a decision maker. Lincoln was no facilitator of some national consensus, seeking to give shape to other people's wants and aspirations. He was an inner-directed man, interested in the opinions of others not as a source of his own decisions but as an important constraint on the pace and form to be applied to the carrying out of his own agenda. He may have been as close to Moses or Bismarck in that respect as to any so called "democratic leader" that one might possibly mention. Lincoln was not averse to shedding blood or putting people in jail without legal charges or trial. His most important war decisions had no prior Congressional authorization. His Emancipation Proclamation, by executive decree, was also the single biggest confiscation of property in the history of the Republic. Lincoln could be ruthless when he believed that he needed to be ruthless.[36]

The critical question is how could Lincoln, a minority President in 1861, behave as arbitrarily as he did, and, yet, die a hero in 1865 and remain one of the Nation's most revered figures forever after? Part of the reason is in the vindication of Lincoln's purpose through the course of time. That slavery is a moral wrong and a fundamental contradiction of the principles of the Declaration of Independence was a controversial opinion in 1860 but increasingly less so since that time. That preserving the United States as one great nation, granted the heavy price paid for it, was worth doing is not much disputed in our time.

Yet, it is clear that Lincoln does not owe his good name to mere victory in the Civil War. For Lincoln, victory could be described as a necessary but not sufficient condition for the maintenance of his great historic reputation. Stalin, too, was a victor in a major war – World War II – and he died surrounded by the public praises of sycophants. But it did not take long to put his reputation into a very negative perspective. Lincoln's name continues to be associated with some of the most treasured human values.

The forbearance of the American people toward Lincoln and their reverence for his memory owe a great deal to his accomplishments and also to his moral character. Lincoln's whole life, public and private, communicated a credibility rarely achieved in the political world. Not one or two elements of it, but the sum of the parts argued Lincoln's cause. Millions of Americans during his Presidency, and even more millions afterwards, understood that Lincoln "did not do it for the money;" that he did not seek the

185

Presidency to "meet girls"; that he would not and did not abuse great personal powers for selfish, private ends; that he was a truly disinterested man whose whole life was a definition of what civic and private virtues are, or ought to be; that here was a powerful and resolute man but no tyrant; that here, indeed, was a thoughtful and kind man, humble before God, but unalterably dedicated to the causes of Freedom and Union; and if therefore Lincoln said that he must violate some laws in order to save more important other laws, or, in fact, act autocratically in order to preserve the country's democratic institutions for the future, he would be followed and believed , even when others might not be so followed and believed.

The paradox of Abraham Lincoln was that in his person he united the most benevolent and high-minded aspirations with a disposition to use power decisively, and if need be, even ruthlessly. Ordinarily, such a disposition toward power is something that people in the Western, and especially American culture, identify with tyranny and cruelty. The genius of Lincoln, however, managed to combine an unlikely mix of personal qualities.

The benevolent aspect of Lincoln was most clearly evidenced by his rhetoric, by his public presentation of himself. The content of Lincoln's speeches, from the earliest beginnings of his career as a politician, stands in stark contrast, with a virtually 180 degree difference, from that of his notable twentieth century opposite, Adolf Hitler. Lincoln's speeches were never built on themes of anger, violence, fear, contempt, hatred, envy or resentment. They were, whatever the subject, the communications of a thoughtful and sensitive human being. They were never coarse and vicious. There was no bullying or gloating in them. Lincoln's speeches were remarkably free of accusations, threats or slanders directed at particular opponents or categoric entities. Characteristically, during the many years of conflict, Lincoln never succumbed to the temptation of labeling his Democratic opposition the party of treason and subversion. He never publicly impugned the motives, interests or associations of those who challenged him for high office. Lincoln never whipped up a mob or held anyone up to vilification.

Some of the more interesting aspects of Lincoln's rhetoric are examined in the work of Lois J. Einhorn in her recent book.[37] As Einhorn points out:

> "Somewhat in contrast to the rigor, often elegance, of his logic, Lincoln portrayed himself as simple, humble and unassuming.... Throughout his public life he tended in speeches to minimize and downplay his authority and ethos." He portrayed himself as an "honest, ordinary person."[38]

Einhorn concurs in Richard Hofstadter's judgment that "the first author of the Lincoln legend was Lincoln himself."[39] There was also a certain sense of the abstract, and later even an impersonal element, in Lincoln's presidential speeches, she observes, which suggested that Lincoln meant to address not only his contemporaries but also future generations. As James G. Randall shows, even in instances where the national policies were brutally tough, Lincoln managed to convey a sense of identification with ordinary people:

> "His humane sympathy, his humor, his lawyerlike caution, his common sense, his fairness toward opponents, his dislike of arbitrary rule, his willingness to take people into his confidence and to set forth patiently the reasons for unusual measures -- all these elements of his character operated to modify and soften the acts of overzealous subordinates."[40]

Lincoln's application of harsh measures usually reflected a significant concern with prudence and morality.[41] People who were arrested and detained by the military were rarely held for long periods of time. For the most part, they were not subjected to brutal treatment which modern observers might identify with the Gestapo or the KGB, such as beatings, torture, starvation, or isolation from all contacts with immediate family, relatives and friends. The President was notoriously, one might say, generous with pardons and commutations on a case by case basis. Even more importantly

187

perhaps, Lincoln was careful not to construct any special, independent and autonomous police agencies or bureaucracies for the purpose of resisting treasonable activities within the Union. He allowed military commanders to exercise this function temporarily and obviously in conjunction with their other military duties and obligations. No Heinrich Himmler or Lavrenti Beria emerged out of the American Civil War.

In his book, *Lincoln's Herndon*, Professor David Donald has referred to Lincoln as the "first among the folk heroes of the American people" and took note of the proposition that "the history of any public character involves not only the facts about him but what the public has taken to be the facts". Nowadays, one would probably refer to this as a person's image. Donald's definition of what the Lincoln legend, or image, has been in American history explains much about the success that Lincoln achieved as perhaps the greatest American role model and image projector. To Donald, the Lincoln legend is " as American as the Mississippi River... essentially national, it is not nationalistic. It reveals the people's faith in the democratic dogma that a poor boy can make good. It demonstrates the incurable romanticism of the American spirit.... The fundamental qualities of legendary Lincoln reveal the essential dignity and humanity of our nation's everyday thinking. Americans can be proud that to the central figure in their history their folklore has attributed all the decent qualities of civilized man: patience, tolerance, sympathy, kindliness, sagacity and humor."[42]

In his Diary, Navy Secretary Gideon Welles referred to Lincoln as the "good and gentle, as well as truly great man." When he saw Lincoln mortally wounded on the evening of the 14th of April, Welles subsequently observed that "his features were calm and striking. I had never seen them appear to better advantage than for the first hour, perhaps, that I was there. After that his right eye began to swell and that part of his face became discolored."[43]

The peaceful visage of Lincoln may well have reflected the great statesman's semiconscious realization that he had completed his journey precisely as he had always hoped to complete it, earning his rightful place   in the immortal company of Washington and Jefferson, a father of his country, and forever the greatest role model for his fellow citizens.

REFERENCE

1. Dwight G. Anderson observes in his <u>Abraham Lincoln, The Quest for Immortality</u> (New York: Alfred A. Knopf, 1982) p. 12. ..."Lincoln's quest for immortality was rooted in a profound anxiety about death which had personal and political dimensions, and which revealed itself in his premonitions and his dreams, his poetry and his public speeches." He also says that "to win immortality is to live on in the memory of subsequent generations, and thus to be out of the ordinary, to disdain the beaten path, to seek regions hitherto unexplored." P. 95. Ambition as Anderson points out, was only a vehicle through which "immortality could be attained" but simply holding office, even the Presidency, was not enough in that respect. <u>Ibid.</u> More on Lincoln's dreams as premonitions of death, and in Anderson's view, anxiety about his own guilt, see pp. 198-204.

Note also George W. Forgie, <u>Patricide in the House Divided: A Psychological Interpretation of Lincoln and His Age</u> (New York: W.W. Norton, 1979). In describing Washington's life-long effort to master his own impulses and temperament in order to live a virtuous life, the author suggests the model followed by Lincoln. P. 39. He concludes, however, that Lincoln's political achievement, in effect, freed Americans from their obsessive need to follow the precedents of the original founders. Pp. 280-281.

2. Congressman George W. Julian recalled that "perhaps the most charming trait in the character of Mr. Lincoln was his geniality. With the exception of occasional seasons of deep depression, his nature was all sunshine." Allen T. Rice, <u>Reminiscences of Abraham Lincoln by Distinguished Men of His Time</u> (New York: North American Publishing Company, 1886) p. 59. As E.B. Washburne put it: "He was a man of the most social disposition and was never as happy as when surrounded by congenial friends." <u>Ibid</u>, p. 13.

3. Basler, vol. I, pp. 8-9.

4. Allen T. Rice, <u>op. cit.</u>, p. 169.

5. Rufus Wilson, <u>Lincoln Among His Friends, A Sheaf of Intimate Memories</u> (Caldwell, Idaho: The Caxton Printers, Ltd., 1942), pp. 342-345.

6. <u>Ibid</u>, p. 360.

7. <u>Ibid</u>, p. 366.

8. Rice, <u>op. cit.</u>, p. 516.

9. Francis Fischer-Browne, <u>op. cit.</u>, p. 197.

10. See Henry B. Rankin, <u>Intimate Character Sketches of Abraham Lincoln</u> (Philadelphia: J.B. Lippincott Company, 1924) for a discussion of Lincoln's "obliviousness to his surroundings" in occasions of great mental concentration (pp. 145-146) and at times of impenetrable melancholy (pp. 148-151) when he was a mystery to all around him, including his "dearest and nearest." P. 149. See also Ervin Chapman, <u>Latest Light on Abraham Lincoln and War Time Memories</u>, Volume I (New York: Fleming H. Revell Company, 1917) p. 76: "No element of Lincoln's character was so marked, obvious and ingrained as his mysterious and profound melancholy." Lincoln was a man who, in a sense, distanced himself from the world around him as few mortals have.

11. As the writer, David R. Locke, observed: "Those who accuse Lincoln of frivolity never knew him. I never saw a more thoughtful face, I never saw a more dignified face, I never saw so sad a face...He said wonderfully witty things but never from a desire to be witty. His wit was entirely illustrative." Rice, <u>op. cit.</u>, p. 442.

12. See John J. Duff, <u>A. Lincoln, Prairie Lawyer</u> (New York: Rinehart, 1960) pp. 228, 367.

13. William I. Curtis, <u>The True Abraham Lincoln</u> (Philadelphia: J.B. Lippincott Company, 1903) estimates Lincoln's income between two and three thousand dollars a year between 1850 and 1860 but his fees were as a rule "less than those of other lawyers of his circuit...avarice was the least of his faults." Pp. 73-74. Note John P. Frank, <u>Lincoln as a Lawyer</u> (Urbana: University of Illinois Press, 1961) "Unlike other lawyers of his time, he was not engaged to any great extent in outside money-making activities." P. 38. ..."his real estate holdings were trifling." P. 39.

14. Richard N. Current (ed.), <u>Mr. Lincoln by J.G. Randall</u> (New York: Dodd, Mead and Company, 1957) notes pp. 26-27 on how "unkempt" Lincoln looked. Even in 1858 he appeared to Stanton as an "uncouth farmer".... P. 27. See J.R. Pole, <u>Abraham Lincoln</u> (London: Oxford University Press, 1964) who describes Lincoln as "untidy." P. 12. "He was the kind of man whose clothes, however carefully made, never seem to fit." P. 14. But Pole also cites the testimony of Lincoln's Assistant Secretary of the Navy, Charles H. Dana, about Lincoln: "The great quality

of his appearance was benevolence and benignity: the wish to do somebody some good if he could. And yet there was no flabby philanthropy about Abraham Lincoln. He was all solid, hard, keen intelligence combined with goodness." P. 59.

15. Note R.N. Current, Mr. Lincoln, op. cit., p. 165. Also Ishbel Ross, The President's Wife, Mary Todd Lincoln (New York: G.P. Putnam's Sons, 1973) pp. 256-257 who observes that despite all of Mary's temper tantrums, and the vexations of her periodic extravagances, "she was greatly and compassionately loved by Abraham Lincoln." P. 342.

16. Duff, op. cit., p. 228.

17. See Jean H. Baker, Mary Todd Lincoln (New York: W.W. Norton, 1987) p. 263 and p. 272.

18. Wilson, op. cit., p. 77 and pp. 77-78.

19. Richard Nelson Current, Speaking of Abraham Lincoln, The Man and His Meaning for Our Times (Urbana: University of Illinois Press, 1983) p. 49.

20. Ibid, p. 140.

21. Ibid, p. 141.

22. Herbert Agar, The Price of Union (Boston: Houghton Mifflin, 1950) p. 389.

23. Fred T. Dubois, subsequently Senator from Idaho, offered this recollection of Lincoln whom he had observed as a youth in the 1840's: "Mr. Lincoln was fond of horses and enjoyed the races...[he] was a good judge of horses and he and his companions would often place a small wager on the result of the race.

"...I never knew of him using tobacco in any form, and he decidedly was not a drinking man but made no fuss about it either.... He never played cards." Rufus Wilson, op. cit., p.97.

Note Isaac N. Arnold The Life of Abraham Lincoln (Chicago: A.C. McClurg Company, 1896) in which a contemporary acquaintance and political associate of Lincoln emphasizes his "perfect integrity and reverence for God." P. 20. Comparing him to Washington, Arnold concludes that Lincoln was "as pure, as just, as patriotic, as the father of his country but he also had more faith in the people and the future of the nation." P.454. Note also the contemporary account of Henry J. Raymond, The Life and Public Services of Abraham Lincoln (New York: Derby and Miller, 1865) in which the President's integrity and his reputation for it are heavily emphasized themes of his personal background. See also George H. Putnam, Abraham Lincoln, The People's Leader in the Struggle for National Existence (New York: G.P. Putnam's Sons, 1911). "It was Lincoln's principle to impress upon himself at the outset the full strength of the other man's position. It was also his principle [as a lawyer] to accept no case in the justice of which he had not been able himself to believe." P. 26. See also Chapter 2, pp. 12-28 on Lincoln's character as his political qualification. Note also William E. Barton The Soul of Abraham Lincoln (New York: George H. Doran Company, 1920) on the religious beliefs of the Sixteenth President. The author's conclusion, based on extensive research, was that Lincoln was no theologian but he was a deeply religious person nevertheless.

24. Note discussion in Alexander J. Groth, "Lincoln and the Standards of Presidential Conduct," Presidential Studies Quarterly vol. xxii, No. 4, Fall 1992, pp. 765-777.

25. See Emerson David Fite, The Presidential Campaign of 1860 (Port Washington, N.Y.: Kennikat Press, 1967) p. 213. As the author reports, it was being publicly suggested, as in the New York Herald on August 16, 1860, that William Seward expected to be the de facto leader of a Republican administration behind a mere Presidential figurehead of Abraham Lincoln. In his memorandum to Lincoln of April 1, 1861, when he was already Secretary of State, Seward had the temerity to suggest to Lincoln that the latter ought to turn over the executive leadership of the government to him. P. 214, fn. 1.

26. Richard Nelson Current, Speaking of Abraham Lincoln, op. cit., p. 141.

27. Lincoln's letter to William Herndon of February 3, 1862 read: "Yours of January 30th is just received. Do just as you say about the money matters. As you well know, I have not time to write a letter of respectable length. God bless you. Says your friend...A.L." See Basler, vol. V, p. 118.

To Mary Todd Lincoln on August 8, 1863, the President wrote: "My dear Wife: All is well as usual, and no particular trouble any way. I put the money into the Treasury at five per cent, with the privilege of withdrawing it any time upon thirty days' notice. I suppose you are glad to learn this. Tell dear Tad, poor 'Nanny Goat' is lost: and Mrs. Cuthbert and I are in distress about it...." Basler, vol. VI, p. 371.

28. Consider Lincoln's advice to a young man, Captain James M. Cutts, who got into some trouble in the army over a personal quarrel: "No man resolved to make the most of himself can spare time for personal contention. Still less can he afford to take all the consequences, including the vitiating of his temper, and the loss of self-control. Yield larger things to which you can show no more than equal right; and yield lesser ones though clearly your own. Better give your path to a dog, then be bitten by him in contesting for the right. Even killing the dog would not cure his bite." See Basler, vol. VI, October 26, 1863, letter to Captain James M. Cutts.

29. Note e.g. Don C. Seitz, <u>Lincoln the Politician</u> (New York: Coward-McCann, 1931) on Lincoln's aspiration, since boyhood, to be President. Pp. 255-256. See also the interesting account by Paul Simon, <u>Lincoln's Preparation for Greatness: The Illinois Legislative Years</u> (Norman: University of Oklahoma Press, 1965) in which he concludes about Lincoln's eight year Illinois service that: "No legislator was more honest. Perhaps none was more popular with his colleagues [though] others were more creative [and] had more background...." P. 293. Note Frank, <u>op. cit.</u>, p. 350 and also Duff, <u>op. cit.</u>, p. 64. Duff remarks that Lincoln was "excruciatingly, almost pathologically sensitive...to the plight of others."

30. Note Francis Fisher-Browne, <u>The Everyday Life of Abraham Lincoln</u> (Chicago: Brown and Howell Company, 1913) p. 478: "He was a religious man in spirit and by nature; yet he never joined a church -- no man on earth had a firmer faith in Providence than Abraham Lincoln." In a revealing comment to Thurlow Weed of March 15, 1865, Lincoln observes as follows about his Second Inaugural Address: "I expect the latter to wear as well -- perhaps better than -- any thing I have produced, but I believe it is not immediately popular. Men are not flattered by being shown that there has been a difference of purpose between the Almighty and them. To deny it, however, in this case, is to deny there is a God governing the world. It is a truth which I thought needed to be told; and whatever of humiliation there is in it, falls most directly on myself, I thought others might afford for me to tell it. Yours truly, A.L."

Note also Glen E. Thurow, <u>Abraham Lincoln and American Political Religion</u> (Albany: State University of New York Press,1976). He points out that in the Gettysburg Address Lincoln was expressing a national viewpoint but in the Second Inaugural he was expressing a politics of transcendence -- something above and beyond mere popular judgment. In the President's words: "As was said three thousand years ago, so still it must be said, the judgments of the Lord are true and righteous altogether." P. 115. Quite appropriately, Thurow observes: "Lincoln teaches us that it is...necessary for the citizens of the democracy to have a perspective transcending the nation. Only by seeing themselves as standing under the judgment of God will the intoxication of their own sovereignty be sobered by awareness of human limits. Only then may the principles of democracy result in justice rather than injustice." P. 116.

31. Fellow lawyer and long time political associate, Elihu B. Washburne, described Lincoln, the state legislator, thus: "Mr. Lincoln was not particularly distinguished in his legislative service. He participated in the discussion of the ordinary subjects of legislation, and was regarded as a man of good sense, and a wise and practical legislator. His uniform fairness was proverbial. But he never gave any special evidence of that masterly ability for which he was afterward distinguished, and which stamped him, as by common consent, the foremost man of all the century." Allen T. Rice, Reminiscences of Abraham Lincoln by Distinguished Men of His Time (New York: North American Publishing Company, 1886) p. 8.

On the other hand, Donald W. Riddle Lincoln Runs for Congress (New Brunswick: Rutgers University Press, 1948) gives Lincoln this credit for some show of political promise during his service in the Illinois state legislature concluded in March 1841: "In recognition of his ability as a parliamentarian he had become the recognized floor leader of the Whigs in the lower house; twice put forward as candidate for speaker, he had once narrowly missed election...." P. 4. Lincoln was also apparently widely credited with helping to move the state capital from Vandalia to Springfield. Ibid.

32. See Herbert Mitgang (ed.), Abraham Lincoln: A Press Portrait (Athens: University of Georgia Press, 1989) p. 181.

33. In "presidential polls taken by Life Magazine in 1948, The New York Times Magazine in 1962, and The Chicago Tribune Magazine in 1982, historians and political scholars ranked Lincoln as the best chief executive in American history." Stephen B. Oates, Abraham Lincoln, The Man Behind The Myths (New York: Harper and Row, 1984) p. 57.

34. William H. Herndon and Jesse W. Weik Abraham Lincoln, The True Story of A Great Life Volume II (New York: D. Appleton, 1896). As one of Lincoln's contemporaries in the practice of law observed: "Any man who took Lincoln for a simple-minded man would very soon wake up with his back in a ditch." P. 3. An extended quotation from Herndon is worth

citing here on the issue of Lincoln's character and mind: "Lincoln is a man of heart -- aye, as gentle as a woman and as tender -- but he has a will as strong as iron. He therefore loves all mankind, hates slavery and every form of despotism." P. 185. According to Herndon, Lincoln could fail, and follow the advice of others, on issues that he viewed as doubtful or questionable. Interestingly, Herndon cited "political economy" as just such an issue, but when acting on questions of "justice, right, liberty, the Government, the Constitution, and the Union, then you may all stand aside: he will rule then, and no man can move him -- no set of men can do it. There is no fail here. This is Lincoln and you mark my prediction." P. 185. Herndon was quoting himself here from a letter he had written to Vice President Henry Wilson on December 21, 1860.

With respect to his legal practice, Herndon recalled that Lincoln's "confidence in his own ability...was so marked that his friends never thought of tendering their aid...." P. 189. Lincoln listened to everybody but he "rarely, if ever, asked for opinions. I never knew him in trying a case to ask the advice of any lawyer he was associated with." P. 247. "No man ever kept his real purposes closer or penetrated the future further with his deep designs." Pp. 247-248.

35. Bruce Miroff, Icons of Democracy, American Leaders as Heroes, Aristocrats, Dissenters, and Democrats (New York: Basic Books, 1993) p. 124.

36. Gore Vidal's fictional account of Lincoln's qualities as a leader perceptively addresses the President's grim determination to pursue the struggle against the Confederates no matter the cost. Note the remarks Lincoln allegedly directs to Seward expressing the willingness to "burn Baltimore to the ground" in order to keep Maryland in the Union. Gore Vidal, Lincoln, A Novel (New York: Random House, 1984) pp. 152-153, 153-154.

37. Lois J. Einhorn, Abraham Lincoln the Orator, Penetrating the Lincoln Legend (Westport, Conn.: Greenwood Press, 1992).

38. Ibid, p. 25.

39. Ibid, p. 41. See also Waldo W. Braden Abraham Lincoln, Public Speaker (Baton Rouge: Louisiana State University Press, 1988) who offers this conclusion as to the basis of Lincoln's popular appeal: "Lincoln relied heavily upon the element of persuasion that the ancient rhetoricians called ethos; he won support by demonstrating that he was a man of common sense, good moral character, and good will." P. 115.

40. James G. Randall, <u>Constitutional Problems Under Lincoln</u>, Rev. Ed. (Gloucester, Mass.: Peter Smith, 1963) pp. 519-520.

41. Future Speaker of the House of Representatives, Schuyler Colfax, recalled of Lincoln: "No man clothed with such vast power ever wielded it more...forbearingly. No man holding in his hands the key to life and death ever pardoned so many offenders, and so easily. Judge Bates of Missouri, his Attorney General, insisted that lack of sternness was a marked defect in Lincoln's character. He told Mr. Lincoln once in my presence that this defect made him unfit to be trusted with the pardoning power. Any touching story, especially one told by a woman, was certain to warp if not control his decision." Rice, <u>op. cit.</u>, p. 338.

42. See David H. Donald, <u>Lincoln's Herndon</u> (New York: A.A. Knopf, 1948) p. 373. See also Donald's <u>Inside Lincoln's Cabinet, the Civil War Diaries of Salmon P. Chase</u> (New York: Longman's Green and Company, 1954) for this, now somewhat amusing appraisal of Lincoln by General David Hunter whom Chase regarded as "very well read": "A man irresolute but of honest intentions -- born a poor white in a Slave state, and, of course, among aristocrats -- kind in spirit and not envious, but anxious for approval, especially of those to whom he has been accustomed to look up -- hence solicitous of support of the Slaveholders of the border states, and unwilling to offend them -- without the large mind necessary to grasp great questions -- uncertain of himself and in many things ready to lean too much on others." P. 172.

43. Howard K. Beale (ed.), <u>Diary of Gideon Welles, Secretary of the Navy Under Lincoln and Johnson</u> Volume II (New York: W.W. Norton and Company, 1960) p. 283 and p. 287. Note also the provocative, and not unpersuasive account of Lincoln's assassination by Dwight G. Anderson, <u>op. cit.</u>: "Lincoln seems to have known that for him there could be no reprieve or salvation." P. 207. "By his death, Lincoln became the savior of the Republic, the one who, by his sacrifice and atonement redeemed the sins of the fathers and gave to the nation a new life, a life everlasting." <u>Ibid.</u>

197

VI

THE MEANING OF THE LINCOLN EXPERIENCE AND SOME MODERN RELEVANCIES

People who are ideologically indoctrinated, the firm believers in any particular creed, have a tendency to insulate themselves from the lessons of experience. Whatever happens around them, or to them, must be made to fit into a preconceived ideological framework, no matter how odd. In modern times, this tendency to "bending" experience in order to fit an ideological perspective was a frequent characteristic of Soviet Marxists. People living outside the former Soviet Union often wondered how so much self-deception, as was evident from the various official Soviet sources, was, in fact, possible. But, for a long time, and for a great many people, self-deception was not only possible, it was the face of Soviet reality.

If collective farms seemed almost obviously wasteful and unproductive enterprises, it was not the fault of the Soviet system -- its lack of individual incentives or its excessive bureaucratic centralization, for example. It was because of all sorts of extraneous, temporary, about-to-be-overcome reasons, and perhaps also the fault of harsh nature itself. Whatever it was, it had nothing to do with any fundamental assumptions of the Soviet regime. The same rule applied to any other observable problem, whether it was crime, drunkenness, ethnic strife, corruption, or the surprising persistence of religious attachments among the broad masses of people. The ideology of Marxism-Leninism posited the Soviet system, axiomatically, as an ultimately inevitable human success. No "pathology" could possibly attach to it.

Somewhat analogously, it was characteristic of people imbued with Nazi ideology of antisemitism that if they encountered Jews who did not fit their stereotypic conceptions of "the Jew," they would either deny that such persons were Jewish (as Alfred Rosenberg denied the Jewishness of Christ, for example) or they would reinterpret the observed conduct so as to vindicate the treasured stereotypes. Thus, for example, if the Jews were seemingly behaving "decently", "bravely", "honorably", etc., it was probably only as a pretense or ruse, or because the behavior was somehow compelled by some external source and therefore did not really reflect the true dispositions of the particular actors.

Although he was a great man and a great statesman, Abraham Lincoln was also a lifelong believer in the ideology of American democracy, especially, of course, as explicated by Thomas Jefferson. When he spoke at the dedication of the military cemetery at Gettysburg in 1863, he provided an interpretation of the Civil War, and implicitly of his own role in it, very much in accord with the tenets of America's liberal creed. In Lincoln's rendition. the War seemed to be a vindication of political democracy in the United States. Given the American cultural experience both before and after the War, this interpretation found almost universal favor with posterity. Its acceptance undoubtedly fulfilled Lincoln's own life-long aspiration to be the instrument of redemption for the principles of 1776.

In fact, however, a somewhat different conclusion from the accepted formula of the Gettysburg Address may be reasonably drawn from the Lincoln experience. American democracy, on the eve of Lincoln's election, was a system on the verge of breakup and bankruptcy. If the resolution of America's problems in 1860 were left to a genuine majority decision, the November election amply demonstrated that there was no majority to lean on in any direction for the country as a whole. There were only regional, local majorities. It appears highly likely that if the very divided American people were somehow all brought together for the purposes of a political dialogue, whether through a referendum or some process of representation, what they would have agreed upon, if they could agree on anything, would have been very different from the Lincoln solution imposed by a President chosen by less than 40 percent of the electorate.

Apart from the more or less reasonable might-have-beens, we know that Lincoln seized the levers of American political power with a remarkable unilateralism. Stripped of conciliatory phraseology, Lincoln offered the Southern slaveholders a choice between force and submission. He would not let them secede and he would not allow them to extend the institution of slavery. The President did not retreat an inch from the positions he articulated in the debates with Stephen Douglas in 1858. And while he did not formally suspend the Constitution, or the Congress, or the courts, his method of waging war against the Confederacy owed very little to the institutions and processes generally identified with political democracy. Lincoln did not rule by committee; he did not emphasize consultation, negotiation, bargaining, dialogue or consent. His most important strategy vis a vis the Congress was to adjourn it and confront it with a fait accompli of assorted war measures. The jurisdiction of courts Lincoln limited by the invocation of military tribunals and the suspension of habeas corpus. In some cases, he directly defied the courts. When there was an outcry in the country, stimulated by the unexpectedly large casualties and defeats of the Union armies, Lincoln ignored the groans expressed in the press, in public meetings, in riots and demonstrations, and, very clearly also in the congressional election results of 1862. He pursued a policy of tough perseverance in a cause he viewed as just, not responsiveness to fluctuating currents of public opinion as modern politicians might.

All the losses on both sides notwithstanding, Lincoln would not give the South a ceasefire short of full fledged surrender. And he did not shrink from waging a very harsh, bitter, all-out war against the Confederacy, despite his obviously kind and generous disposition toward individual appeals for help addressed to him during the conflict.

To be sure, Lincoln did not use his war measures to *destroy* the institutions of democracy in the United States. His temporary measures were just that, emergency expedients to save the Union in its hour of mortal danger. They were the acts of a faithful fiduciary agent.

But none of this can deny that the means of salvation which Lincoln employed in the Civil War were largely authoritarian. And it is precisely this fact which calls for a reevaluation of the meaning of the Lincoln experience in American history and world politics.

Lincoln was very conscious of the importance of public opinion and he sought, often successfully, to influence it. But he did not draw upon it as the source of his inspiration and his moral sanction. He had rejected Douglas popular sovereignty doctrine, and, with all his professions of respect for the law, he had also rejected the Supreme Court's Dred Scott decision. Like Winston Churchill and Charles de Gaulle in later times, Lincoln was a man who marched to the beat of his own drummer. In at least one respect he limited the sphere of American freedoms after his own time, by making it clear, through victory, that no state could ever, on its own volition, however overwhelming, leave the American federation. By the abolition of slavery, however, he enormously advanced and expanded the sphere of American freedoms in still another direction, and by preserving the Union he left to all Americans a far richer and greater opportunity for self-development than they might have had otherwise. Thomas Bailey in his study of the American Presidency, pictures Lincoln's role in these terms:

> "Lincoln acted greatly in great times: he possessed the inner fortitude to see the horrible ordeal through to the last corpse. The task of bringing the South back into the Union was overpowering enough, but he had to complete it under incredibly harrowing conditions. Imagine a captain in a hurricane whose ship, nearly broken in half, is being blown rapidly onto the rocks. Below in the cabin his beloved son lies dead and his wife is having hysterics. On deck, nearly half the crew is firing mutinous shots; the rest of the crew is firing back; many of the passengers are screaming contradictory orders; others are demanding a new captain or conspiring to take his place; while still others are below trying to scuttle the ship. Yet 'My Captain' in Walt Whitman's

words 'weathered every rack' and came safely to port, 'cold and dead', past the shoals of secession and emancipation, and the rocks of copperheadism and disunion."[1]

The Lincoln experience in American politics was, above all, a remarkable example of a historically recurring bail-out of a failed or failing democracy by an outstanding, resolute, and far-sighted individual, one who could do for "the People" what "the People" most evidently could not do for themselves: conceive, decide, implement and persevere.

The American crisis of 1860 and the Lincoln solution of 1860-1865 illustrate but a larger question. The qualities ascribed to democracies by their ideological proponents are sometimes lacking, or put in another way, they sometimes fail.[2] Indeed, it is remarkable that the ideological self-deception of its proponents should have been so successful in disguising what is, after all, a generic problem of the liberal democracy. To view the rectitude, wisdom, courage, and sundry other attributes of "the People" as always superior to those of particular individuals, or groups, within the body of the people is a logical absurdity. An averaged aggregate is always higher than the lowest sum or sums which compose it, and, of course, it is always lower than the highest sum or sums which contribute to the make up of this aggregate. To admit the truth of this proposition is not to endorse necessarily the universal virtue of an autocratic or oligarchic form of government or to unconditionally repudiate democracy.

The criteria of politically rightful authority involve very complex matters. If within a given community, for example, many people, perhaps most people, wise or foolish, moral or wicked, aspire to share in political power, exclusion may be both difficult and impractical. There may not be a self-evident system of political authority with which to replace political democracy. After all, how could and should our autocrats and oligarchs be chosen? Could political power be distributed, for example, on the basis of the highest I.Q. test score in the nation? What if that score belonged to an inmate of a maximum security prison? Who would make up the test? If something we called "moral excellence" were to be made a criterion of power, would someone like Mother Theresa make a good Finance Minister or even President of a properly constituted polity?

There may be no general, universal answers to questions like these. But the difficulties of answering them should not keep us from identifying particular, specific malfunctions of the democratic political systems or from appreciating the contributions of their occasional individual rescuers. Here we may recall a famous observation of Machiavelli's recorded in his Discourses:

> .... "where the body of the people is so thoroughly corrupt that the laws are powerless for restraint, it becomes necessary to establish some superior power which, with a royal hand, and with full and absolute [authority] may put a curb upon...excessive ambition and corruption...."

Democracy may be, formally at least, a very popular form of political association in modern times because it is all but impossible to get people who participate in politics to agree to any alternative formula. But that does not make it immune to all sorts of malfunctions. In Lincoln's time, as in ours, and with virtual certainty in the future as well, democracies may suffer from failures of morality, competence and harmony. All three were evident in America of Lincoln's time. [To be sure, such failures may surface because of various underlying dissynchronizations between emergent challenges to the political system and its particular social, economic and cultural legacies. What is ultimately important is that they do surface....].

It had been the President's judgment prior to his 1860 election that if slavery was not wrong, nothing was wrong. Yet, it is virtually certain in any reasonable retrospective, that if the fundamental decision on America's future in 1860 or 1861 were left to the actual majority of the whole American electorate, slavery, at least in the short run, would have been vindicated. If the southern states were allowed to secede, naturally, they would have continued to cultivate their peculiar institution undisturbed by the Congress or any other Federal agency. Although in 1861 the Confederacy had agreed to desist from the overseas importation of slaves, sovereignty certainly would have enabled it to change its mind in subsequent years. Another likely alternative would have been the acquiescence of the American majority of 1860-1861 in some form of extension of the rights of slavery to new territories and to heretofore free states. These were far more likely alternatives than a majority decision to stand firm and fight a civil war in order, if we may use Lincoln's words, to put the institution of slavery on the road to extinction. In 1860 this position was widely identified with abolitionism, and relatively few Americans were prepared to go to war on its behalf. The last probable alternative would have been a kind of 'non-decision' in the form of squabbling and wrangling among people who apparently lacked consensus on the great issue of their time. And squabbling and wrangling would have favored American fragmentation as a de-facto process of human accommodation to impasse. States and regions would have likely drifted into different local solutions, probably including ultimately a Southern withdrawal from the Union with slavery intact.

All this can be attributed to some very understandable human dispositions. The Lincoln alternative to the North-South impasse of 1860 involved, at first, an enormous risk: war and destruction. Once implemented, it involved enormous suffering, calamitous loss of life, pain, prolonged disruption of the people's existence, and huge material costs. Most people do not like to suffer great risks and costs if they can possibly avoid them. The advantages and benefits to future generations do not carry the same weight with people as the immediate consequences of things to themselves in the here-and-now. Life has always been short and never equipped with a second chance. To many, the conflict with the South seemed to be personally irrelevant, over matters in which they themselves had no stake. Indifference and very narrowly focused self-interest have always been very important forces in the conduct of human affairs.

The particular facts and the time were different but, in basic outline, this was also the situation confronted by Winston Churchill and the British people in the 1930's. Criticized as an adventurer and an eccentric, Churchill recognized the moral and practical threat posed by Hitler's totalitarian regime in Germany, to Britain, Europe, and the world at large. Before others realized it, Churchill somehow, almost intuitively, sensed that it would never be possible to make a satisfactory, lasting settlement with the Nazi dictator. And, if he was right about Hitler, then it was necessary for Britain to begin immediately spending a far larger share of her resources on war preparations and also to undertake measures which might ultimately risk war itself.

Yet, in the 1930's British democracy seemed incapable of recognizing and thwarting Hitler's aggression in Europe. It was not simply a matter of Mr. Neville Chamberlain and his famous umbrella, both symbols of a failed British appeasement policy toward Hitler. It was virtually a national, consensual policy that Britain was pursuing in trying to avoid confrontations with the Nazis.[3] Both the Conservative and the Labour Party spoke the language of illusion and appeasement. Neither was prepared to support vigorous rearmament policies in the early or even middle 1930's. Both hoped to resolve differences with Germany through collective security, the League of Nations, and diplomacy. Both feared the possibility of war and rejected the use of force in curbing Nazi aspirations to hegemony in Europe. Naturally, there were significant reasons for these British positions. The bloody losses of World War I were still remembered and mourned. Strong currents of pacifism, isolationism, and a sense of national weakness, combined to create an atmosphere of acquiescence in Hitler's repeated provocations.

Nazi repudiation of the Versailles Treaty disarmament clauses in 1935 was seen as justified by the alleged unfairness of the Treaty as a whole; the military reoccupation of the Rhineland in 1936 in violation both of Versailles and Locarno treaties was seen as no more than a restoration to Germany of what was German. Austria, too, in 1938 was said to be a Germanic area. The Nazi claim to the Sudetenland was similarly justified on the grounds of affinity

205

between the Sudeten Germans and their ethnic brethren in the Third Reich. As for the fate of Czechoslovakia, Mr. Chamberlain argued that here was a place most British people had not even known existed. Why should it be important to them?

A few years earlier, the previous Conservative Prime Minister, Mr. Stanley Baldwin, openly admitted his opinion that no party pledged to an onerous rearmament program could hope to win a national election. The people would not accept this sort of policy, he argued. Indeed, when Mr. Chamberlain returned from Munich in September 1938, and waved the famous piece of paper with Hitler's signature on it as a guarantee of peace, he was greeted by enthusiastic, deliriously happy crowds and received as a hero in the House of Commons. Whatever virtues British democracy may have possessed, it was not capable of facing up to the trap that was being sprung for it in Berlin.

Winston Churchill's role was to transform a polity prepared to yield to Hitler's aggression to one that was determined to resist it at virtually any cost. For this historic role--- which proved critical not only for the British but for the destiny of the world as a whole -- Churchill had prepared himself somewhat like Moses prepared to lead the people of Israel out of Egypt: he spent the 1930's in the political wilderness. Although a member of parliament and nominally a Conservative, he had become a persona-non-grata, an outcast with the likes of Baldwin and Chamberlain. After Hitler's accession to power in 1933, Churchill became singularly unwelcome to Conservative Party leaders. He persisted in warning Britain about the danger of Nazism and called for extremely unpopular measures of rearmament and vigorous opposition to Hitler's expansionism. Not only was Churchill excluded from office but in a period when most people in Britain wanted to believe that peace could be maintained by concessions to Hitler, he was regarded as a political eccentric, a dangerous man of doubtful judgment and an adventurer not to be trusted.[4] Public opinion saw Stanley Baldwin and Neville Chamberlain as sensible and solid politicians. Churchill was the marginal maverick.

Until March of 1939, when Hitler violated his own pledge given in Munich to respect the sovereignty of Czechoslovakia by sending in the German army to occupy that country, Churchill continued in the role of political outcast. The collapse of the Munich agreement changed the perception of Churchill among the British people. At last, the eccentric had become a prophet. It was finally beginning to become clear that it was Neville Chamberlain and not Winston Churchill who had lived in a world of dangerous illusions.

Chamberlain proceeded to issue his controversial guarantee to Poland and when Hitler unleashed his panzer divisions on the Poles in September of 1939, Britain declared war on Germany. The Prime Minister asked Churchill to join the War Cabinet in his old, World War I post of First Sea Lord. But it was becoming increasingly clear that the man who had led Britain in appeasement of Hitler was not, and could not be, the man to lead the country in the all-out struggle to follow. Politically and psychologically, Chamberlain was haunted by a sense of failure and inadequacy. Early in 1940, following British setbacks in Norway, and despite a large Conservative majority in the House of Commons, Chamberlain resigned, paving the way for the installation of Winston Churchill as Prime Minister of a national unity government. He would lead Britain through the gravest crisis since the Napoleonic wars of the early nineteenth century.

Capitalizing on his unique reputation, Churchill set about inspiring and "energizing" the British to an effort which was only at the margin of rational calculation. It is true, of course, that by 1940 Hitler had amply demonstrated his ruthless and callous disregard for treaties and for peace and his brutally aggressive appetite. The blueprint of Mein Kampf was beginning to unfold. But this was a time when Hitler's major crimes had not yet been committed. The Final Solution and the extermination of millions of people in such camps as Auschwitz, Majdanek and Treblinka were still many months away.

The balance of power, especially with France out of the war in June 1940, was heavily in Hitler's favor. British prospects in resisting the Nazi onslaught -- in the face of crippling submarine warfare and aerial bombardment -- were rather bleak. The United States was still neutral, substantially demilitarized, thousands of sea miles away in an age which did not yet know of intercontinental missiles or even air-refueled airplanes. Hitler's resources, with all Europe at his feet, were enormous.

Emerging out of a period of prolonged appeasement, British public opinion was hardly a mirror image of Churchill's own tremendous resolve. Moreover, people who -- understandably-- may have had their doubts about the prudential aspects of fighting Hitler in 1939 or 1940 were likely to be reinforced in those doubts and vacillations by the steady course of allied defeats. The marvel of Churchill's work was that at its best it coincided with the most unfavorable military and political prospects for Britain. When the British army fled the coast of France at Dunkirk, Churchill gave perhaps his most famous speech on June 4, 1940:

> "We shall fight in France, we shall fight on the seas and oceans, we shall fight with growing confidence and strength in the air, we shall defend our island, whatever the cost may be, we shall fight on the beaches, we shall fight on the landing grounds, we shall fight in the fields and in the streets, we shall fight in the hills; we shall never surrender."

A few days later France collapsed, leaving Britain the sole major power confronting the Nazis. Churchill's public response was the celebrated radio address in which he told the British people:

> "Let us therefore brace ourselves to our duties, and so bear ourselves that, if the British empire and its Commonwealth last for a thousand years, men will still say: 'This was their finest hour'."

In praising the Royal Air Force for its efforts against the Nazis in the Battle of Britain in 1940, Churchill said that never in the field of human conflict have so many owed so much to so few. With all the prudent discount of hyperbole, it is possible to say that rarely did so many people owe so much to one person as in the case of Winston Churchill during the Second World War.

Among Western examples of democracies being "bailed out" by the efforts of outstanding individual leaders, the only known "multiple" case is that of General Charles de Gaulle. He did it in 1940 and again in 1958. In the first instance, de Gaulle, like Winston Churchill in the 30's, stood virtually alone against the overwhelming majority of French popular opinion and the edicts of France's legitimate democratic institutions. The prevailing opinion was to promote collaboration with Hitler in a Nazi-dominated Europe. De Gaulle opposed it on both moral and pragmatic grounds, and risked his life in offering to France, from London, an alternative to collaboration with Nazism.[5]

One of the consequences of the defeat of French armies by the Nazis in June of 1940 was an astonishing abdication of French democracy. Meeting in the little provincial town of Vichy, the French National Assembly (Chamber of Deputies and Senate) on July 10 delegated the powers of the Republic, by an overwhelming affirmative vote, to Marshal Henri Philippe Petain. He was given a virtual blank check to reshape French institutions. Moreover, the grant of power was given in the context of an unmistakable understanding that Petain would abandon the regime of parliamentary democracy which France had had since 1871 and devise a new regime, more acceptable to and consonant with the new Nazi hegemony in Europe.

Most of the people who voted these powers for Petain had been heretofore considered -- using the terminology of modern American politics -- quite "liberal." Petain had the support of Radicals, Moderates, and quite a few Socialists, not to mention Conservatives and neo-Fascists. The Communists were spared a potentially embarrassing test since they had been expelled from parliament in 1939 as traitors to the nation. Stalin's pact with Hitler concluded in August 1939 would have put them in an awkward position in 1940. Still, much of the Left and Center of French politics rushed onto the Nazi bandwagon, all past rhetoric notwithstanding. It was argued that France had to accommodate itself to the "new realities" of European political life. The old regime was condemned as corrupt and ineffective.

One can only speculate on this tremendous "about face" by French politicians -- all freely and democratically elected. Did they act out of fear of the Germans? Were they eager to lay down the burdens of power in the face of national calamity? Were they looking for personal advantages within a new, and perhaps inevitable, pro-Nazi regime? On the whole, France in 1940 was in no mood to continue the war and to defy the Nazis. She was weary and, by and large, beaten in spirit as well as in battle. Accommodation to the "New Order" in Europe was a genuinely popular theme. But not all Frenchmen were prepared to give up.

General Charles de Gaulle, with that wonderful and almost unbelievable sense of ego which allowed him to identify France with his own person, was not about to give up the struggle. He defied the lawfully constituted French government, now headed by the capitulationist Marshal Petain. De Gaulle flew to London and began to create the Free French movement so as to continue the fight against the Nazis at the side of the British. He had made his famous (though little noticed at the time...) broadcast to France from the British capital on June 18, 1940 asking the French people to rally around him for the cause of continued resistance until ultimate victory and liberation.[6]

Like Churchill before him, de Gaulle seemed frankly quixotic in his stance. What hope was there of defeating the Nazis in the summer of 1940? "Sensible" Frenchmen ignored de Gaulle. Many considered him a rebel and a traitor. But, like Churchill earlier, de Gaulle had an important moral vision for his compatriots. Like Churchill, he had a certain understanding of the consequences of Nazism which eluded most of his contemporaries. He sensed that no majority of French parliamentarians could sanctify collaboration with the Nazis without accepting moral abasement and national slavery. And like Lincoln, de Gaulle understood that no majority could make wrong right. De Gaulle's foresight, like Churchill's and Lincoln's, was linked to his character. It was not only that he knew how to choose sides unequivocally, and that in these choices he was vindicated by history. He was also willing to stand alone and to suffer rejection, scorn, ridicule, and censure in order to adhere to what he believed to be right.

It did not take very long to reveal the true face of Nazism in its day to day impact on France. Hitler's rule soon demonstrated all its familiar characteristics-- brutal force and secret police, mass reprisals, executions, concentration camps, deportation of Frenchmen to forced labor in German war factories, censorship, confiscation and legalized insecurity. Simultaneously, the fortunes of war had begun to turn against Hitler. Victory yielded to defeat. Resistance to Vichy and Nazism in France itself continued to mount. Reckoning was approaching. By mid 1944, there was very little by way of benefits that any rational Frenchman could expect of Hitler. When Charles de Gaulle returned to France to lead a victory parade down the Champs Elysee, he was welcomed as an authentic national hero. He had saved the national honor and preserved France's place among the victors of the Second World War. As Provisional President of the Republic, de Gaulle was the consensual choice of all the parties of the Resistance.[7]

In the immediate post-war period, de Gaulle sought to reform French institutions with the objective of somehow avoiding the repetition of the kind of politically divided, fragmented regime France had had before the Second World War. But in this design, de Gaulle failed. De Gaulle's reform movement, the so-called Rally of the French People, could not attract majority popular support in the 1940's and early 50's. The General's response was withdrawal from active political life in 1953 to the seclusion of his country home at the village of Colombey des Deux Eglises. Politically, he appeared to be "washed up" and was so treated by newspaper pundits and commentators.[8] But de Gaulle's political obituaries proved premature. In 1958 he would be needed once again.

211

The Fourth Republic which had experienced more than twenty governments in a period of twelve years (1946--1958) disintegrated under the stress of its colonial wars. The war of independence waged by Communist guerrillas against French rule in Indochina began in 1948 and ended in 1954 with a humiliating French defeat in the battle of Dienbienphu. The partition of Indochina at the Geneva Conference in the same year followed and so did the outbreak of an Algerian Moslem struggle for independence from France. Frustrated by its failure in Indochina and the lack of political support at home, the French Army in Algeria grew increasingly impatient and embittered. Its tactics against the Algerian rebels -- or freedom fighters -- became increasingly savage and reckless without, however, yielding the desired result of victory for the French.

The Algerian war proved to be the undoing of the Fourth Republic. The political parties proved unable to crystallize a consistent policy, either quitting Algeria altogether, or settling on a course of military and/or political victory over the insurgents. In May 1958 the French armed forces effectively rebelled against their own government. The army in Algeria refused to obey orders from Paris and there were several simultaneous seizures of control in various locations by the military. A paratroop division under the command of General Jacques Massu was rumored to be readied for the seizure of Paris and the ouster of the civilian government of France. The country appeared on the brink of a military coup or, failing one, the beginning of a civil war. It was widely expected that the unions and the Communists would take up arms against a military insurrection. It seemed as if France was about to repeat the scenario of the Spanish Civil War of the 1930's.[9]

Under these circumstances, the President of the Republic at the time, Rene Coty, called upon General de Gaulle to take over the leadership of the French government. The hero of French resistance to Nazism and a general, de Gaulle seemed the only possible incumbent whom both the military and the civilians were likely to obey. De Gaulle extracted the quintessential political condition from the majority coalition which he required in return for his services: a virtual blank check to frame fundamental reforms of French political institutions and the right to submit them to the approval of a popular referendum, bypassing the deeply divided, multi-party parliamentary assembly. At last, apart from the Communists, there was widespread recognition in France that the country needed to be pulled back from the abyss. De Gaulle's reforms -- tilting the balance from the legislative to the executive branch of government-- were precisely the sort which French parliamentarians had been unable to agree upon for almost a century.

The Gaullist political system gave France nearly four decades of relative political stability without any appreciable loss of personal and political freedoms enjoyed under previous Republican regimes. But it has not been without its controversies. Although no one had ever seriously questioned the General's exemplary personal integrity, his use of political power, like Lincoln's, has been controversial.

Did de Gaulle occasionally trample upon his own Constitution? Illustratively, political scientist, William Safran, has offered this bill of particulars:

> "He violated Article 11 a number of times, when he bypassed Parliament before submitting a bill to a referendum -- the most notorious case being the referendum of 1962 regarding the direct election of the President; Article 29, by refusing to accede to the demand of the assembly for a special session in March 1960; Article 38, by unnecessarily asking for special decree powers in May 1967; and Article 50, by refusing to dismiss Pompidou as premier in 1962, after the latter had been ousted by a vote of censure in the Assembly."[10]

According to Safran, one could also charge de Gaulle with an excessively "political" interpretation of Article 16, conferring emergency powers on the President, because de Gaulle meant to use emergency powers not simply against "civil disorders, insurrections or wars" but largely for political purposes, "especially in order to overcome a hostile parliamentary majority."[11]

On the other hand, Jean Blondel has observed:

> "Much has been written about the authoritarianism of de Gaulle, which was undeniable. But, even under de Gaulle, the main features of the liberal democratic system were in existence. The provisions of the Constitution of 1958 have given the president and the whole executive very strong powers. But these are not without checks and the people have had a say in the life of politics. Broadly, the regime has been based on consent -- and it was in some ways based more on consent under de Gaulle than it had been previously. Since 1965, the president of the Republic has been elected by universal suffrage, and the election was truly competitive; de Gaulle won because, after a free and clear contest, he obtained more votes than his opponents...(and) de Gaulle always put his authority in the balance in the referendums which he proposed...."[12]

Before condemning his constitutional excesses, one may wish to consider, and appreciate, de Gaulle's role in making French democracy -- with all its particularistic problems -- a viable enterprise. As in historic crises elsewhere, the General acted as the charismatic savior of a democracy which was not always up to the job of governing itself.

The emergence of democracy's saviors is a highly idiosyncratic event. There is no "counting on it." De Gaulle was not a member of any political party or movement in 1940. A general and minor Cabinet official, he simply stepped forward to assume a role no one else sought to fill. Churchill, though a Conservative M.P. and former Cabinet member, was not identified with any larger political stratum. Properly speaking, he would have been disclaimed by every branch, left, right or center, of each of the major parties before 1939.

The election of Abraham Lincoln as President of the United States was one of the more spectacularly fortunate accidents or coincidences of history.[13]   It was, to all appearances, an act of Providence. Despite the debates with Douglas and Lincoln's well received Cooper Union speech, relatively few Americans knew who Lincoln was in 1860 and even among the activists of the Republican Party he was hardly a "household name", let alone consensual choice for the Presidency. Joseph Barrett, who had been asked by Party leaders to write a campaign life story of the 1860 nominee, recalled the situation as follows:

> "Before the meeting of the Republican National
> Convention of 1860 I had undertaken, not of my
> own motion or at first willingly, to write a campaign
> biography of its nominee for the Presidency. I was
> confident that my subject would not be Mr. Seward,
> but had no presentiment that the choice of the
> convention would be Abraham Lincoln, whom I had
> then never met."[14]

Indeed, on the first ballot at the Convention, Lincoln received only 102 votes out of 464, i.e., less than 22 percent of all ballots cast. Lincoln' principal opponent, William H. Seward, received 173 votes.   Between them, Simon Cameron and Salmon P. Chase received 99 votes, virtually equal to Lincoln's total.[15]   The President was not nominated until the third ballot, when delegates began to invoke their second and third choices in light of some fairly complex deals and maneuvers between and among various state delegations. The switch by Pennsylvania to Lincoln was especially significant, since its large bloc of delegates created a huge sense of momentum for the man from Illinois. According to Barrett, the Pennsylvania decision, reached by a majorlty-driven caucus, was actually very narrowly   determined in Lincoln's favor over the candidacy of Edward Bates.[16]

What Lincoln, Churchill and de Gaulle shared, was a sense of personal vision or mission, which severely limited, if not precluded, their disposition to engage in what may be termed "committee government." On the major questions of policy, these leaders did not seek a consensus of their associates, political or bureaucratic, in order to move forward. They paid minimal homage to the democratic customs of collective, drawn out consultations and discussions as sources of policy inspiration. If anything, such procedures were reserved by them either to the lesser details of policy, or alternately to the provision of some decent minimum of symbolic and psychological gratification for those who expected this sort of procedure as a matter of constitutional propriety. Among the three, Lincoln and de Gaulle clearly resorted to more manifest illegalities or constitutional infractions in the management of state policies, but, despite all the blemishes, they both shared an ultimate, underlying respect for constitutional government and popular consent. Their measures did not aim at, or result in, the derailing of political democracy in either France or America. They were also generally free of the mass brutalities associated with the notorious dictators of the twentieth century. That Churchill was the more scrupulous observer of constitutional norms than either Lincoln or de Gaulle may be credited not only to his own sense of restraint, but most importantly to the much higher degree of domestic disunity faced by the latter.

Had it not been for Abraham Lincoln, the American democracy of the 1860's would have turned into a great failure, not only in domestic consequences but international ones as well. The great influence which the United States was to have in world affairs during the twentieth century would have been inconceivable for some conglomeration of small or middle-sized states squabbling among themselves on the North American continent. The savior was providential. He happened upon the scene when he was most sorely needed. In many democratic political systems, crises have occurred without the intervention of saviors to bring about a restoration of stability, with liberty and a regime of orderly popular participation.

In the 1920's many democratic regimes in Europe failed, most conspicuously in Italy in 1922, but also in Poland, Hungary, Romania, and Yugoslavia. In the 1930's Spain succumbed to dictatorship as did Portugal. In the 1970's calamity overtook the well established democracies of Chile and Uruguay. But perhaps the greatest single failure occurred in Germany in 1933 when President Paul von Hindenburg called upon the leader of the Nazi Party, Adolf Hitler, on January 30, 1933, to assume the office of Chancellor and constitute a new government for the Weimar Republic.

In the midst of a great economic depression, and with tremendous political divisions at home, the German experiment in political democracy was in the throes of what proved to be its mortal crisis. The constitutionally elected President of the Weimar Republic was an old man, undoubtedly a very tired man, and one who had only a little more than a year of life left to him. In January of 1933 Hindenburg gave up; he did something that he had resolutely refused to do earlier, i.e., he called upon Hitler to head up the German Cabinet. This single decision turned out to have enormous, evil consequences for Germany and for the whole world. Yet, it was an eminently avoidable decision, if only Hindenburg would, like Lincoln, faithfully adhere to certain reasonable moral and political principles implicit in his Presidential oath of office.

In April of 1932 Paul von Hindenburg had defeated Adolf Hitler for the Presidency of the German Republic by 19,359,642 votes to Hitler's 13,417,460. The Communist candidate, Ernst Thalmann, polled 3,706,388 votes. Hindenburg was thus the choice of some 53 percent of the German electorate in the second round of the presidential elections. It was also noteworthy that in the first round of voting, a month earlier, with the field open to all, von Hindenburg missed the necessary 50 percent-plus one by only about 0.4 percent of the national vote. He had achieved a seemingly significant mandate. If he had chosen to resist Nazi demands for political power, the President would have been possessed of numerous important assets.

217

To begin with, the Nazis did not have majority support in parliament. In fact, they had declined from the high tide of their popular backing of 37.3 percent in the parliamentary elections of August 1932. At the time of Hitler's elevation to the Chancellorship, the Nazi vote had slipped to 33.2 percent. Two thirds of the German electorate was outside the Nazi fold. On the other hand, President von Hindenburg, like Lincoln, had available to him the important moral resource of his oath to defend the Constitution of the Republic, and by and large, the loyal support of the German Army.

If one were simply juggling numbers, it was perfectly reasonable to say that by adding some 33 percent of Hitler's deputies in the Reichstag to the roughly 8 percent controlled by the conservative Nationalists and perhaps, by some possible bargain, the 10 percent or so of the Catholic Center Party, a parliamentary majority behind Hitler could be created. But here, alas, an important qualitative judgment was clearly necessary. What sort of parliamentary government could be established in Germany under the leadership of Adolf Hitler? Who was Adolf Hitler and what did he and his Nazi Party stand for?

The Constitution of the Weimar Republic in its explicit enumeration of the various rights of citizens and principles of political conduct was most evidently incompatible with the whole known philosophy, program and practice of Hitler's so called National Socialism.[17] In fact, based on contemporaneous knowledge, not hindsight, it would be difficult to imagine anything more contrary to it.

According to Article 42 of the Constitution, the President on assuming office was required to take an oath swearing to "devote all my energy to the welfare of the German people (and) to preserve the Constitution and the laws of the Commonwealth"....[18] The Constitution contained both domestic and international provisions which stood in stark contrast to almost everything that the Nazis preached and practiced. The section on the Fundamental Rights and Duties of Germans declared all citizens to be equal before the law.

It demanded   equal rights and equal duties for all citizens; it specifically demanded protection of German citizens who might speak a foreign language;   it declared personal liberty to be inviolable. It also protected the right of freely expressing opinions "by word, in writing, in print, by picture, or in any other way"; it guaranteed freedom of association, petition and peaceable assembly; it protected the right of religious beliefs and prohibited state discrimination against citizens on grounds of their religious affiliation.

With respect to international affairs, the Constitution explicitly acknowledged that "the generally recognized principles of the law of nations are accepted as an integral part of the law of the German Commonwealth"   (Article 4).   Significantly, the preamble to the Constitution declared that the German people were united ... "by the determination to renew and strengthen their Commonwealth in liberty and justice (and) preserve peace both at home and abroad...."

In 1933 Hitler stood before Germany and the world   as a convicted felon for his abortive, violent coup of 1923, and as a man who, in word and deed, was opposed to all the articulated values of the German Constitution and its democratic society. Hitler's whole career had consisted of the glorification of force and violence in human relations, and of whipping up racial hatreds and aggressive appetites.[19] Von Hindenburg had ample reason to deny executive power to this man. In fact, he had denied it to Hitler on August 13, 1932 when Hitler's claim, in terms of popular backing, was actually much stronger than it was in January of 1933. On that earlier occasion, Hindenburg had received Hitler in his presidential office without even asking him, or allowing him, to sit down, and rather summarily rejected his bid for power. The President's subsequent public statement addressed the question of giving the Nazis control in a democratic republic in these terms:

> "The President cannot conscientiously, and with due
> regard to his responsibility toward the fatherland,
> appoint Herr Hitler chancellor and intrust him with
> the guidance of German destinies."

How much pain and anguish would have been spared to Germany and to the whole world, if President von Hindenburg had only invoked his constitutional oath against Hitler in 1933! The actions of a single individual, strategically placed, could have had an enormous impact for the good on the whole future course of world developments. But, alas, what Providence had made available to America in 1860 was denied to Germany in 1933.[20]

To think that another Lincoln, or someone like Lincoln, might yet again appear on the American horizon is perhaps asking too much. What is more likely, however, is the eventual repetition of the crisis conditions which, in one possible version, Lincoln so brilliantly mastered.[21] Granted that there is a very wide range of underlying causes for democratic failure, material and cultural, the symptoms often follow a pattern. There may be a great deal of readily perceptible tension, unrest and turmoil. In systems plagued by pathological polarization, the procedural rights of democracy are likely to be mobilized -- paradoxically -- for great social mischief. The rights of free expression, petition, assembly, and association combined with the usual legal guarantees of individual safety and the due process of law, are all likely to translate into tumultuous demonstrations and serious disruptions of the ordinary life of the community. Rumors of plots and counterplots are likely to be quite common. There may be widespread rioting, terrorism, assassinations, bombings and arson.

Given the magnitude of such behavior, one is likely to witness the failure of duly constituted authorities to protect the life and limb and property of citizens. There may be palpable failure to keep order in the streets, random seizures or destruction of land, buildings and other objects. Access to public facilities for work, recreation, trade, or provision of services, may all be impeded. And all these, in turn, may promote an atmosphere of chaos and insecurity. These were the realities of Spain in the 1930's, Italy in the 20's, Germany both in the early 20's and early 30's, and in the 1970's of Chile and Uruguay. In fact, such symptoms of conflict and disintegration have figured in the collapse of many would-be democratic regimes of the twentieth century, whether in Europe, Latin America, Africa or Asia.

Some symptoms of democratic failure are so manifest that they can be seen and experienced, and in a sense properly "appreciated" by virtually anyone. Certainly, the worlds of Lincoln, de Gaulle and Hindenburg knew a great deal about them. But there can also be -- concurrently or not -- more subtle symptoms not so readily apparent to the naked eye or ear. The society may be somehow unable to muster sufficient foresight, skill, heart, and conscience to deal with problems that in one way or another need to be addressed if the collectivity is to survive and prosper beyond its immediate present.

In the case of Winston Churchill, Britain's crisis of the 1930's represented this kind of less easily perceptible situation. The danger to Britain, and the world, was not apparent in the streets of London, Manchester, or Glasgow on any given Spring afternoon of 1939. It lurked beyond the horizon. The symptoms of failure were invisible to the eye.

In mid nineteenth century, America was fortunate to produce a leader in the person of Abraham Lincoln who could boldly resolve its historic crisis of freedom and union. Whether a leader as extraordinary as Lincoln might again appear in the American, or indeed world experience, is not nearly as likely as the occurrence of great socio-political emergencies in which such a leader might be desperately needed.[22]

REFERENCE

1. Thomas A. Bailey, Presidential Saints and Sinners (New York: Free Press, 1981) p. 320.

2. As John Hallowell observes in his work The Moral Foundation of Democracy (Chicago: University of Chicago Press, 1954) "There is no democratic institution which is not subject to perversion, and the spirit in which we employ these institutions...is as important as the institutions themselves." P. 65. See also Roland Pennock, Democratic Political Theory (Princeton: University Press, 1979): "individualists often say that each individual knows his own interest best. 'Only the wearer,' the saying goes 'knows where the shoe pinches.' But the argument thus stated overlooks an important distinction. Granted that only the wearer can feel, and therefore locate, the pinch, perhaps someone else could have predicted better than he that that particular shoe would pinch the foot." P.103. Note also John Plamenatz, Democracy and Illusion (London: Longman, 1973). He concludes that "democracy can neither be explained nor justified as a political system that maximizes the satisfaction of wants better than other systems." P.181. See Michael Crozier, Samuel P. Huntington and Joji Watanuki, Crisis of Democracy (New York: New York University Press, 1975) for the following diagnoses of the ills of present day European democracies: "The European political systems are overloaded with participants and demands, and they have increasing difficulty in mastering...their...economic growth and development.... There is a breakdown of consensus...." P. 12.

3. Among others, see especially William Manchester, The Last Lion, Winston Spencer Churchill, Alone 1932-1940 (Boston: Little, Brown and Company, 1988) pp. 417-418 on just how bipartisan British appeasement of the 30's was.

4. As a psychiatrist wrote about Churchill, "The kind of inspiration with which Churchill sustained the nation is not based on judgment, but on an irrational conviction independent of factual reality. Only a man convinced that he had a heroic mission...could have conveyed his inspiration to others." See Anthony Storr in A.J.P. Taylor et al., Churchill Revisited : A Critical Assessment (New York: The Dial Press, 1969) pp. 251-252. A recent biographer, John Charmley, goes so far as to characterize Churchill's "We shall never surrender" speech as sublime nonsense in light of the realities of the British situation, Churchill: The End of Glory (New York: Harcourt, Brace and Company, 1993) p. 411. See Ronald Lewin, Churchill as Warlord (London: B.T. Batsford, 1973) p.23. During the 1930's a critic

observed: "What sensible man is going to place confidence in Mr. Churchill in any situation which needs coolheadedness, moderation and tact?" P. 95.

5. As one author puts it, "On June 18th 1940 the most famous living Frenchman was Marshal Petain. He had his feet on the ground, while de Gaulle's head was in the air." Oliver Coburn, Petain and de Gaulle (London: Heinemann, 1966) p. 114.

6. See William L. Shirer, The Collapse of the Third Republic, An Inquiry into the Fall of France in 1940 (New York: Simon and Schuster, 1969) who notes that in the wake of de Gaulle's speech "not one single military or political figure of any consequence, even in London, offered to join the defiant general. He was utterly alone." P.860. As for the French parliamentarians, "the fever to surrender was contagious." P. 932. The vote of the National Assembly on July 10th was 569 in favor of Petain's mandate to abandon the Republic; 80 against and 17 declared abstentions. P. 942.

7. On de Gaulle's return to France in 1944, see e.g. Bernard Ledwidge, De Gaulle (London: Weidenfeld and Nicolson, 1982). "Everywhere he was greeted with enthusiasm and his authority was accepted without question. His tour was a triumph. Liberated France had recognized him for what he was, the man who could give her a place of honor among the victorious powers and abolish the heritage of Vichy. American and British reporters...sent the news around the world." P. 172. ...the effect was a political consecration, 'ratifying de Gaulle' claim'... P.173. In the latter part of 1945, no one in France "openly disobeyed de Gaulle"... P. 185. His election by the National Assembly as President on November 13, 1945 was unanimous. P. 207.

8. A few years after the Second World War, "de Gaulle had suddenly become a pathetic figure...he was shunned by many of his old admirers, deserted by those who had sought to use him, derided rather than feared by his opponents; the men who spoke most loudly in his favor were either adventurers or belonged to the anti-Republican right-wing splinter groups which he had always mistrusted and despised." Aidan Crawley, De Gaulle (Indianapolis: Bobbs-Merrill Company, 1969) p. 309. When he resigned as President in 1946 de Gaulle said: "I wasn't made for this system...I am worn out by parliamentary skirmishes...I must go so as to hold myself ready for the big events which must be expected."

9. French Army Chief of Staff, General Paul Ely wrote to de Gaulle on May 12, 1958: "The army is cut off from the nation. It is menaced with subversion. It is open, in case a government of abandonment (of Algeria)

is formed, to secession from the homeland. Your high authority must intervene to save the country, the national unity, and that of French forces." Orville D. Menard, The Army and the Fifth Republic (Lincoln: University of Nebraska Press, 1967) p. 118. When he returned to power in 1958, de Gaulle was asked if he would abolish public liberties. His reply was "Have I ever done so? On the contrary, I restored them when they had disappeared..." Crawley, op. cit. p.343.

10. William Safran The French Polity (New York: David McKay, 1977) p. 168. See Also p. 204, fn. 43.

11. Ibid, pp. 168-169.

12. Jean Blondel, The Government of France, Fourth Edition (New York: Thomas Y. Crowell, 1974) pp. 35-36. William G. Andrews in his Presidential Government in Gaullist France (Albany: State University of New York Press, 1982) speaks of a Gaullist dictatorship in France in 1958-59 as an "interim regime that concentrated legislative authority in executive hands to a degree rarely exceeded in a major democratic state." P. 127. Simultaneously, however, Andrews expresses this judgment of de Gaulle's stewardship of power: ..."the dictatorship never breached constitutionality. It observed all the substantive and procedural limitations of its various grants of authority. Furthermore, the Parliament elected in November 1958 could have disavowed de Gaulle's measures by withholding its confidence from the Debre government. Nothing prevented that except de Gaulle's popularity, parliamentary acceptance of his measures, and the atmosphere of crisis that continued to hang over the land." P. 132.

13. See Rufus Rockwell Wilson, Lincoln Among His Friends, A Sheaf of Intimate Memories (Caldwell, Idaho: The Caxton Printers, Ltd., 1942) who cites this view of newspaperman, Horace White, a Lincoln contemporary: "After the contest of 1858 was ended, although ended in defeat, Lincoln was certainly elevated in public estimation to a good place in the second rank of party leadership. It was not until the beginning of 1860, however, that certain persons in Illinois began to think of him as a possible nominee for the Presidency. Lincoln did not think of himself in that light until the month of March, about ten weeks before the convention met." Pp. 173-174.

14. Joseph H. Barrett, Abraham Lincoln and His Presidency, Volume I (New York: D. Appleton and Company, 1930) p. iii.

15. Ibid, p. 218.

16. Ibid, p. 222.

17. See Rene Brunet, The New German Constitution (New York: A.A. Knopf, 1922) pp. 323-329. References here are to Articles 109, 110, 113, 114, 118, 124, 126, 123, 135, and 136.

18. Ibid, p. 297.

19. In January of 1930 (merely one example, of course...) Hitler expressed his ideas publicly in the following manner: "We Germans have no reason to wish, even in the slightest degree, that through events, no matter of what nature they might be, a so called 'World Peace' should be preserved which makes possible, indeed confirms...the most terrible plundering and extortion as the only possible fate for our people.... Germany can have only one ardent wish, namely, that the spirit of misfortune should hover over every conference, that discord should arise therefrom, and that finally a world peace which would otherwise ruin our nation should dissolve in blood and fire...."

The goal of foreign policy is the preservation of a people's means of subsistence... The path to this goal will, in the final analysis, always be war....

If men wish to live, then they are forced to kill others.... One is either the hammer or the anvil. We confess that it is our purpose to prepare the German people again for the role of the hammer.... There is only power, which creates justice."

...Insofar as we deliver the people from the atmosphere of pitiable belief in possibilities which lie outside the bounds of one's own strength--such as the belief in reconciliation, understanding, world peace, the League of Nations, and international solidarity -- we destroy these ideas. There is only one right in this world and this right is one's own strength."

These quotations from the Nazi paper, Voelkischer Beobachter, are collected and cited by Gordon W. Prange, Hitler's Words: Two Decades of National Socialism 1923-1943 (Washington, D.C.: American Council on Public Affairs, 1944) pp. 9-41.

20. See John W. Wheeler-Bennett, Wooden Titan: Hindenburg in Twenty Years of German History 1914-1934 (London: Archon Books, 1936) p. 409. How and why Hitler was ultimately invested with the Chancellorship on January 30, 1933 is still far from clear. That Hindenburg was being blackmailed has been advanced as a reason by some authors. See Emil Ludwig, Hindenburg (Philadelphia: John Winston Company, 1935) pp. 487-

225

91 and 514-15. Konrad Heiden, Der Fuehrer (Boston: Houghton Mifflin, 1944) p. 439. Alan Bullock, Hitler: A Study in Tyranny (New York: Harper and Brothers, 1952) pp. 223-224, among others.

21. Carl Sandburg in his Abraham Lincoln, the War Years, volume vi (New York: Charles Scribner's Sons, 1948) reports this response to Lincoln's Second Inaugural Address by Charles Francis Adams, Jr.: "Once at Gettysburg and now again on a greater occasion he has shown a capacity for rising to the demands of the hour which we should not expect from orators or men of the schools.... What will Europe think of this utterance of the rude ruler of whom they have nourished so lofty a contempt? Not a prince or minister in all Europe could have risen to such an equality with the occasion." P. 96.

22. In his American Politics: The Promise of Disharmony (Cambridge: Harvard University Press, 1981) Samuel P. Huntington describes one possible scenario of the future of American politics as, first, a "weakening of government in an effort to reform it (followed by....) replacement of the weakened and ineffective institutions by more authoritarian structures more effectively designed to meet historical needs." P. 232. With a view to developments apparent in American society at the beginning of the 1980's, Huntington quotes Plato's observation that in the constitution of society any excess brings about an equally violent reaction. So the only outcome of too much freedom is likely to be excessive subjection... "the culmination of liberty in democracy is precisely what prepares the way for the cruelest extreme of servitude under a despot." Pp. 232-233. As far back as 1969, Samuel Beer, in writing about the future of British politics, declared "Caesarism based on technocracy as the first possible alternative to present regime of parties....incapable of producing among the people the understanding and acceptance that will yield the decisions necessary for planning." British Politics in the Collectivist Age (New York: Vintage Books, 1969) p. 430. Obviously, many different scenarios of democratic failure are possible and many are historically recorded.

According to Professor Philip Shaw Paludan, "if one compares Lincoln's use of power with executive actions before 1861, popular and even scholarly use of a word such as 'dictatorship' makes limited sense." p. 316.

Paludan's assessment of the Lincoln achievement, however it may have been produced, is quite consonant with the view offered here. see pp. 318-319.

INDEX